Conspiracy Theories

ALSO BY AARON JOHN GULYAS

*Extraterrestrials and the American Zeitgeist:
Alien Contact Tales Since the 1950s* (McFarland 2013)

Conspiracy Theories

*The Roots, Themes and
Propagation of Paranoid Political
and Cultural Narratives*

AARON JOHN GULYAS

McFarland & Company, Inc., Publishers
Jefferson, North Carolina

LIBRARY OF CONGRESS CATALOGUING-IN-PUBLICATION DATA

Names: Gulyas, Aaron John, 1975– author.
Title: Conspiracy theories : the roots, themes and propagation of paranoid political and cultural narratives / Aaron John Gulyas.
Description: Jefferson, North Carolina : McFarland & Company, Inc., Publishers, 2016 | Includes bibliographical references and index.
Identifiers: LCCN 2015050422 | ISBN 9780786497263 (softcover : acid free paper) ∞
Subjects: LCSH: Conspiracy theories—History.
Classification: LCC HV6275 .G85 2016 | DDC 001.9—dc23
LC record available at http://lccn.loc.gov/2015050422

BRITISH LIBRARY CATALOGUING DATA ARE AVAILABLE

ISBN (print) 978-0-7864-9726-3
ISBN (ebook) 978-1-4766-2349-8

© 2016 Aaron John Gulyas. All rights reserved

No part of this book may be reproduced or transmitted in any form or by any means, electronic or mechanical, including photocopying or recording, or by any information storage and retrieval system, without permission in writing from the publisher.

On the cover: 1952 FBI declassified Office Memorandum; all other images © 2016 -MG-/Lingbeek/Pobytov/iStock

Printed in the United States of America

McFarland & Company, Inc., Publishers
  Box 611, Jefferson, North Carolina 28640
  www.mcfarlandpub.com

For Commander X

Acknowledgments

Love and appreciation, as always, to Cindy and Matthew for their time and patience while I was working on this project. Thanks as well to innumerable friends and colleagues who remained fairly good-natured I when spent way too much time explaining just why underground bases were so fascinating. Special mention should go to Jessica Himstedt at the Mott Library for handling all my research needs efficiently and for being a good sport about promoting my work to the campus community.

Table of Contents

Acknowledgments	vi
Preface	1
Introduction: The Nature of Conspiracy	5
1. Secret Societies	21
2. New World Orders	45
3. They Came from Outer Space	70
4. Mind Control	98
5. Mad Science and Forbidden Knowledge	134
6. The Hidden World of the Nazis	172
Conclusion	196
Chapter Notes	203
Bibliography	215
Index	225

Preface

Many of us have been conspiracy theorists at some point in our lives. That does not necessarily mean we have holed up in a bunker, wearing an aluminum foil hat, or we've insisted that our primary care physician scan us for implanted mind control or alien tracking devices. Conspiracy theories, sometimes, can be much more subtle. A conspiratorial frame of mind may result from a series of real or perceived slights against us or others. It can come to us through unrelated conversations that—when squinted at in just the right way—dovetail in enlightening ways. A series of events may cause us to wonder if some kind of causal relationship existed where none actually did. Humans often seek patterns and connections between disparate ideas, concepts or events. Storytelling is part of human culture. Combine these two ideas and it is not surprising that narratives emerge that created connections and patterns. During the second half of the twentieth century citizens of the western democracies (particularly the United States) began to lose confidence in their national governments. As real incidents of secrecy and cover-ups were conflated with long lived paranoid stories, many of the "conspiracy theory" narratives with which we are familiar began to emerge. As access to print media, television and, eventually, the Internet spread during that time, conspiracy narratives multiplied. Every story has a beginning. While it may be true with regard to history, it is not always the case that we can find that beginning. When historical evidence becomes diluted through the depredations of popular culture, finding the roots of a narrative becomes more difficult still. Conspiracy theories are a prime example of this phenomenon. Despite the tiny kernels of historical truth and circumstance that often serve as the launching point of various conspiracy theories, finding and evaluating those bits and pieces of truth is often challenging.

Conspiracy theories and the complex narratives produced by those who believe in them can often vary greatly. They emerged from both the political right and the political left. The belief systems of their adherents include the atheistic and secular as well as the fundamentalist and theocratic. Some conspiracy theories are extremely limited in their scope, alleging cover-ups and hidden agendas relating to specific contexts such as a stolen election, instances of political-corporate collusion, or a war initiated via deceit. Others are vast and complex, taking those seemingly isolated incidents and weaving them into a narrative that spans decades, centuries, or even millennia.

Given their outrageous, unbelievable, and extremist nature one might reasonably conclude that a prudent observer of politics and culture should dismiss conspiracy theories out of hand. One could argue that there are many issues that are demonstrably much more important and fact-based with which one should engage. Despite the fringe position these theories occupy, they persist and continue to evolve in response to new political, social, and cultural concerns. Because of this, conspiracy theories (and theorists) are important. Despite the corrosive effect that some conspiracy theories have sometimes had on public discourse, particularly during the late twentieth and early twenty-first centuries, understanding their origins and development is crucial for navigating the dangerous currents of politics and culture in the twenty-first century. While conspiracy theories exist in the shadows, they have noticeable effects on discourse in the real world.

No book can adequately explore, dissect, and analyze every extant conspiracy theory and this book does not intend to. Rather, this study will delve into several prominent and specific manifestations of conspiracy theory and paranoia with the intention of exploring the roots of these narratives and explicating the historical context which has surrounded the development of these theories. This context, of course, includes any factual basis for the historical claims of these narratives. While any historical basis should not be overstated, the connections between conspiracy and history (as well as conspiracists' casual misuses of historical sources and other evidence) are crucial for understanding both the development of conspiracy theories and narratives over the decades. Complicating this use of history and historical context is the propensity of conspiracy theorists to extend their theories backwards through time, presenting readers and viewers with manipulated, selective historical narratives to provide proof for their assertions. The resulting pseudo or alternative histories are among the most the most quickly expanding genres of conspiracy theory, commanding hours-long blocks of television time on cable channels. The following chapters will discuss a number of conspiracy theories and narratives that have become prominent over the past fifty years as well as the more general nature of conspiracy theory and current trends in the scholarship surrounding conspiracy theories and conspiracy thought.

It is not the goal of this book to delve deeply into the critical and cultural theory approaches to conspiratorial thinking and political paranoia. There are numerous excellent scholars who have addressed the theoretical aspects of conspiracy culture. Rather, my purpose is to explore in greater depth and detail the development of the actual conspiracy narratives themselves as well as the nature of the cultures and communities that emerged around different theories and worldviews. Conspiracy theories are stories and these stories (and the changes they have undergone over the decades) reflect their political, social, and cultural context. A fascinating and frustrating fact about them, however, is that conspiracists have often applied the same basic narrative to a variety of contexts. Thus, it is difficult to apply blanket labels to conspiracy theories. Theorists of the political left, right, or center can (and often do) use the very same narratives to promote their political viewpoints and agendas.

My reason for taking this approach is informed by my main vocation as a classroom history teacher at a large community college. As discussed above, given the range of pop cultural treatments of conspiracy theory—many of which invite and encourage viewers and readers to accept their claims uncritically—I am encountering more and more students of all age groups and backgrounds who believe strange, unsupportable stories on the flimsiest evidence. In a related way, both in the classroom and on the Internet, people who are exposed to some conspiracy narratives for the first time react as though they are seeing (and relating to others) previously unavailable, groundbreaking information.

The ultimate goal is for this book to serve as something of a primer. It is my hope that it is useful both for general readers interested in the variety of conspiracy theories and narratives that have emerged over the past half century as well as those who desire background information on the historical roots of these theories. Books by Mark Fenster, Michael Barkun, Lance deHaven-Smith, and others do an admirable job providing deep analysis of the theoretical approaches to a broad array of conspiracy theories. They do not, in most cases, delve deeply into the changing nature of these theories or discuss how they have developed from often modest, more low-key beginnings.

Introduction:
The Nature of Conspiracy

Conspiracy theories and narratives that attribute an unfeasibly generous number of events to the actions of shadowy and malign forces have been part of the fabric of human history for centuries. Formal scholarly analyses and dissection of these theories—their origins, development, and deeper meaning and importance to politics and culture—on the other hand, have emerged relatively recently. Political scientists, sociologists, communications scholars, historians, and others have framed and interpreted conspiracy theories and narratives. Like these theories and narratives themselves, scholarly interpretations and analyses have changed over time, reflecting the political and academic contexts in which scholars operate. Despite these changes over time, some commonalities do exist among various scholarly treatments of conspiracy writing. In general, there is a significant level of skepticism toward many conspiracy claims. Scholars have a tendency to view those who promote such theories and narratives as having motivations and intentions beyond the promulgation of their particular and peculiar version of "truth" such as class envy, racism or religious prejudice. Scholarly observers and analysts have, generally, viewed the effects of paranoid and conspiratorial viewpoints as irrational and unfortunate. That characterization, however, has shifted over the past decade.

Since the late 1960s, revelations of documented and significant cover-up and conspiracy have increased in frequency. The speed with which information and misinformation, interpretation and misinterpretation spread around the globe continues to increase. Scholars have, as a result, delved more deeply into the ways in which these stories emerge and propagate as well as the effects they have on political and cultural discourse. Literary and cultural studies scholars have increasingly focused on aspects of the phenomenon such as the creation and alteration of narratives—and the creation of narratives as being, to a certain degree, a political act and an attempt at political or cultural agency for groups that are either marginalized or that, at least, perceive themselves as marginalized.

Another increasingly significant factor in the study of conspiracy narratives has been the increased attention scholars have paid to issues of class, gender, and ethnicity in their examinations. Broadly speaking, the study of conspiracy theory has benefited from the turn toward analyzing politics, society, and culture through a wider array of lenses than in the past. This has led to a more nuanced approach to the issue of political paranoia, an acknowledgment that there is value in examining a multitude of contradictory narratives from a variety of creators. This approach, however, has produced works that are less scholarly and aimed at a broader audience—particularly television documentaries and radio programs—presenting all narratives of historical or political events as being potentially valid. While this may be a useful mindset when evaluating and analyzing the cultural impact of various ideas it has also served to obfuscate those historical narratives that are more fully supported by factual evidence.

I do not intend the following summary of some of the significant works and approaches to the study of conspiracy theory to be exhaustive (or exhausting). My goal, rather, is to provide a sampling of the various representative themes within the scholarly study of conspiracy theory. At one end of this spectrum is the pioneering work of Richard Hofstadter during the early 1960s, a period that was the climax of an era in which a broadly liberal consensus held sway, an era in which conspiracy theory was seen as destructive and divisive. At the other end of this spectrum is the twenty-first century work of Lance deHaven-Smith, who examines the pejorative and rhetorical uses of anti-conspiracy invective as a tool to ultimately perpetuate the secrecy surrounding government misdeeds.

Historian Richard Hofstadter's 1964 *Harper's Magazine* essay "The Paranoid Style in American Politics" engaged with political paranoia and conspiracy theory within the particular contest of the Cold War. In the aftermath of the anti–Communist hysteria wrought by Joseph McCarthy and the House Un-American Activities Committee, Hofstadter drew parallels between modern anti–Communist sentiment and prior outbreaks of paranoia in the history of the United States. These included the anti–Masonic movement, fears of Roman Catholic subversion, and anti–Semitic international banking conspiracies, all of which would persist into conspiracy theories and narratives.

Hofstadter's summary of the nature of political and cultural paranoia rings as true in the early twenty-first century as it did in the mid-twentieth. No cover-up is ever limited in scope; no one on Earth escapes the evil wrought by the conspirators:

> The paranoid spokesman sees the fate of conspiracy in apocalyptic terms—he traffics in the birth and death of whole worlds, whole political orders, whole systems of human values. He is always manning the barricades of civilization. He constantly lives at a turning point. Like religious millenialists he expresses the anxiety of those who are living through the last days and he is sometimes disposed to set a date for the apocalypse.[1]

This apocalyptic thread runs through conspiracy narratives from their origins to their present configurations. If anything, as we will see in the following chapters, these theories and narratives have become ever more eschatological, predicting (and sometimes longing for) end times both secular and spiritual. While Hofstadter's assessment of these theories' scope is keen and even prescient, his explanations of their origins and significance is less flexible. Hofstadter's conclusions paint conspiracy and paranoia as an often, if not exclusively, right wing expression ("In recent years we have seen angry minds at work mainly among extreme right-wingers").[2] He judges this paranoia and the "style" of political rhetoric it produces to be the result of alienation from the political process, evidence of political and cultural disharmony. Those outside the system cannot possibly understand how that system works. The believers and promoters of this paranoia, Hofstadter claims, have "no access to political bargaining or the making of decisions" and as a result "they find their original conception that the world of power is sinister and malicious fully confirmed." Being outsiders, without access to the corridors of power, "they see only the consequences of power—and this through distorting lenses—and have no chance to observe its actual machinery.... Circumstances often deprive him of exposure to events that might enlighten him—and in any case he resists enlightenment."[3] For Hofstadter, the paranoid political actor is not truly part of the machinery of government and, almost certainly, does not wish to be. Scholars, however, are just as bound by their historical and cultural context as anyone else. The decade following the publication of "The Paranoid Style in American Politics" saw a remarkable shift in the American public's willingness to place trust in the federal government. The public's confidence was eroded by misleading information about the depth of American involvement in Vietnam, the Watergate break-in and cover-up, as well as revelations of intelligence and security agency malfeasance toward targets as varied as civil rights workers and South American politicians.

A Gallup/University of Michigan study illustrates this decline during the period following the appearance of Hofstader's essay (1964). Responses to the question "How much of the time do you think you can trust government in Washington to do what is right—just about always, most of the time, or only some of the time?" provide some insight into the descent of Americans' confidence in the moral rightness of their government. The percentage of respondents answering "just about always" or "most of the time" was 73 percent in 1964. By 1968 this had fallen to 61 percent and 1972 saw those answers drop to 53 percent. In 1974, the Watergate investigation and Richard Nixon's resignation from the Presidency coincided with a drop to 36%. These figures would reach a low point (25 percent) by 1980 before rebounding slightly by 1982 (33 percent).[4] While it would be unsupportable to equate answers to broad questions like "How much of the time do you think you can trust government in Washington to do what is right?" with acceptance of or belief in conspiracy theories, they do provide some context for the world in which these theories would increasingly flourish.

As that flourishing took place during the 1980s and 1990s, other scholars emerged to challenge aspects of Hofstadter's analysis of paranoid politics. While the vast majority of these scholars did not give credence to such conspiracy theories and narratives, the political developments of the late 1960s and 1970s provided a broader context for understanding the rapid dissemination and development of stories that were becoming simultaneously less credible and more widespread.

Mark Fenster's 1999 book *Conspiracy Theories: Secrecy and Power in American Culture* is emblematic of the increasing wave of critique aimed toward Richard Hofstadter's "consensus" approach of the 1960s (and adopted by thinkers and commentators for decades afterward). Fenster questions this conception of the place of paranoia and conspiracy in American politics and society, characterizing Hofstadter's definition of political paranoia as being "a pathology suffered by those existing outside of the pluralistic consensus."[5] Fenster argues that this approach—paranoia as a diagnosable disorder—was an understandable one within the context of the "consensus" approach to history and politics in the post-war era. This approach sought to enshrine a historical narrative that defended and promoted America's dominant political, social, and cultural values. Political and intellectual leaders often coopted dissent and criticism, folding them into a hegemonic narrative of American greatness, if not actual infallibility.

Hofstadter's approach, according to Fenster, "implied a continuum between proper politics and pathology." Conspiracy theory and paranoia, being on the "pathology" end of this spectrum could not truly be considered political in any useful or proper sense. In this way, he "applied a theory of individual pathology to a social phenomenon … problematic if … one is attempting to produce a concept that can be used across history to explain, for example, populist political dissent in the 1990s."[6] Far from being a symptom of political or institutional breakdown, Fenster asserts that "conspiracy must be recognized as a cultural practice that attempts to map, in narrative form, the trajectories and effects power; yet it not only does so in a simplistic, limited way, but also continually threatens to unravel and leave unsettled the resolution to the question of power that it attempts to address."[7] This issue of developing and, ultimately, disintegrating narratives is a crucial one to bear in mind. Fester sees these narratives as being useful tools for understanding the complexities of American cultural and politics at the close of the twentieth century. Hofstadter, in contrast, merely used the details of these narratives as tools to confirm the diagnosis of a theory or view point as sufficiently "pathological" to exclude.

As we will see in the more recent work of later scholars, a significant point of departure from the earlier work of Richard Hofstadter is shown in Fenster's cautious acknowledgment that "there *are* elements of secret treachery in the contemporary political and economic order."[8] This observation does not exempt the truly outlandish and extreme theories from scrutiny. It does, however, present an indication that the mere existence of conspiracy theories is not an indicator of an unhealthy political system. On the contrary, Fenster speculates that some aspects of conspiracy culture could point the way to a "populist possibility, a resistance to power that implicitly imagines a better, collective future."[9] This opportunity for change and progress Fenster glimpses is visible in the various calls to action presented by conspiracy researchers and writers. Whether they are urging their readers to protest american involvement in the United Nations or advocating for support and compensation for victims of government medical and psychological experimentation, there is often a desire for political change that transcends the conspiracy genre and illustrates a broad applicability to non-conspiratorial politics.

Mark Fenster was not alone in critiquing Richard Hofstadter's conception of "paranoid" thinking and its role in both shaping and reflecting American society. Authors such as Michael Barkun and Lance deHaven-Smith have also examined conspiracy theories and the culture that surrounds them within the context of post–Vietnam and post–Watergate history as well as through a variety of theoretical approaches. While not excusing or ignoring the often extreme, unreasonable, and bigoted nature of some aspects of conspiracy culture, scholars like Fenster and his contemporaries acknowledge that so broad an array of ideas and writings cannot be dismissed as summarily as Hofstadter did in 1964.

A Culture of Conspiracy: Apocalyptic Visions in Contemporary America opens with its author, political scientist Michael Barkun, recounting the fascination held by Oklahoma City bomber Timothy McVeigh for flying saucers and the ephemera of UFO conspiracy theories. McVeigh visited the semi-mysterious Area 51 in 1994, protesting the base's lack of public accessibility and accountability. Barkun also details McVeigh's interest in right-wing conspiracy talk show host Milton William Cooper, a figure who got first gained prominence on the UFO lecture circuit. These anecdotes, Barkun argues, illustrate the increasing overlap between political paranoia and conspiracy theories that focused on the notion that the government was hiding "the truth" about extraterrestrial visitation to the Earth.[10]

Barkun positions his examination of conspiracy culture by outlining common threads tying together various theories and narratives. In conspiracy theories there are no accidents, nothing is truly as it seems, and everything is connected. He also posits that conspiracy theories fall into three broad categories: "event conspiracies," "systemic conspiracies," and "superconspiracies." These categorizations illustrate Barkun's approach which, unlike Richard Hofstadter's, focuses to a greater degree on the makeup and organization of conspiracy narratives, examining the stories told by conspiracy theorists and how these stories reflect the changing nature of the cultural and political contexts of conspiracy theory.[11]

Like Mark Fenster, Michael Barkun critiques Richard Hofstadter's approach to understanding conspiracy theory. Barkun questions Hofstadter's use of the term "paranoia." While Barkun acknowledges that Hofstadter used the word in a manner that was "metaphorical rather than literal and clinical" he argues that "Hofstadter, partly by the force of his writing and argument, introduced clinical terminology into the stream of discourse, were it could be employed more broadly by others." Barkun asserts that Hofstadter's use of the word "paranoid," with the accompanying connotation (if not denotation) of mental illness was a calculated move. That "Hofstadter utilized it precisely because of its judgmental quality. Its overtones are such that its use, even in careful hands, runs that risk of merely labeling people whose ideas we disapprove of."[12]

As its title suggests, Barkun's study focuses on the apocalyptical and eschatological nature of many conspiracy narratives that emerged during the late twentieth century as well as examining the connections between them. Barkun goes into much deeper background on the historical roots and details of many conspiracy theories than many other conspiracy analysts but he often fails to track the many changes over time undergone by the various narratives. He does, however, acknowledge that the age of widespread public access to the Internet has led to confusion over the details of these stories:

> Copyright and intellectual property appear to count for little among many who engage in Internet posting. Multiple versions of the same document are likely to appear in various places, some identical, some slightly different, some with

annotations by the poster. The result is not unlike the variant accounts of urban legends that circulate by word of mouth. Unlike oral versions, however, all of the variants may in principle be simultaneously available to the Web surfer, who may then be tempted to judge the credibility of a story by the number of times it is told. Here repetition substitutes for direct evidence as a way of determining veracity.[13]

This issue is one with which we will have to contend as we move forward in this study. Barkun's well-developed sense of the importance of narrative is echoed by Fran Mason, who writes that

> every conspiracy theory provides a narrative to legitimate its account of contemporary society, offering a view of how things got to be as they are. Conspiracy theory provides archaeology in narrative form, locating causes and origins of the conspiracy, piecing together events, connecting random occurrences to organize a chronology or sequence of sorts, and providing revelations and denouements by detailing the conspiracy's plans for the future. Narrative provides a form of mapping for conspiracy theory, offering not only an explanatory history but also a map of the future that is to come.[14]

It is an examination of narrative that is all too often lacking in conspiracy research and analysis, a gap that this study hopes to fill. The essential importance of narrative to conspiracy theory is complicated by the variable nature of those narratives. Over time, stories change, as theorists weave new evidence and new theories into existing stories. In a similar way, certain long-lasting themes or tropes persist and serve, in a manner of speaking, as building blocks for new variations on familiar narratives.

Political scientist Lance deHaven-Smith's *Conspiracy Theory in the United States* breaks with the approach traditionally taken even by modern scholars who examine the political and cultural significance of conspiratorial thinking. DeHaven-Smith, in the first paragraph of his book, asserts that readers assume it "is simply another addition to the long list of books criticizing conspiracy theories" and that they "probably expect the book to blame the popularity of these theories on some flaw in American culture or character."[15] However most critiques of conspiracy theory and theorists, he claims, are "based on sentimentality about America's political leaders and institutions rather than on unbiased reasoning and objective observation."[16] Far from being a critique of conspiracy theory or conspiracy theorists, *Conspiracy Theory in the United States* seeks to reframe and reorient the discourse about such theories, with deHaven-Smith injecting what, in his view, is needed balance on the subject. Indeed, "the literature's hasty dismissal of antigovernment suspicions is not merely an incidental attitude." Rather, it is the result of the "loaded language" of the phrase "conspiracy theory" and the meaning attached to it in use and application.[17]

This loaded language did not emerge accidentally. DeHaven-Smith traces the origins of the term "conspiracy theory" to attempts to deflect criticism of the 1964 Warren Commission report on the assassination of President John F. Kennedy and cites CIA dispatch #1035–960, a 1967 set of instructions that highlight the negative effect that questioning of the Commission's might have on American government and society. Officials within the CIA feared that "innuendo ... affects ... the whole reputation of the American government." In response, dispatch #1035–960 aims to "provide material countering and discrediting the claims of the conspiracy theorists." The dispatch suggests that CIA agents "point out ... that parts of the conspiracy talk appear to be deliberately generated by Communist propagandists."[18]

The long-term effect of this official denigration of any criticism of the Warren Commission's findings, according to deHaven-Smith, has been that "conspiracy beliefs are associated with mental illness, including paranoia, obsession, psychosis ... with being antisocial, including crackpots and despicable and bigoted people." he also observes that the "conspiracy theory" label has become "arbitrary and defensive" with those on the political right and the political left using the term to deride their critics. This derogatory characterization has "undermine[d] popular vigilance against abuses of power."[19]

It is these abuses of power on which deHaven-Smith spends a great deal of his analysis. In critiquing the cultural, social, and psychological definitions of "conspiracy theory," he focuses on what he believes gets "lost" in the scholarly debate: "the empirical questions about the events at issue, events that are gravely important and about which people everywhere want to know the truth." DeHaven-Smith addresses this through the concept of the State Crime Against Democracy (SCAD). This is a term that he believes should displace the term conspiracy theory in a variety of contexts. SCAD, he writes, "is a name for the type of wrong-doing about which the conspiracy-theory label discourages us from speaking" (emphasis in original). There is, deHaven-Smith asserts, a "conspiracy-theory conspiracy," an attempt by those in power to "suppress mass suspicions that inevitably arise when shocking political crimes benefit top leaders or play into their agendas."[20]

Conspiracy Theory in America blurs the line between scholarly analysis and activism. DeHaven-Smith calls for "an American *glasnost*" which would involve "revisiting all major investigations in which public officials were dubiously exonerated."[21] His introduction of the "State Crime Against Democracy" category places a boundary between unsupportable paranoid political or cultural narratives and historically documented events that have been, for a variety of reasons, ignored or diminished by the political and media establishment. DeHaven-Smith's treatment focuses solely on those "conspiracy theories" that fall under the SCAD umbrella. There is no discussion of secret technology kept at Area 51 nor does he give space to theories of a secret government colluding with the extraterrestrials from whom some conspiracy theorists believe we acquired that technology. While that is a relatively extreme example of the paranoia deHaven-Smith excludes from his "conspiracy theories that aren't" model others are less outrageous. He spends no time on CIA mind control experimentation, one of many documented historical episodes that have become deeply intertwined with the lurid ephemera of conspiracy culture.

DeHaven-Smith's goal, however, is to rescue legitimate historical crimes and cover-ups from the pejorative purgatory of the "conspiracy theory" label. Thus *Conspiracy Theory in America* is not necessarily an analysis of conspiracy culture or the genre of written, visual, and audio media that culture has produced. By the same token, it does not fall into the category of works that actively promote unsupportable conspiracy theories. Despite deHaven-Smith occasionally lapsing into conspiratorial conjecture (he asserts that John F. Kennedy's support of the military coup themed film *Seven Days in May* indicated that he "knew he was in danger" in the months leading up to his assassination[22]), there are few incidents he examines that are not supported by evidence and, often, are within the bounds of conventional historical scholarship.

Since the 1960s, scholars such as Hofstadter, Fenster, Barkun, deHaven-Smith, and others have done a tremendous amount of work examining the political, cultural, sociological, and theoretical roots and implications of conspiracy theory. What has often been missing from their works, however, has been an in-depth, longitudinal examination of the narratives themselves. They will often address the narratives in whatever form they took at the time a particular scholar wrote. I do not believe this to be an inappropriate approach, given the scholarly and theoretical approaches these authors took.

However, for the student of history, such an approach runs the risk of removing these narratives from the totality of their contexts. The paired notions of continuity and change in conspiracy narrative are important, as are whatever factual bases these tales may possess. Clearly, no conspiracy theory exists in isolation from other conspiratorial narratives. Indeed, the same basic theory or narrative told over and over again across the decades, gains new strands and new meanings depending on its political, social, and cultural milieu.

Hofstadter's approach has been thoroughly criticized by later scholars but it is a useful one for understanding the viewpoint of those who seek to debunk conspiracy theories. While the "consensus" viewpoint of the 1950s and 1960s has faded, adherence to unsupported and paranoid narratives does carry the risk of putting various social or political groups needlessly at odds. Similarly, deHaven-Smith's State Crimes against Democracy terminology, while often based in accepted historical evidence, opens the door to an uncritical approach to theories and narratives that are not nearly as well-supported as deHaven-Smith's examples.

While not every conspiracy theory and narrative I will discuss in the following chapters is necessarily a "history conspiracy." Historical conspiracy theories trade upon the premise that the accepted historical narratives developed by scholars (both professional and avocational) are not merely incorrect but have, in fact, been deliberately and maliciously constructed to be misleading. The reasons for these historical misdirections usually center on the need of those in power to keep the truth about history hidden lest their role become widely known. As we will see, "those in power" are a varied collection comprised of Nazis, Communists, Freemasons, Roman Catholics, Jewish financiers, extraterrestrial overlords, the United Nations, and dozens of others. While not all conspiracies are history conspiracies, the notion of history permeates conspiracy culture. Conspiracy theories, like everything else, have changed and developed over time.

Lance deHaven-Smith's perspective on the use of "conspiracy theory" as a politicized pejorative is a useful model as we examine conspiracy theories of all types. This approach—which encourages us to acknowledge a distinction between theories about possible or probable conspiracies in history and politics on the one hand and the volumes of written, spoken, and filmed media that conspiracy theorists have produced. The former are, of course, subject to debate and historical scrutiny. The latter serve as primary sources, raw material for understanding how conspiratorial thinking and, more broadly, conspiracy cultures and the narratives that those cultures have developed over time. For example, it is well-established through declassified documentation and Congressional testimony that the Central Intelligence Agency, working with universities and other research institutions, explored the use of hallucinogens and psychological trauma in interrogations and conditioning. There are, however, narratives that have built on that well-established foundation, reflected in the lurid autobiographies of alleged "government mind control slaves." This book explores that and similar journeys from lurid and unsavory historical fact to lurid and unsavory contemporary fantasy.

The historical development of the various narratives is an important consideration when dealing with conspiracy culture. Political scientists, cultural theorists and scholars in other fields have long recognized conspiracy theories as being a useful reflection of the deeply held views of those who profess them. The fears and aspirations embodied in various conspiracy theories provide a window into political, social, and cultural aspects of the times and places in which they originated and thrived. To study conspiracy theories only as an expression of fear entails a risk of overlooking important aspects of these theories. Any given conspiracy theory, while existing within a particular context, has also often built on pre-existing narratives and events, not all of which are necessarily paranoid or conspiracy driven. Conspiracy theories that are prominent today have their roots in historical events. While current conspiracy theories may provide a means to more fully understand the fears and prejudices of the cultural, social and political landscape, we can also trace these theories back to whatever historical basis might exist. The twists and turns of these theories and narratives inform their contemporary shapes as well as providing insight into the transition of accepted historical fact into ill-supported stories propagating on the internet and cable television. While not all conspiracy theories are explicitly about history, even conspiracy theories that are firmly focused on current events have deep roots. Narratives and, often, meta-narratives developed from these roots, their twists and turns affected by the world in which their creators lived. This book aims to illuminate the the long and convoluted path that these stories have taken.

Over the course of my years teaching both United States and World history survey courses I have observed a rise in the number of students in introductory courses to accept conspiracy theory-based claims about history on an equal basis as more thoroughly supported but less sensational claims. While they may not always express blind belief in these theories, many tend to lend them the same weight as the measured, evidence-based judgments of acknowledged experts. From well-worn conjecture about the assassination of John F. Kennedy to startling tales of Nazi bases in Antarctica, students, colleagues, and members of the general public seem to have an increasing interest in what proponents often euphemistically call "hidden history." Critics of these narratives often, on the other hand, call them "pseudo history."

There are several trends which account for the rise of a more paranoid vision of history and current events. Documentary programs which present conspiratorial conjecture about history as established fact have emerged across several cable networks in recent years. Shows like *Ancient Aliens* and *America Unearthed* often have the same production standards as more conventional history and scientific documentary programs. They feature talking-head interviews that, superficially, provide expert content. They use well-crafted and convincing graphics to bolster the views these experts present.

As we will see in the following chapters, a well crafted historical narrative and a well crafted pseudo-historical conspiracy narrative often look and sound very similar.

Conspiracy theories and the narratives produced by conspiracy theorists are often distinguished by the way in which they—at least on a superficial level—leave no questions unanswered. Conspiracy promoters marshal vast amounts of evidence are marshaled to support the narrative presented. Out of context quotations and inappropriately applied statistics can sound like evidence, especially in the compressed format of a television series. While a historian or archaeologist might acknowledge that we know little about an ancient civilization like that of the Indus River Valley, the pseudo-historian has no compunction about filling the gaps in the historical record with ill-considered applications of archaic myth and poetry. This certainty can be very appealing to viewers, particularly those who might not be familiar with the very uncertain nature of some historical knowledge. On the face of it, the "expert" who is able to tell the most complete story carries more weight with viewers. Conspiratorial thought often emerges in pseudo-historical narratives when explaining why mainstream historians and archaeologists refuse to acknowledge the truth of their extraordinary claims. Pseudo-history promoters will often assert that professional academics are engaged in a conspiracy to protect their positions and reputations—reputations that would not survive the revelation of their particular historical "truth." Like most conspiracy theories, the cover-up at the heart of pseudo-historical paranoia reflects the anxieties of the paranoid about their own lack of power and prestige. Besides conventional academics there are also shadowy forces—the Freemasons, the Knights Templar, and others we will see more of in these pages—who could be damaged if those things which were hidden in our history were to become widely known.

History-based conspiracy theories, while only one of several paranoid genres, tend to hover in the background of many other narratives which at first glance, may appear unrelated. We must also bear in mind that not every conspiracy theory that makes use of historical information is necessarily a historical conspiracy theory. Authors, speakers, or television presenters may use historical information that is completely in line with widely accepted and well supported interpretations and use that to build a case for a theories that are far afield from reality.

This book, then, takes an approach that is less focused on critical theory—as those threads have been well-explored by scholars throughout the 1990s and early twenty-first century—than on the development and propagation of paranoid interpretations of both historical and current events. In keeping with that goal, I will be presenting a survey of conspiracy theory. Within the broad "conspiracy theory" genre there are a number of storylines that emerge in a notably consistent and persistent way. This book aims to outline the most prominent strands of narrative that have emerged over the past half century, examine the historical context in which they emerged, and trace the connections between these conspiracy theories and the wider mass culture.

If one were to ask the stereotypical "average American" to name a prominent conspiracy, her answers would probably be unsurprising. The ever-present assassination of John F. Kennedy would likely be high on the list. Other political assassinations, such as those of Martin Luther King, Jr., Robert F. Kennedy, or Malcolm X, would also rank highly. Further afield, but still present would be suspicions that the United States government—particularly the military and intelligence services—have been covering up evidence of extraterrestrial visitation to the Earth. From well known cases such as the supposed "Roswell Incident" to less over-exposed stories like the supposed underground base near Dulce, New Mexico, alien invasion fears have circulated within the conspiracy community for decades.

JFK and the aliens might be high on the public's list of conspiracy prone categories but there are others that might appear. Paranoia about the perceived role of the United Nations in the internal political affairs of the United States—along with other "globalist" conspiracy theories—have been a staple of conspiracy thought since the close of the second World War. The more general notion that outside powers seek to subvert American sovereignty date back to the earliest days of the republic. Closely tied to these fears are those of mad science and technology run amok. While it might not rank highly on our person-in-the-street poll, malicious manipulation of scientific data to drive policy in evil directions is a leading notion in many conspiracy theories. Mind control—whether referring to the clandestine programming and control of individuals or the use of mass media to condition large swaths of the public—also appears prominently. To these relatively well-known theories we may add secret Nazis who wield power in the corridors of American government long after the end of the Third Reich and the free-will destroying properties of popular food additives. Many of the most popular conspiracy narratives tend to fall into these broad categories. Often, these categories are combined, the connections between them creating ever larger and more sprawling conspiracies.

While examining the historical context of various conspiracy claims, theories, and narratives gives valuable insight into the reasons why certain theories may look like they do, it also incurs some risk. It is very easy to dismiss conspiracy theorists and their ideas by asserting that they were, perhaps, unable to think any other way given their historical context including such factors as class, gender, or political ideology. Assuming that *of course* a white, heterosexual, working class man in the 1950s would think a certain way about this, that, or another situation is problematic. History, however, is deeply important for understanding the development of these theories and narratives.

Rather than using history and historical context as a means through which to explain away conspiratorial thinking, my aim is to shed some light on the historical roots of the ideas encapsulated and expanded upon by various conspiracy theories. Many, if not most, conspiracy narratives have a kernel of historical truth buried under layers of conjecture, paranoia, and outright lies. One goal of this book is to investigate these stories to determine the point at which the commonly accepted and documented historical record becomes unable to bear the weight of sensationalism. Put into simpler terms, we know that the CIA and other elements of the U.S. government engaged in mind manipulation experiments with LSD and other substances and techniques. How does the narrative evolve from that starting point—which is well-documented—to lurid books, magazine articles, and late night radio interviews with individuals who claim that were a mind-controlled CIA sex slave for the likes of Bill Clinton, Dick Cheney, and Bob Hope? Can we pinpoint the moment where the narrative goes off the rails? Are we able to find where, why, and how it moves from an odd and, often, dark page of American history to a paranoid sideshow?

Each chapter of this book will also present the background, historical context, and development over time of the most prominent and significant conspiracy narratives which have emerged over more than half a century as well as some of the figures who have promoted them. The examples of these narratives are, often, vast in number. As a means of illustrating the variations on the themes present in the conspiracy genre, each chapter will also present a number "case studies" which will delve into and analyze specific claims, often those encapsulated in discrete works by prominent conspiracy authors or—especially in the case of mind control conspiracy claims—by those who assert that they are victims of the conspiracy. Generally, these chapters will be fairly discrete. One exception to this is the concept of conspiracy theories that fear some sort of entity establishing a tyrannical global government. This topic is so large that I have broken it into to chapters—one focusing on secret societies and another that addresses more specifically political conspiracies.

Sometimes, these case studies center on a particular topic. Secret technologies developed by the Nazis, the underground base at Dulce, New Mexico, that is jointly operated by the United States and our sinister alien overlords, a number of books that—while not well-known—encapsulate the major themes of the "New World Order" paranoia of the 1990s. Other times they will be more specific and personal, such as the accounts of self-proclaimed mind controlled sex slaves Cathy O'Brien and Brice Taylor; the saga of political scientist and "remote viewer" Courtney Brown and his claims about the Hale-Bopp comet; or the stories circulating around the so-called Georgia Guidestones and its dicta on population control.

These case studies are not intended to be exhaustive or exclusive. Rather, they serve as guideposts on the endlessly winding trail of conspiracy narrative. They are also not going to be the only pieces of evidence or example I provide in these chapters. They will, however, be this into which I delve with the most depth and detail. Like conspiracy theories themselves, the analysis and explanation of conspiracy theories run the risk of overwhelming the reader with a deluge of supporting evidence. While less is not always more, concise and well-organized information makes these convoluted topics more manageable. As tempting as it may be to present every possible variation on the CIA mind control meme, a few representative samples will go further in promoting a deeper understanding of these topics.

A common assumption of conspiracy thought—as pointed out by Michael Barkun—is the assertion that everything is connected. No event happens in isolation. Similarly, no event is truly insignificant, random, or merely unlucky. Every death is suspicious, every utterance of prominent government or business figures is freighted with sinister meaning, and every act of government is part of a wide web of deceit designed to enslave humanity. This propensity to see connections everywhere is at the heard of one additional concept I will examine. This is the deep connections between different strands of conspiracy thought—even those that, on the surface, may not appear to be related in any way. Each chapter will explore key examples of the ways in which these narratives tie together.

Conspiracy theories about the persistence of Nazi ideology at the highest levels of government connect to narratives about extraterrestrial invasion and the cover-up of that invasion. Those same alien-based conspiracy theories tie into fears about globalist and the New World Order. The many narratives that invoke a New World Order—shorthand for a one-world governmental, economic, and religious system have deep connections to theories about government mind control operations, climate manipulation, and population control.

Unsurprisingly, some of these connections are too prominent to be limited to one chapter. As we move through the world of conspiracy theory we will encounter figures and concepts that wend their way through a variety of often unrelated tales. The words of perhaps lesser-known figures such as conspiracy theorist William Cooper or journalist, investigator, and theorist Jim Keith will haunt these pages as well as more prominent conspiracy celebrities like David Icke. Conspiracy theories and stories, as well as the questions that drive them will be explained in a variety of ways by a variety of theorists, all staking a claim to significance. A key example is political assassination.

Given the vast amount written by scholars on assassinations and the political implications of them (including conspiratorial thinking), I am making a difficult, but necessary choice, to not head down a rabbit hole of assassination theories in and of themselves. The quagmire of accusations, counteraccusations, and allegations is particularly difficult to cop with in the case of JFK's death. This is not to say that I will not address assassinations and conspiracy theories surrounding them at all, for they are a perfect example of the connectedness of conspiracy narrative. John F. Kennedy's assassination, for instance, has been explained and "solved" many times over by a variety of conspiracy theorists. He was killed for threatening to expose the truth about the Roswell crash; for threatening to end the CIA's reign of terror (including its mind control experiments); for standing up to the hidden Nazi leaders in the American government; and for daring to oppose the growing power of globalist elites. The list goes on. His brother Robert has been the subject of similar conspiratorial hagiographies, as has (although to a lesser degree) Martin Luther King, Jr.

The following chapters will detail a number of broad conspiracy theory subjects that have gained prominence in American culture during the twentieth century. While many of these narratives and memes had some sort of basis in historical fact, it is important to bear in mind that historical facts are not necessarily neutral and that standards of evidence tend to vary when ideology becomes involved. These realities will confront us several times throughout the course of this book. The most innocuous, banal, or dull correspondence, Congressional resolution, or Defense Department memo takes on new and exciting meaning when viewed through the prism of paranoia. Thus, the conspiracy-minded student of history sees additional, significant meaning where others might not. These straightforward artifacts, freighted with meaning when addressed by conspiracy-minded researchers, are the bedrock of the genre's enduring thin veneer of a factual basis.

1

Secret Societies

> After thousands of years of evolution, the reptilian network is now a vast and unfathomable web of interconnecting secret societies, banks, businesses, political parties security agencies, media owners and so on. [They] operate mostly in the background from underground bases and overwhelmingly by possessing the reptilian-human bloodstreams which resonate most closely to the reptile consciousness of the lower fourth dimension.[1]

So wrote prominent conspiracy author, lecturer, and celebrity David Icke in his 1999 book *The Biggest Secret*, immodestly subtitled *The Book That Will Change the World*. Icke's vision of a global conspiracy is rooted in humanoid reptile beings from the "lower fourth dimension" and represents a particularly vivid example of the wide array of conspiracy theories and narratives that focus on global control and domination.

One of the most consistent and nearly all-pervading themes in conspiracy literature, these theories express a fear that sovereign nations will be subverted and supplanted by foreign or international forces. There are variations on this broad theme: spiritual, religious, and cultural expressions are also significant factors in these theories. However, from the mid-twentieth century and extending into the early twenty-first century, these have usually taken the form of "globalist" conspiracies and they have increased in popularity since the establishment of the United Nations following World War II. The end of the Cold War in the early 1990s saw another surge in the prevalence of such fears. Like many conspiracy theories, however, these ideas are not recent developments. Particularly since the European intellectual Enlightenment of the 18th century, there have been fears of a dominant global force threatening not only national sovereignty but the freedoms and lives of those living within those nations. These threats have come from a variety of sources and have ranged from largely spiritual to mostly secular and they have occupied nearly every point on the political spectrum.

While a political subversion of national governments is a key feature of these conspiracy theories, there is also a strong spiritual (if not always a religious) element to many of these narratives. Even when the conspiratorial antagonist is a religious entity (such as the Jesuit order or the Roman Catholic church as an institution), the conspiracy theorist sees him or herself as engaged in a righteous cause akin to a religious crusade. Politics and religion are inextricably bound together. Another key religious or spiritual feature in these conspiracy narratives of global control is the presence of secret sects, societies, or otherwise occult organizations. These range from various groups identified as "the Illuminati" to the Jesuit order to any one of a number of "new age" organizations or movements. Mysterious, hidden, and heterodox organizations are often the driving forces beneath the political and economic machinations of these narratives.

These fears of plots and schemes that are set on drastically altering the political, spiritual, cultural, social, and economic landscape of the targeted nations, are as old as the modern age. This chapter will explore why the centuries since the Enlightenment—and especially the past hundred years—have fueled so many conspiracy narratives concerned with secret societies or religious organizations dedicated to the overthrow of established political, economic, and religious orders. The following chapter will examine fears of political subversion and the creation of a tyrannical world government that are grounded in political movements rather than esoteric sources. These two sides of the "global control" coin are a necessary starting point, as these fears tend to lurk in the background of the other, more specific and focused conspiracies we will examine. Particularly in the late twentieth century, fears of a New World Order (whether promoted by secret societies or open political movements) have undergirded conspiracy theories relating to everything from flying saucers to climate change.

Enlightenment Roots

The social, cultural, and political contexts of a particular time are necessary ingredients for conspiracy theories to emerge. Times of considerable change and transition often provide fertile ground for paranoid thinking. The Enlightenment period saw many European political, social and cultural elites shift away from the revealed religions (particularly Christianity) as the sole source of truth. This shift tilted toward rationalism, a school of thought asserting that deductive investigation is the most reliable source of knowledge. In the classical world, Greek philosophers such as Pythagoras, Plato and Aristotle pioneered the use of reasoned proofs and logic. Medieval European theologians such as Thomas Aquinas sought to use Classical thought, such as that promoted by the Greeks, to explain, clarify, and proof elements of Christian doctrine.

By the seventeenth and eighteenth centuries, however, two key events had taken place that would bring a spirit of rationalism more fully into the cultural and intellectual life of Europe. First, writers and artists of the Italian Renaissance had led a return to the world of classical Greek and Roman ideals, with Gutenberg's printing press making copies of writings from all ages much more accessible. Renaissance thinkers would weave Classical ideals into their writings. One example is Giovanni Pico della Mirandola's 1486 *Oration on the Dignity of Man*, in which he argues that "man is the intermediary between creatures, that he is the familiar of the gods above him as he is the lord of the beings beneath him; that, by the acuteness of his senses, the inquiry of his reason and the light of his intelligence, he is the interpreter of nature, set midway between the timeless unchanging and the flux of time." This renewed emphasis on the importance and significance of human reason and inquiry would be one of the foundations of the Enlightenment. A second crucial event that paved the way for the Enlightenment was the Protestant Reformation which broke the monolithic political, spiritual, and cultural power held by the Roman Catholic church in western Europe. In a broad sense, the Church's fears about Reformation's undermining of the existing order in Europe were similar to fears of revolution in later societies. Similarly, Reformer's concerns about the growing power and corruption of the Church resemble current concerns about power mad conspirators seeking to impose their control over the masses.

As secular and spiritual elites in German, England, and other states broke away from the Church so did their institutions and key intellectual figures. The investigation of the natural world, using guidelines for experimental procedures and frameworks outlined by the eleventh century Arab philosopher Alhazen (c. 965-c.1040) and thirteenth century English cleric Roger Bacon (c. 1214–1292)—the roots of the "scientific method"—would accelerate. Thinkers such as René Descartes (1596–1650) would refine the essential elements of rationalism as a philosophical system as opposed to simply a means for understanding the natural world. Applying rationalism as a worldview would be one of the hallmarks of the Enlightenment, one that would extend to the rationalization of political systems—questioning the traditional sources of political authority such as monarchs that claimed to rule by divine right. Events such as the so-called "Glorious Revolution" of 1688 in which elements of the English Parliament deposed King James II and installed William and Mary as his replacements were justified by the writings of Enlightenment-inspired philosophers such as John Locke.

Opposition to the tenets of the Enlightenment emerged, unsurprisingly, from the exponents church and state they questioned and, often, sought to undermine. Throughout Europe, thinkers were denounced as heretics or traitors. This, in turn, fueled the writing of satire—some of it quite pornographic—directed at the political and religious power structures of the day. Increased freedom of the press allowed a wider array of ideas to permeate European society and by the time of the 1789 revolution in France—which would be often serve as a clear line dividing the early modern and modern ages of European history—the ideas of the Enlightenment were well established in the minds of elites. The earliest revolutionaries in France saw the birth of the United States as a model for their new republic to follow and, indeed, some of them (like the Marquis de Lafayette) had personally supported the American cause. As it radicalized, however, and became more indiscriminately violent, the French Revolution and the wars it spawned threatened to engulf Europe in chaos.

Throughout the nineteenth century conservative forces sought to reassert the world that had existed before the French Revolution as nationalism and other political expressions of the modern age threatened to overwhelm Europe. The Revolution had, for the nobility and ruling classes of Europe, been a disaster and they were fearful that such a crisis might erupt again. In evaluating the period of the French Revolution and the wars that emerged in its wake, conspiratorial thinking came to the fore. Secret societies dedicated to radical change along the lines laid down by Enlightenment principles had developed and grown during the eighteenth century. Surely, conservatives reasoned, some manner of devious machination had been responsible for the devastating destruction of the Revolution. As Jonathan Israel, in his book *Democratic Enlightenment: Philosophy, Revolution, and Human Rights, 1750–1790*, argues it became "a commonplace" to blame radical secret societies for the French Revolution and prevalence of supposedly dangerous Enlightenment philosophies. "The idea that the radical wing of freemasonry ... was the root from which the French Revolution arose ... persisted as a potent mythology among segments of the Catholic Church, and finally, in the early twentieth century, in the fevered minds of Fascist, Falangist, and Nazi propagandists." While much of this blame may be "obsessive exaggeration," Israel acknowledges that "there really was a network of radical conspiracy stretching across central Europe ... and, while less potent and sensational than reactionary mythology would have it, it did exert a certain political and cultural impact."[2] From the roots of this basic historical event grew an immense number of branches. Conspiracy theories persisting until the present day. As journalist Daniel Pipes writes, "In an almost innocent fashion, eighteenth-century thinkers developed themes of subterfuge, inner secrets, and overlapping secret societies that largely defined the subsequent career of conspiracies. One might say that just as the European philosophical tradition consists of a series of footnotes to Plato, its tradition of world conspiracy theories consists of footnotes to the Enlightenment."[3] This assumption, that secret societies would use their influence to rule the world, would become embedded within a wide variety of conspiracy theories. In the United States, in particular, concern about secret societies would blend with religious prejudice.

Secret Societies and Religious Paranoia in American History

Secret societies and centuries-old religious orders—such as the Freemasons, Bavarian Illuminati, or Knights Templar—have long played a significant role in conspiracy theories and political paranoia since the nineteenth century. From being blamed for the destruction and political upheaval of the era of the French Revolution to their supposed culpability in bringing about the New World Order, a wide variety of secret societies have served as able scapegoats for conspiracy theorists. These organizations' own origin myths have provided links to a deep historical past, bolstering their critics' fears that they represent an evil that has existed from before the dawn of recorded history. This gives such organizations an aura of almost supernatural power that, as we will see, conspiracy theorists use to instill fear in their followers.

The origins of the organized Freemasonry that emerged in the eighteenth century supposedly lie in smaller organizations that were descended from medieval guilds of stonemasons and texts from medieval England established a mythology for these groups that extended back to ancient times. One of the most significant of these is the Matthew Cooke Manuscript, dating to the mid-fifteenth century. This document traces the dawn of various technologies, recounting the Biblical stories of Jubal, Tubal Cain, and Naamah inventing and promoting the crafts of music, metal working, and weaving respectively as found in the book of Genesis. Knowing that the flood of Noah would destroy mankind, the keepers of these skills and schools of knowledge carved what they knew on stone pillars. Thus, crucial wisdom would be successfully preserved from the pre- to post-diluvian worlds:

> And this flood was called Noah's flood, for he, and his children, were saved therein. And after this flood many years, as the chronicle telleth, these 2 pillars were found.... A great clerk that [was] called Pythagoras found that one, and

Hermes, the philosopher, found that other, and they taught forth the sciences that they found therein written.

In this way, scientific knowledge passed from the Biblical to the classical worlds.[4]

This mythic origin would remain a significant aspect of Masonic tradition. Modern organizations emerged in 1717, with the formation of the Grand Lodge of Freemasons. This was "ostensibly the product of four founding lodges seeking a structure for their mutual governance." However, Ric Berman argues that while this organization intended to be local to London, "within a few years, the Grand Lodge of England was positioned as a self-professed national governing authority for freemasonry and the principle force behind the movement's development in England and elsewhere."[5] As a secret society, however, Masonic lodges were sometimes viewed with suspicion. As the Enlightenment expanded into central Europe, however, some began to believe that secret societies should have a more active role in spreading new philosophies of liberty. One of these was German philosopher and dramatist Gotthold Lessing.

Lessing had been a freemason since 1771 but, according to Jonathan Israel, soon came to believe that "minimizing religious, national, and class rifts ... should be the undeviating aim of all freemasonry." German freemasonry as a whole, however, did not necessarily share Lessing's lofty goals. In many cases, the lodges were reactionary rather than revolutionary, and did not seek to challenge the social, economic, and political status quo. Adam Weishaupt, a law professor from Inglestadt University, established a new group which became known as the Bavarian Illuminati in 1776. It was "the first of what were to became nation-wide reform-oriented underground networks opposing conventional freemasonry." Philosophically, they were atheistic and materialist, asserting that "everything that exists is matter, that God and the universe are one, that all organized religion is political deception devised by ambitious men."[6] These were, for the time and place, fairly radical ideals and the extent of the group's opposition to the existing religious and philosophical order was kept hidden from outsiders and low-ranking members of the organization. The illuminati were, of course, far from the only secret societies in central Europe at the time. The leaders of the Illuminati viewed the various freemason groups, as well as the Rosicrucian order as either potential or actual enemies, their more mystical views conflicting with the stark rationalism of the illumined ones. They were also in conflict with more explicitly religious groups, such as the Jesuit order. A number of government edicts in the 1780s which aimed to suppress the Illuminati succeeded in triggering a decline and, combined with the number of enemies they had cultivated in other secret groups led to the decline of the organization.

1. Secret Societies

The first extensive attacks on the Illuminati (and other Enlightenment figures) accusing them of planning and carrying out the French Revolution emerged in the 1790s. Writers such as French Jesuit priest Augustin Barreul posited that a conspiracy of Enlightenment thinkers and organizations was the key cause of the revolution. Scottish scientist John Robison's 1798 book *Proofs of a Conspiracy* described the Bavarian Illuminati as something far more devious than a simple secret lodge. "Weishaupt," he wrote, "had long been scheming the establishment of an Association or Order, which, in time, should govern the world."[7] Robison outlined a complex plot by the Bavarian Illuminati to instigate the French Revolution as part of their overall goal to undertake this global control. It is this image of the Illuminati—a devious hidden force bent on global domination—that would persist into the twenty-first century.

The violent revolt of the 13 American colonies from Britain and their establishment of the United States of America was thoroughly based in the ideals of the Enlightenment. The United States's revolutionary beginnings possessed, according to Lance de Haven-Smith, patterns of thought and reasoning that would—in the twentieth century—be considered hallmarks of conspiracy theory. DeHaven-Smith cites letters from John Dickinson, a lesser-known but significant member of the founding generation, English friends in which he explains that "as wrongs against the colonies accumulated, Americans began to connect the dots and recognized ulterior motives in the pattern of Great Britain's actions," what Dickinson referred to as "parts of a system of oppression." This, deHaven-Smith argues, "is the essence of conspiratorial suspicion, which reconstructs hidden motives from confluent consequences in scattered actions."[8] Following the establishment of independence, paranoia continued. The political development of the early republic is, to a degree, a reflection of the fears of various factions that the new American state could be undermined by powerful cabals; such fears hovered in the background of early party politics as Federalists and Republicans vied for power. Following the defense of its independence in the War of 1812–1815 and the proclamation of what would eventually become known as the "Monroe Doctrine," asserting American diplomatic domination of the Western Hemisphere, fears that the British—with the help of disloyal Americans—sought to retake the United States began to fade. Similar concerns, however, would soon take their place: fears that the United States was under threat from external and internal forces were never far from the surface.

During the 1830s and 1840s in the United States, suspicion of secret societies, particularly the masonic orders, led to the development of the Anti-Masonic political party. Freemasonry in the United States had grown in popularity in the early decades of the nineteenth century and, with it, resentment of the perceived privileges of its members. Fears of their power to flout the law, however, emerged after William Morgan, a disgruntled freemason in New York, threatened to reveal the secrets of the Lodge. He was arrested for nonpayment of a loan in 1826 and disappeared shortly after being released on bail. Widely thought to have been murdered by the masons whose secrets he threatened to expose, his book *Illustrations of Masonry by One of the Fraternity* was posthumously published in 1827, and gained notoriety due to Morgan's disappearance. In his foreword to the book, publisher David C. Miller asserts that

> masonry gives rogues and evil-minded characters an opportunity of visiting upon their devoted victim, all the ills attending combined power, when exerted to accomplish destruction. It works unseen, at all silent hours, and secret times and places; and, like death when summoning his diseases, pounces upon its devoted subject, and lays him prostrate in the dust. Like the great enemy of man, it has shown its cloven foot, and put the public upon its guard against its secret machinations.[9]

The moral decay Miller associates with masonry was only part of the problem with the organization and other, similar, secret societies. A second issue was the damage such secret societies might do to the still-young American republic. The growing influence of masonry, its ranks full of judges, lawyers, and politicians might be a threat to the United States:

> The day we trust will never arrive here, when ranks in Masonry will be stepping-stones to places of dignity and power—when this institution will be a machine to press down the free born spirit of men ... high in our elevation, and invincible in our strongholds, we put at defiance secret cabals and associations. The public opinion is like a mighty river, and gigantic in its course it will sweep every interposing obstacle before it.[10]

In a similar vein, in 1830 an anonymous poet published a book entitled *Free Masonry: A Poem in Three Cantos*. Full of numerous historical and classical allusions, the poet describes an angel descending from above who commissions him to write of the dangers of Masonic lodges to the United States:

> Hear then the pleasure of the Power Divine:—
> Mortal, to thee the duty is assign'd,
> To render one great service to mankind;
> Who long have yielded to the lawless sway
> Of those whose deeds are hidden from the day;
> Long by a secret institution curst,
> Robb'd of their rights, and trampled in the dust.
> Know't thou the worst what masonry designs?
> Thy country's welfare, freedom, fast declines
> Beneath its sway; it threatens to o'erthrow
> And lay the pillars of her glory low.

The poet also positions these Masonic forces as antithetical to the founding principles of the republic:

> Vain that thy fathers fought, and all in vain
> Were countless heroes number'd with the slain,
> The boon of freedom for their sons to gain,
> If now that freedom shall be filch'd away
> By *Kings* and *Priests* who seek insidious sway.[11]

The use of "kings" and "priests" as pejoratives illustrates one root of anti-masonic feeling—concern that the United States would fall prey to some manner of "foreign" power. Fear and suspicion of monarchic government was a persistent feature of early American politics while "priests" demonstrates a degree of conflation between anti-masonic sentiment and the anti-Catholicism that would build over the course of the nineteenth century.

In order to combat this influence, in 1828, the Anti-Masonic party emerged partially in response to Morgan's disappearance and presumed murder and was partially a product of the religious revivals known as the Second Great Awakening. The party experienced some limited success in the 1830s, spreading to states adjacent to New York and being particularly effective in Vermont and Pennsylvania (which both elected Anti-Masonic Governors). As the sectional conflict over the expansion of slavery became the predominant political issue of the United States, narrowly-focused parties like the Anti-Masonic party faded into obscurity. Anti-Masonic sentiment would persist in the United States, however, blurring into a wider conspiracy culture during the twentieth century.

While not a secret society in the same manner as the Bavarian Illuminati or the masonic lodges, the Roman Catholic church was subject to similar scrutiny and suspicion during the nineteenth century. The Protestant roots of the United States as well as persistent concerns about foreign infiltration and subversion of American politics and government found in Catholicism a suitable target. While not entirely analogous to the freemasons, the Jesuit order, with its focus on evangelism and education, served a similar purpose. Anti-Catholicism was also deeply connected, during the nineteenth century, to the increasing rates of immigration from Ireland and the German states. Many of these immigrants were Roman Catholic and suspicion among some Americans their growing numbers reflected both a nativist, anti-immigrant stance (that would fuel political parties such as the American party or "Know Nothings") as well as an anti–Catholic position. These positions, in turn, reflected the view of some American protestants that the United States was the "promised land" in a nearly literal sense. These sentiments have persisted from John Winthrop, in 1630, proclaiming the Puritan colony in Massachusetts Bay to be a City on a Hill to the present day.

Lyman Beecher, a prominent evangelist and temperance activist, in 1835, predicted that if the United States was "destined to lead the way in the moral and political emancipation of the world, it is time she understood her high calling.... Soon our character and destiny will be stereotyped forever." Beecher, like many Americans in the early 1800s, saw their county's destiny as being decided beyond the western frontier. During the 1840s and 1850s, the national debate over the settlement of the west would be inextricably bound up with the question of the expansion of slavery. In 1835, however, Beecher predicted the west would be the center of "a conflict of institutions for the education of her sons, for purposes of superstition or evangelical light; of despotism or liberty."[12] Much of Beecher's argument is centered on the need for robust educational and religious institutions in the western lands, with a view toward garnering donations for the Lane Seminary in order for it to be able to undertake the evangelization of the frontier. The dangers of an uneducated citizenry was, according to Beecher, "augmenting daily by the rapid influx of foreign emigrants, the greater part unacquainted with our institutions, unaccustomed to self-government, inaccessible to education." These new arrivals suffered from "inveterate credulity and intrigue" and were "easily embodied and wielded by sinister design."[13] This sinister design had been undertaken by European governments in collusion with the Catholic church. Beecher reports that "it is the testimony of American travelers that the territorial, civil and ecclesiastical statistics of our country, and the action and bearing of political causes upon our institutions are more familiar at Rome and Vienna than with us" and that these dark powers are circulating "tracts and maps" which detail the "most fertile soils and most favored locations" in order to bring about a "stimulated expatriation." This influx of Roman Catholic emigrants would enable the United States to be conquered. Beecher speculates that "if, upon examination, it should appear that three-fourths of the foreign emigrants whose accumulating tide is rolling in upon us are, through the medium of their religion and priesthood, as entirely accessible to the control of the potentates of Europe as if they were an army of soldiers, enlisted and officered, and spreading over the land; then, indeed, should we have just occasion to apprehend danger to our liberties." These "soldiers" would usher in

> the union of church and state in the midst of us. The church and the state both in Europe, and the pliant colonial church here. Her priesthood educated under the despotic governments of Catholic Europe, and dependent for their office support, and honors upon a foreign temporal prince, on whose sanction to their laws and doings they are as dependent as the colonies were upon George the Third.[14]

For Beecher, the political factors at work in the United States were just as dangerous, if not more so, as the spiritual ones. Catholicism, Beecher implies, cannot coexist with political liberty.

The "Catholic system," Beecher asserts, "is adverse to liberty, and the clergy to a great extent are depended on foreigners opposed to the principles of our government, for patronage and support."[15] The Catholic clergy, moreover exercised a "decisive" amount of influence over the political views of Catholic lay people. This puts the Protestant denominations at a distinct disadvantage within the American political system for

> the ministers of no Protestant sect could or would dare to attempt to regulate the votes of their people as the Catholic priests can do, who at the confessional learn all the private concerns of their people, and have almost unlimited power over the conscience as it respects the performance of every civil or social duty.[16]

Beecher does not support the suppression of Catholic civil rights, however, wishing to rely upon educational and cultural institutions to, over time, encourage these new Catholic Americans to fully assimilate into the American system and, one suspects, convert to Protestantism which he positions as a Christianity more fully suited to life in the United States.

Beecher's *Plea for the West*, while an important piece of anti–Catholic literature, receives far less attention than Father Charles Chiniquy's 1886 book *Fifty Years in the Church of Rome* which would become a lynchpin of anti–Catholic conspiracy theory in the United States. One of the crucial pieces of of Chiniquy's work is his assertion that the American Civil War was, in fact, the doing of the Catholic church and, in particular, the Jesuit order. Chiniquy was not he only American who saw connections between the Vatican and the Confederate States of America. Pope Pius IX had written a December 1863 letter to Confederate president Jefferson Davis which became known to the wider public in 1876, nearly a dozen years after the war's end. This letter addresses Davis as "Illustri et Honorabili Piro Jefferson Davis, Praesidi Foederatarum Americae Regionum": "Illustrious President." While this letter, which largely extolls the virtues of peace, has been taken by some as evidence that the Vatican officially recognized the Confederacy that using the title "President" represented a solid diplomatic tie is questionable. The *New York Times* article which presented the letter proclaimed it as "nothing less than a recognition of the Government of the Confederate States."[17]

Chiniquy, a Canadian Catholic priest who converted to Protestantism, reported in *Fifty Years in the Church of Rome* that he met with Abraham Lincoln many times. At first, these meetings took place in Illinois early in Lincoln's career. Later, Chiniquy met with President Lincoln and Lincoln presented his views of the Catholic Church. The United States, like other nations, had "committed a suicidal act by allowing Popery to put a foot on their territory with the privilege of citizenship. The power of life and death is the *supreme power*, and two *supreme powers* cannot exist on the same territory without anarchy, riots, bloodshed and civil wars without end." Lincoln's actions against the Church, Chiniquy alleges, led the Pope and the Jesuits to orchestrate Lincoln's assassination. The president, says Chiniquy, was destined "to fall by the hand of Jesuit assassin, for his nation's sake."[18] The killing of Lincoln, was hardly the first assassination carried out by Jesuit order. According to Chiniquy, "Admiral Coligny, Henry III, and Henry IV, and William the Taciturn" were all taken out "by the hired assassins of the Jesuits." There were parallels between those murders and Lincoln's assassination, he argues and readers who compare them would discover "that one resembles the other as one drop of water resembles another." These assassins were "selected and trained by the Jesuits" and lived lives "of the most exalted Roman Catholic piety, living in the company of priests, going to confess very often, receiving the communion the day before, if not the very day of the murder." The assassins believed themselves to be "the chosen instruments of God, to save the nation by striking its tyrant; that they firmly believed that there was no sin in killing the enemy of the people, of the holy church, and of the infallible Pope!"[19] Chiniquy's conspiracy theories would have a long career, persisting into the twenty-first century, with evangelical Protestant pamphleteers like Chick Publications citing him as an authority on Lincoln's assassination by the Jesuits.[20]

This anti–Catholic sentiment would survive into the twentieth and twenty-first centuries, as would ongoing concerns about secret societies such as the masonic lodges. While the conspiracy theories of the nineteenth and early twentieth centuries were fairly compact—addressing the baleful influence of one or another group or organization, those that would emerge in the post–World War II world would be more all-encompassing, tying together a variety of organizations and movements in the process, portraying vast coalitions of the sinister as being arrayed against the forces of freedom and morality. Conspiracy theorists would latch on to the mythic histories of groups like the freemasons and fashion narratives that stretch back millennia.

Edith Starr Miller's Occult Theocrasy

One of the key figures in the development of secret society-oriented conspiracy theories is Edith Starr Miller. Miller, an American socialite who married into the British aristocracy in the 1920s, had interest in the occult as well close connections with British nobles who were connected to the

British Union of Fascists and other right wing organizations. Miller died in 1933, but her posthumously published *Occult Theocrasy* would lay the foundation for later conspiracy theorists such as William Cooper. Miller's book "endeavoured to expose some of the means and methods used by a secret world, one might almost say and underworld, to penetrate, dominate and destroy not only the so-called upper classes, but also the better portion of all classes."[21]

Miller first examines Freemasonry within the context of nearly every organized religious tradition produced by humanity from ancient India to European Catholicism and various sects emerging out of the Reformation. The Freemasons, she argued, have their roots in the depths of history and have infiltrated all of these organizations. She moves century by century, from the sixteenth to the twentieth, exploring the interconnections between the freemasons and the wider occult conspiracy. For example, when discussing the role of the Anti-Saloon League, Miller explains that alcohol is "recognized by occultists as a deterrent to hypnotic influences. Thus the annulling of the receptivity of mediums, conscious and unconscious, by the general use of alcohol among the masses must create serious difficulties to such powers, if such indeed there be, who seek to rule by thought transference and absent suggestion."[22] Other organizations and movements, ranging from organized crime to the various forms of international communism were, according to Miller, tools of an ancient conspiracy. Keeping in mind Miller's association with right wing groups, it is not surprising that she describes the origins of the Italian Fascisiti in a triumphalist manner. She explained that, "after the European War of 1914 certain banks, conscious of the menace of Satanism, ultimately rechristened Bolshevism, fearing that the monster might get out of hand, selected certain men whose integrity, patriotism, and bravery they trusted and, but paying them a stipend, kept them as a nucleus, ready, when the signal was given, to rally to a leader." This group, once in power, "summarily dealt with" Italian communist leaders and "put an end to the activities of the terrorist society known as the Mafia."[23]

Miller's identification of Bolshevism as a key player in this global conspiracy was a common one following the first world war and Russian Revolution. In the United States Attorney General A. Mitchell Palmer's raids of supposed subversive and communist infiltrated organizations challenged the notion of free and open political discourse. Following the second world war as well as the uncovering of a fairly large Soviet espionage Organization with in the United States government fear of Soviet and communist infiltration became commonplace during the late 1940s and 1950s. By the 1960s American right wing writers had begun to recognize what they thought were clear signs that communist organizations had successfully infiltrated American politics, society, and culture. Much less common, however, were Starr's conclusions linking burgeoning communism to ancient secret societies.

David Icke: Invasion of the Lizard People

Perhaps no conspiracy theorist of the past twenty years has captured the public's imagination to quite the same degree as David Icke. His claims—crucially, that evil forces bent on our spiritual destruction are subjugating humanity—are not entirely unique. Icke masterfully weaves the entire universe of conspiracy theory into his work and his claims are not particularly provable in any conventional sense. Writer Jim Keith (1949–1999), a promoter of some astounding conspiracy theories himself, said that "like many other unworthies who couldn't string together a grammatical sentence for love nor money … somehow happened into the awful truth about the alien invasion," Icke has discovered a secret to conspiracy fame and success. As Keith explains, Icke's key research technique is to "believe every goddamn weird thing anybody, anywhere ever said."[24] Icke's conspiracy work and writing, however, underwent significant evolution during the 1990s, moving from quite standard New Age spirituality to something much darker. As this transition took place, Icke's work displayed a strong influence from earlier theories who expressed concerns about a global takeover and the subjugation of humanity, particularly focusing on the influence of secret societies and ancient forces of evil on human affairs.

Born in England in 1952, David Icke first came to public attention as a professional footballer. After retiring due to rheumatoid arthritis, he became a sports journalist for various outlets including the BBC. Getting involved in politics, he served as a spokesperson for the British Green Party in the late 1980s, rising to a leadership position which he held until 1991.[25] In 1990, he wrote the book *Truth Vibrations* (which would be revised and republished several times) which dealt with "the transformation of mankind." This transformation involves "the earth and all the life she supports" undergoing "changes of an incomprehensible magnitude. Nothing and no one will be the same again." A key component of these changes are "new energies … encircl[ing] the planet." These truth vibrations, wrote Icke, would "explain how you can tune into these higher energies and how we, as a human race, can reduce the impact of the physical events the earth is due to undergo." Lest the reader think that Icke was inventing these significant changes, he assures us that "these truths have been given to me by some of the most evolved beings in this solar system. We are not alone or even nearly alone. Every planet and star is pulsating with life and we on earth in physical bodies are only a tiny part of the wonder that is Creation."[26] Icke's alleged encounters with extraterrestrial beings echoed the stories of the UFO Contactees of the 1950s and 1960s, which developed into tales of channeled communication from advanced space beings, often with ecological messages similar to Icke's.

Icke discusses his spiritual development during the late 1980s and early 1990s, recounting what he perceived as his growing enlightenment as he encountered various teachers and experienced encounters that led him to believe in the power of karma and the reincarnation of the soul. He explains to the reader that western religious traditions have erred in their discounting of reincarnation, asserting that the trouble may have begun with the Roman Emperor Constantine ("I feel it was during his reign that references to reincarnation were taken from the Bible"[27]) and details a first millennium conspiracy within Christianity to eliminate all teachings of death and rebirth from Christianity. Icke then discusses what he has learned about his past incarnations. He had "lived many simple lives worshipping 'the Great Mother,' and gaining attunement with the cycles of the Earth." Icke goes on to discuss well-worn New Age and esoteric topics such as Atlantis, reporting that "Atlantis itself disappeared under the sea and it was this that allowed the Gulf Stream to flow northwards to warm the British Isles.[28]" This, and other information, was conveyed to Icke from extraterrestrial beings via psychic channeling and automatic writing, techniques that had been part of the fringes of UFO and extraterrestrial belief since the 1950s.

Icke's increasingly esoteric and spiritual approach to issues as well as a March 1991 public appearance in which Icke announced he was a "Son of the Godhead" led the British Green Party to dispense with his services. A subsequent appearance with television talk show host Terry Wogan in which Icke seemed to reiterate his claims to some kind of divinity as well as his predictions of Earth-shaking calamities that he had been sent to prevent (a recurring theme of *Truth Vibrations*) led to laughter from the audience and the British press. Icke would persist in these claims and continue to speak and write about the coming disasters which could destroy our civilization just as Atlantis had been destroyed.

In 1994, Icke published *The Robots' Rebellion: The Story of the Spiritual Renaissance*, a book that would begin the process of connecting Icke's New Age ideas to well-established conspiratorial trends. *The Robots' Rebellion* surveys all of human history through Icke's lens of conspiracy. This conspiracy has been undertaken by dark forces since the beginning of time in order to manipulate humanity and keep it from knowledge of its true self—a powerful, spiritually-realized self. For "if we can be encouraged to switch off the connection with our personal Mission Control, the higher self, and the manipulators can at the same time control the flow of information coming in through the eyes and ears, we can quite easily forget who we really are and what we are doing here."[29] Pulling from authors such as Zecharia Sitchin, who developed pseudo-historical stories of aliens who created humanity as a slave race and served as the inspiration for beings such as the Annunaki in ancient Sumerian and other Mesopotamian literatures as well as the Nephilim from the book of Genesis in the Hebrew Bible. Icke weaves a story in which the Earth and humanity in their present, post–Atlantis forms, have undergone a series of indoctrinations in the form of political and—especially—religious dogma. Humanity, Icke argues, is under the domination of "an organization, which I will call the Brotherhood" which "has been used over thousands of years to manipulate the human race."[30] From the ancient Sumerians, to the Egyptians, Greeks, and Romans, humanity has been under the control of priests, adepts, and emperors. They all "had the same secret codes, symbols, and initiations" and, in modern times, they take the form of secret societies. Like Edith Starr Miller before him, Icke links religious traditions from all times and places into a unified system, believing that "all of these apparently opposing religions were started by the same non-physical manipulatory—Lucifer in his many forms.[31]" He also takes at face value the mythic origins of Masonic lodges, reporting as historical fact that "one of the most active Brotherhood organizations today are the Freemasons and they would seem to have their origins in Sumer and Egypt in the guilds of the stonemasons and craftsmen." Their goal, "like the whole infiltrated Brotherhood through the centuries," is "to keep spiritual knowledge from the general population."[32]

In *The Robots' Rebellion*, Icke begins to link more prosaic political and technological conspiracy theory elements to the more esoteric discussion of secret societies. When discussing the dawn of Islam, Icke speculates that Muhammad's revelations (as well as earlier spiritual events such as the Apostle Paul's conversion) may have been been the result of mind control technology. While Icke thinks that extraterrestrials in the service of Lucifer might have done this, "the CIA today have the ability to abduct someone, implant a micro-chip in their brain, and so hypnotize them that another version of what happened can replace the actual experience in their memory." Like many conspiracy mongers before him, Icke is careful to hedge his bets on this point, conceding, "I am not saying that this happened, I don't know. But it would be naive to dismiss the possibility out of hand, in the light of what we know about mind-controlling techniques today."[33]

Icke's adeptness at making outrageous claims and then, sometimes within the same sentence, backing away from them is crucial for any conspiracy theorist. As the story of *The Robots' Rebellion* reaches the modern age, Icke would embark down a path that would, in some ways, overshadow many of his later claims. Icke presents the often violent political and social upheaval of the eighteenth and nineteenth centuries as "inspired" by the Brotherhood, reporting that "sometimes the monarch would hold on, more often the revolution would usher in a people's dictatorship or 'democratic government.'" Another goal was to "replace religion with the Godless version of science called materialism" in order to "persuade people they were just physical, one-life, accidents with no spirit or eternal purpose."[34] While the Bavarian Illuminati held materialist positions similar to this, Icke recasts an eighteenth century philosophical view on reality as a millennia-long secret plot to undermine humanity.

This line of reasoning and narrative is not too different from what had come before in the book and bears similarities to other conspiracy narratives. Major events and turning points are often attributed to malign manipulative forces. In this discussion of the emergence of the modern age, Icke moves further down the path of well-worn conspiracy theory by invoking *The Protocols of the Elders of Zion*. This book, a well-worn anti–Semitic hoax, emerged in early 20th century Russia and claims to be the record of a meeting of Jewish leaders planning to dominate the world by fomenting war and undermining the morality of western civilization. Though repeatedly debunked, the Protocols persist in popularity within some conspiratorial circles.[35]

Icke claims that "almost everything these documents proposed to do has happened in this century" and that they may have been made public "for the purposes of disinformation, not least in using a title that blames it all on the Jews." Icke argues that the *Protocols* should be referred to as "the Illuminati Protocols."[36] Icke implies that the *Protocols* were made first public and subsequently exposed in order to discredit anyone citing them or ideas contained in them. Thus, if a writer claimed that anything "predicted" by the Protocols was the truth, then that writer could be denounced for taking those Protocols seriously. For the Illuminati, revealing their plan is, paradoxically, a key part of concealing their plan.

As *The Robots' Rebellion* moves into the twentieth century, Icke addresses such common American conspiracy tropes as the Federal Reserve Act ("The Federal Reserve system has refused to be audited since the day it was formed") and the supposedly questionable legality of the 16th Amendment to the Constitution that provided for an income tax:

> Only two states agreed to the Federal Income Tax Amendment and it required at least thirty-six if it was to be legally ratified. When this was obviously not going to happen, the Secretary of State, Filander [sic] Knox, simply told Congress in 1913 that the amendment had been ratified even though it had not.... All the money that people have been forced to pay to the IRS has been a theft![37]

Icke continued to use the *Protocols* to explain the development of the two World Wars (they had been manipulated into existence by the Illuminati)[38] and the Cold War following 1945. In fact, everything has been a manipulation by the Illuminati or Brotherhood. Every political leader, every religious tradition, every historical event is a lie. The goal of these lies is, according to Icke, to establish a New World Order. If the reader is unable to fully accept what Icke is saying, that is because their "consciousness is being challenged to reject the accepted history of humankind, and to see through the smokescreen that much of it is. This is not easy when you have been through the education (indoctrination) system."[39] Icke, using selections from the *Protocols* as well as the well-worn writings of his fellow conspiracy theorists, moves further into the quagmire of the standard conspiracy narrative that had emerged in the late 1980s and early 1990s. Despite adding occasional bits of evidence that he claimed to have "channelled," *The Robots' Rebellion* sees Icke set a course that begins to drift away from the New Age, Green-politics orientation of his first books. Icke does spend the final portion of the book discussing such topics as the need for humanity to overcome the mainstream science establishment and free itself from the destructive need for fossil fuels ("The knowledge of how to tap into the non-physical, sub-atomic, energies that surround us is available today, but the scientific establishment and the system in general does not want to know"[40]). Even the topic of renewable energy, however, is as freighted with conspiracy theory standards as the first part of the book. Among other narratives, Icke invokes tales of the supposed UFO crash at Roswell as well as the Philadelphia Experiment, a convoluted tale of a World War II invisibility experiment which resulted in time travel. Both of these stories had been a fixture in the paranormal and conspiracy theory communities since the early 1980s.[41]

Icke closes *The Robots' Rebellion* with a call to action, imploring concerned readers to take such steps as boycotting "all banks which create money out of nothing charge interest on it" and "refus[ing] to pay interest on their loans." That step, however, "needs to be well coordinated so that millions do it at the same time." Icke also encourages "a refusal to cooperate with and in schools, universities, and government departments in every country, until we have the free flow of information about what is really going on in secret and all the knowledge available."[42] He concludes the book by declaring, "We are here to change the world.... Our time has come. We cannot and we will not fail."[43] Icke emphasizes the need for nonviolent protest, with boycotts and sit ins contrasting sharply with the overtones of violent resistance beginning to take shape in some corners of the conspiracy world in the 1990s.

David Icke's subsequent books, *And the Truth Shall Set You Free* (1995) and *I Am Me, I Am Free* (1996), largely reiterated the key points of *The Robots' Rebellion*, discussing the ancient roots of the Brotherhood/Illuminati and their plans for world domination. It is possible, however, to see further shifts in Icke's approach. Just as *The Robots' Rebellion* moved away from the preponderance of New Age discussion of "truth vibrations," in these later works, Icke is moving toward the fringes of the conspiracy world. He will, through the end of the 1990s, increasingly make that fringe his own. While the earlier book, *And the Truth*, makes references to the most controversial aspects of *The Robots' Rebellion*, particularly *The Protocols of the Elders of Zion*, these are few and far between. *I Am Me, I Am, Free* makes no reference to the *Protocols*. It does, however, point the way forward to Icke's later works and the claims that would garner him as much attention as when he claimed to be the son of the Godhead in 1991.

That book would appear in early 1999. Entitled *The Biggest Secret: The Book That Will Change the World*, it would launch Icke into a much higher public profile as his appearances outside of the UK—particularly in the United States and Canada—would coincide with the debut of his argument that the Brotherhood or Illuminati force that he had discussed in his earlier books were, in fact, not actually human. The earth, in fact, has been invaded by beings from another reality. They are humanoid reptilian beings. Their origins are complex, with Icke presenting three options: "They are extraterrestrials; they are 'inner' terrestrials who live within the Earth; they manipulate humanity from another dimension by 'possessing' human bodies." Icke believes all three of these potential origins are true.[44] In general, however, he focuses on the extra-dimensional aspect of the Reptilian menace. These Reptilians are humanoid, Icke observes, but can "shape shift" in and out of their seemingly human forms. Major political leaders and important cultural figures are, in fact, Reptilians in disguise. Icke connects this Reptilian issue with a long-standing piece of conspiracy lore—the theory that nearly all United States presidents have been related to each other and connected to the British royal family. Harold Brooks-Baker, who published *Burke's Peerage*, a directory of British aristocracy, made predictions in U.S. presidential elections choosing winning candidates based on which one had a closer genetic collection to the royal family. In a 1988 *New York Times* article, for example, Brooks-Baker predicted George H.W. Bush would win over Michael Dukakis. Bush, he reported, was a thirteenth cousin of Queen

Elizabeth II while Dukakis because he was "the son of a Greek immigrant" thus "the chance of getting very far with him is remote."[45] Brooks-Baker's last prediction came shortly before his death in 2004 when he wrongly predicted that John Kerry would defeat President George W. Bush.[46] The ruling classes of humanity, Icke asserts, are the descents of

> a race of interbreeding bloodlines, a race within a race in fact, were centred in the Middle and Near East in the ancient world and, over the thousands of years since, have expanded their power across the globe. A crucial aspect of this has been to create a network of mystery schools and secret societies to covertly introduce their Agenda while, at the same time, creating institutions like religions to mentally and emotionally imprison the masses and set them at war with each other.[47]

The members of these bloodlines are "the reptilian crossbreeds who run the world today and it this profusion of reptilian genes which allows such people to shape-shift into reptilians and back into an apparently human form."[48] As evidence, Icke relies heavily on Cathy O'Brien's stories in *TRANCE Formation of America* as well as other people who have reported encounters with these shapeshifting beings. One unnamed man Icke met in the United States reported that he could detect the hidden lizard people thanks to his fairly heavy drug use:

> He "tripped" on large amounts of LSD in the 1960s and in his seriously mind-altered state he would see some people as humans and others as humanoid lizards and other reptiles. For a while he believed that he was merely hallucinating, but as a regular "tripper" at high doses he began to realise that what he was seeing, usually by the third day of a five-day "trip," was not an hallucination, but the vibratory veils lifting which allowed him to see beyond the physical to the force controlling the person.[49]

Zulu shaman Credo Mutwa is also one of Icke's sources. Icke's interpretation of Mutwa's teaching places the notion of the extraterrestrial roots of humanity within an African context and is a logical extension of Icke's approach. Icke reports spending a day with Mutwa in South Africa during which he learned that "the word Zulu means People from the Stars because they believe they are a royal race that originates beyond this planet. We talked about the global manipulation and his belief that an extraterrestrial race is behind the global Brotherhood of monarchs, politicians, bankers and media owners." Icke also uses elements of popular culture to bolster his argument. Like Bill Cooper did in 1997, Icke suggests that the 1988 horror film *They Live* as a useful illustration of his theories. Further, he urges study of the early 1980s television movie and miniseries *V*, which also featured villains who were reptilian beings disguised in human form.[50]

Beside more thoroughly introducing and explaining the Reptilian angle into his conspiracy framework, *The Biggest Secret* signals the beginning of a new pattern for Icke's books. As noted, Icke spends much of each book reiterating—often in exhaustive detail—the key tenets of his system, particularly the deep historical manipulation of political and religious systems. Each subsequent David Icke book is basically the same, with new information added to keep the books topical. *The Biggest Secret* spends more time tying the British royal family into this narrative never letting the reader forget, of course, that this family is in reality blood-drinking Reptilians from the lower fourth dimension. It also—to emphasize that Icke is engaged in ongoing research—ties the 1997 death of Diana, Princess of Wales, into the wider Reptilian conspiracy. Diana, Icke asserts, undoubtedly knew about the Reptilian truth lurking behind the royal family's facade. Her death, according to Icke, was carefully arranged as an occult sacrifice:

> According to Brotherhood Satanic ritual, Diana had to die in that underground chamber on the ancient sacrificial site and it had to happen at night under the Moon in the goddess month of August, ruled according to legend by the Roman version of Isis, Diana, etc: Juno Augusta. The Satanists in the emergency team simply ensured that Diana would not leave the tunnel (sacrificial chamber) alive. We are told she bled to death and, if this is correct, it was precisely in accordance with their blood rites and sacrificial rites.[51]

This was necessary because, according one of Icke's sources—a woman named Arizona Wilder who claimed to have escaped from mind control torture and slavery at the hands of the Illuminati—the royals had made Diana aware of their true nature before she and Prince Charles were even wed. According to Wilder, "Prince Philip and the Queen Mother then shape-shifted into reptiles to show Diana who they really were. 'Diana was terrified, but quiet,' she said. Diana was told that if she ever revealed the truth about them, she would be killed." Another Icke source, an unnamed, alleged "close confidant" of Diana, recalled that of the Princess's nicknames for the royals was "the lizards" and that "she used to say in in all seriousness: 'They're not human.'"[52]

The title of the book, *The Biggest Secret,* refers to this supposed extra dimensional, possibly extraterrestrial, Reptilian control of humankind. With this claim, Icke seemed to move from being a politian-turned-guru into conspiratorial powerhouse. Speaking engagements and media appearances increased in number. In the midst of this, he would continue publish books in which he reiterated his arguments about the Reptilian bloodlines as well as other aspects of the global conspiracy. Later books would follow this pattern. *Children of the Matrix* (2001) exploits the popularity of the *Matrix* series of movies and appropriates its central them of reality being a construct from which we need to escape, echoing his use of popular media as "evidence" of a global conspiracy. While continuing to develop the story of the Reptilian agenda to subjugate humanity, this installment in the Icke oeuvre largely reiterates what has come before, including the dire waring that this is "the time when we, the people, either bring this hidden dictatorship to an end or face a future, very shortly, in a global fascist state."[53] In his introduction to the book, Icke provides an explanation of this constant restating of his basic points, saying, "Readers of my previous books will see information they already know fused with the latest knowledge and developments because it is important that my books are self contained so that new readers will have all they need to follow the plot."[54]

Innovations in *Children of the Matrix* largely take the form of enhancements and further explanations of information that appeared in *The Biggest Secret*. Icke includes additional information on the various ancient "bloodlines" that rule the world, all of which had their roots in the ancient world. For example, "the Merovingian-Windsor-Bush bloodline and its offshoots include a long list of Pharaohs in ancient Egypt" as well as "the Anunnaki-human hybrids who ruled Sumer, Babylon, Greece, and Troy and which, today, rule the world. In turn, they go back to Atlantis and Lemuria."[55] Icke, following the lead of a great many conspiracy narratives and theorists, includes the Rothschild family as one of these controlling bloodlines. Icke also, in an appendix to the book, discussed the possibility that Adolf Hitler and the Nazi movement was "created and funded" by the Rothschilds and that they, in fact, engineered his rise to power. In fact, Hitler may have even been, Icke asserts, a descendent of the Rotshchilds.[56] Icke also attacks the present-day Rothschilds, describing then-senior family member Guy de Rothschild (1909–2007) as "one of the most grotesque exponents of trauma-based mind control" who "has been personally responsible for the torture and death of millions of children and adults." Additionally, "he conducts Satanic rituals, as all these bloodlines have always done, and goodness knows how many human sacrifices he has been involved in." Icke then dares Rothschild to challenge these accusations in court: "Let's take these claims into the public arena and have you and me in the witness box. Make my day."[57]

Icke has often used this tactic, as journalist Jon Ronson recounted in a 2001 story on David Icke:

> "Why do you think that is?" David Icke had asked me when I interviewed him about this matter in London. Then he turned to my notepad and thundered, "Come on, Ted Heath! Sue me if you've got nothing to hide! Come on, George Bush! I'm ready! Sue me! I'm naming names! Come on, Jon? Why are they refusing to sue me?"

There was a silence. "Because they are twelve-foot lizards?" I suggested, smally.

"Yes!" said David. "Exactly!"[58]

Ronson's story detailed efforts by Canadian activists to notify venues of their concerns about anti–Semitic elements in Icke's work. These warnings had led to radio stations and other outlets refusing allow Icke to present his views. This was not the first time Icke had encountered such trouble in Canada and in *Children of the Matrix* he accused Richard Warman of engaging in a campaign to "preventing me speaking and anyone having the opportunity to hear me anywhere in the world." Icke accuses Warman of being backed by the Bronfman family, one of the "key bloodlines" of the Illuminati. Because Warman worked to—in Icke's view—prevent the spread of truth about the global conspiracy, the world suffered, since "while all this was unfolding, the children went on being abused, tortured, and sacrificed, and the wars and other horrors went on being manipulated as Mr. Warman ... worked so ferociously to stop it being exposed. They have made their priorities very clear."[59]

Warman brought a libel suit against Icke and his publisher in 2002 based on these claims. As part of a 2015 out-of-court settlement, Warman received $90,000 (CDN) from Icke as well as the cessation of sale of *Children of the Matrix* until a new edition could be published with the defamatory claims excised. Warman announced that "this settlement exposes Icke's argument that no one had ever sued him because his allegations were true as nothing more than a fallacy."[60]

Later books would tie Icke's existing claims to current events. *Alice in Wonderland and the World Trade Center Disaster* (2002) and *Tales from the Time Loop* (2003) connected the 9/11 attacks and the subsequent wars into his conspiratorial framework. *Human Race Get Off Your Knees: The Lion Sleeps No More* (2010) and *The Perception Deception* (2013) saw Icke return to his New Age roots, delving into humanity's potential for greatness as well as a continuing emphasis on reality as being an illusion created and manipulated by the Reptilians:

> What I am doing is following the information blueprint for my personal journey in the Metaphysical Universe and bringing it into holographic manifestation. When I was told that all I had to do was "follow the clues" it was another way of saying that all I had to do was stay on the "path" that had been encoded in the Metaphysical Universe.... The Reptilian Control System operates from the Metaphysical Universe and it can see potential challenges before they become a holographic "done deal." The Reptilians work and scheme to make life more difficult for those who are "here" to expose the conspiracy by encoding people and situations into the blueprint to block them, divert them, and generally undermine them.[61]

David Icke continues to be a fixture on talk radio programs and conspiracy theory conferences as well as organizing workshops and seminars and in conspiracy circles on the Internet, he has a substantial following—particularly among newcomers to conspiracy culture, those who are not necessarily aware that many of his claims are not unique. These supporters also accept Icke's claims that he is being persecuted for his efforts to expose the truth. One message board poster (using the handle "M0JFK"), reacting to news of Icke's libel settlement with Richard Warman, paints the settlement as a merciful act on Icke's part, saying, "In other words David let them off when this vile chap Richard Warman should be hung by his ankles from the nearest lamppost. He is a career complainer and gloats often about the poor sods he ruins by his use of lies and distortion and total exaggeration and miss representation [sic] of what people actually say. A vile chap and how he sleeps at night is beyond me."[62] While he seems to be under the impression that Icke filed suit against Warman, M0JFK's ad hominem attacks are telling.

Icke's success continues to rest on two key elements: his charisma and skill as a public speaker and his use of well-worn global-control conspiracy tropes that stood the test of time. Icke's innovative blending of New Age dogma and terminology with alien invasion stories and pseudo-history allowed him to carve a niche that has given him a great deal of prominence in the conspiracy world. While David Icke is not the only conspiracy figure to discuss the concept of "lizard people" being the malign force behind the push for a tyrannical global government, he is arguably the most prominent. In a 2013 study, Public Policy Polling conducted a survey to determine the most widely held conspiratorial beliefs. According to their polling, 4 percent of voters believe "'lizard people' control our societies by gaining political power." This is the least popular conspiracy belief of those listed, falling far behind the 28 percent of voters who believe that a "secretive power elite with a globalist agenda is conspiring to eventually rule the world through an authoritarian world government, or New World Order."[63] The Reptilians, however, probably would not even have been part of the survey without David Icke as a proponent.

Narratives that present the possibility—or, indeed, probability—that forces exist that sought to subjugate humanity represent a significant and persistent theme in conspiracy theories. Cabals of freemasons and Jesuits or reptilians from the lower fourth dimension have populated fears of subjugation for centuries. The targets and suspicions may change over time but overall, they are representative of a pattern of paranoia, one that continues today. Often, as well, fears of secret societies or spiritual subversion tie into more overtly political conspiracies in significant ways.

2

New World Orders

Conspiracy theories concerned with global tyranny became, unsurprisingly, more explicitly political after the Second World War. Communism had already become a favored target of conspiracy theorists. With the advent of the Cold War and the rise of collective security organizations like the United Nations, geopolitical conspiracy theories and narratives became a dominant part of the genre. There would, as we will see, still be connections to those conspiracy theories that relied upon sinister secret societies as a target of fear and suspicion.

John Stormer's 1964 book *None Dare Call It Treason* became a classic of this anti–Communist conspiracism. Stormer asserted that the growth of the communist-controlled world is growing had led to "the hidden tentacles of the communist conspiracy exerting unmeasured influence over the rest of the world. " Asking, "Where have we failed?"[1] Stormer argues that a number of factors contributed to a sense that the Soviet Union could, perhaps, win the Cold War. These included a lessening of anti-communist sentiment since the early 1950s, American involvement in the United Nations, and a lack of public information and education about the goals of international communism have paved the way for a slow but steady communist victory in the United States. Stormer is a bit more ambivalent about the depth of an actual conspiracy, asking,

> Is there a conspiratorial plan to destroy the United States into which foreign aid, planned inflation, distortion of treaty-making powers and disarmament all fit? This question divides many knowledgeable and dedicated conservatives. They waste time and effort and split their ranks with senseless debate. It doesn't really matter whether the "parts" have been planned for an "assembly line revolution" as [Indiana] Senator [William E.] Jenner charged, or if they are the work of well-meaning but misguided idealists.[2]

For Stormer, spending time on determining the exact nature of any extant conspiracy took valuable time and resources away from educating the general public about the dangers of communist influence around the world and in the United States. Later writers would, on the other hand, spend a great deal of time detailing the nature of the conspiracy. Mimicking Stormer's title, Gary Allen's 1971 book *None Care Call It Conspiracy* focuses more extensively on what would become—within two decades—the well-worn paranoid tropes of the central banking conspiracy, pointing to the Rothschild and Warburg families as well as J.P. Morgan as key figures in the effort to create the Federal Reserve System. Allen also adhered to a more conspiratorial view of history than Stormer, asserting, "While all of the standard reasons given for the outbreak of World War I in Europe doubtless were factors, there were also other more important causes. The conspiracy had been planning the war for over two decades."[3]

Gary Allen also contributes another trope to the growing conspiracy conversation. This is the role of political and cultural "insiders" (exemplified for Allen by the Council on Foreign Relations and the Bilderberger organization) in shaping American foreign policy, often in ways that are detrimental to the United States and beneficial to their goals of global control:

> Yes, the *Insiders* have no aversion to working with the Communists whose ostensible goal is to destroy them. While the *Insiders* are serving champagne and caviar to their guests in their summer mansions at Newport, or entertaining other members of the social elite aboard their yachts, their agents are out enslaving and murdering people. And you are next on their list.... It should not be surprising to learn that there is on the international level an organizational equivalent of the C.F.R. This group calls itself the Bilderbergers. If scarcely one American in a thousand has any familiarity with the C.F.R., it is doubtful that one in five thousand has any knowledge of the Bilderbergers. Again, this is not accidental [emphases in original].[4]

Allen observes that prominent members of both the Republican and Democratic parties are members of the Council on Foreign Relations, along with officials from many key corporations, giving lie to the supposed division within the American political system. A key part of this "insider" system was the Rockefeller family. From its roots with John D. Rockefeller (whom Allen connects with the various financially powerful forces such as J.P. Morgan and the Rothschild family) to its contemporary scions and their influence in the Nixon administration, Allen's book identified individuals and organizations that readers could easily track in their daily newspapers, enabling them to become conspiracy theorists in their own living rooms.

The Rockefeller family was a frequent target of conspiracy theory in the United States. One of their detractors was Peter Beter, a conspiracy theorist whose frequently outlandish conspiracy theories also targeted the Federal Reserve system and the Soviet Union. He spread his message through recorded messages distributed on cassette tape to subscribers, released monthly from 1975 to 1982. Beter claimed that the Soviets had planted short range nuclear missiles just off the coast of the United States and that the U.S. and USSR had fought an orbital conflict with space-based weapons which he called the "Battle of the Harvest Moon." It was, however, Beter's tales of assassinated and replaced political figures that remain his most outlandish legacy.

Beter alleged that the Russians had created human duplicates called "organic robotoids." According to Beter, "A robotoid is alive in the biological sense but it is an artificial life form. Robotoids respond to conventional routine medical tests.... Robotoids can also think, but they think only in the sense that a computer does." However, the robotoids only a brief life expectancy, and "die" fairly quickly. Their uses are limited because "organic robotoids are extremely expensive, troublesome creatures to produce and utilize; and robotoid capabilities do not exceed those of human beings. All they can really do is simulate human beings; but, my friends, for intelligence purposes that's all they have to do!"

President-elect Jimmy Carter with Rosalynn and Amy Carter on Inauguration Day, January 20, 1977 (photograph by Thomas J. O'Halloran, Library of Congress Prints and Photographs Division). According to Peter Beter, all three would eventually be assassinated and replaced by "organic robotoids."

Russian operatives schemed with elements of the Rockefeller family to use organic robotoids as replacements for powerful and prominent public figures around the world. They were part of a "war of doubles" between two factions of Russians—one of which was allied with the Rockefellers. Among those American leaders replaced with an organic robotoid was President Jimmy Carter. Peter Beter's evidence was irrefutable: "Only a few months ago Carter had been limping around with what we were told were severe hemorrhoids; but now, out of the blue, here was a Carter who was a powerhouse—hiking, fishing, and jogging ten miles a day, he also looked and sounded younger than before."[5] Just as troublingly, the month before that revelation about President Carter, Beter revealed, "On Friday night, April 20, the real Walter Mondale was being held incommunicado by Bolshevik captors in New Richmond in western Wisconsin. Sometime between 9:30 and 10:00 p.m. local time, Vice-President Walter Mondale was executed!" The American people had not, however, known because "barely an hour later, Mondale's body was dumped into Lake Superior at a point about 12 miles southeast of Taconite Harbor, Minnesota. Meanwhile Air Force II was already on its way westward across the Atlantic with a Mondale 'double' aboard."[6] Beter's approach blended the increasingly prominent targeting of "insiders," be they members of prominent political or financial families as well as those associated with organizations like the Council on Foreign Relations. Organic robotoids were not, however, a prerequisite for shadowy undertakings by political actors.

The United States government engaged in a number of covert activities that ranged from scientific to political during the 1950s and 1960s. Often, these activities were part and parcel of the wider American effort during the Cold War to disrupt, disperse, or otherwise contain the expansion of Soviet- or Chinese-backed communism.

The December 22, 1974, edition of the *New York Times* featured a front page report by journalist Seymour Hersh that exposed wide ranging surveillance operations conducted by the Central Intelligence Agency against a number of activist groups, including anti-war organizations during the Nixon Administration. The investigation, which concluded that "the Central Intelligence Agency, directly violating its charter, conducted a massive, illegal domestic intelligence operation during the Nixon Administration" which involved "intelligence files on at least 10,000 American citizens" collected by agents operating outside of the normal channels of the CIA, reporting directly to Richard Helms, the Director of Central Intelligence.

The impact of this story was significant. While there had been earlier reports and investigations of the U.S. Army engaging in domestic intelligence operations, the involvement of the CIA triggered more incisive and direct action by the federal government. In December 1974 President Gerald Ford established the United States President's Commission on CIA Activities within the United States, usually referred to as the Rockefeller Commission after its chair, Vice President Nelson Rockefeller. On the legislative side, the Senate voted on to January 27, 1975, to establish an investigatory committee under the leadership of Frank Church (D–Idaho), popularly known as the Church Committee. The Committee found a wide array of programs designed to gather intelligence and data. Much of this intelligence was, as Hersh's article indicated, directed at supposedly subversive organizations and—as it took place within the United States—outside the jurisdiction of the Agency.

A number of intelligence related escapades came to light through these investigations. The most exotic and well known of these efforts were often overseas—CIA-backed coups d'état in Iran, Chile, or Guatemala for example. The domestic implications of these investigations, however, would have a significant impact on the conspiracy narratives that developed in the closing decades of the twentieth century. There arose a notion of a dedicated effort by the federal government (or elements of the federal government) to surveil and—potentially—round up and imprison those whose political views were out of line with those of the powerful and influential (the "insiders" as Gary Allen might have called them). This fear would become one of the most prevalent in the conspiracy culture of the 1980s and 1990s.

The United States government had, of course, imprisoned those who were believed to be threats to national security. Executive Order 9066, issued by Franklin Roosevelt on February 19, 1942, ordered the detention of over 100,000 persons of Japanese descent (as well as a far smaller number of German- and Italian-Americans). In the 1980s, however, investigation of the Iran-Contra affair uncovered hints of plans being put in place to suppress political expression and speech. In the July 5, 1987, edition of the *Miami Herald*, Alfonso Chardy reported that "Congressional investigators and administration officials" discovered that Lieutenant Colonel Oliver North "helped draw up a controversial plan to suspend the Constitution in the event of a national crisis, such as nuclear war, violent and widespread internal dissent or national opposition to a U.S. military invasion abroad." The organizational structure developed to implement this potential plan operated like a "secret government-within-a-government." North collaborated with the Federal Emergency Management Agency "from 1982 to 1984" in "revising contingency plans for dealing with nuclear war, insurrection or massive military mobilization." Attorney General William Smith objected to part of the operation that involved "a secret contingency plan that called for suspension of the

Constitution, turning control of the United States over to FEMA, appointment of military commanders to run state and local governments and declaration of martial law during a national crisis." The plan, however, "did not define national crisis, but it was understood to be nuclear war, violent and widespread internal dissent or national opposition against a military invasion abroad." The *Herald* obtained a letter from the Attorney General in which he expressed concern that "the role assigned to the Federal Emergency Management Agency in the revised Executive Order exceeds its proper function as a coordinating agency for emergency preparedness.... This department and others have repeatedly raised serious policy and legal objections to the creation of an 'emergency czar' role for FEMA." The *Herald*, however, acknowledged that "it is unclear whether the executive order was signed or whether it contained the martial law plans."[7] These plans came to more widespread public attention during the July 14, 1987, Iran-Contra hearings when Representative Jack Brooks (D–TX) questioned North about his role in developing the plan. Before North could respond, that line of questioning was interrupted by concerns that any answer North gave could compromise national security. The FEMA-oriented part of this contingency for national emergency was designated REX 84 (an abbreviation for "Readiness Exercise 1984") and such plans were far from unique in American history.

REX 84 and its military counterpart, with the cryptonym "Garden Plot," would be consistent features in a number of New World Order globalist-oriented conspiracy theories throughout the 1990s and early twenty-first century. As we will see, conspiracists such as William Cooper used such contingency plans as a cornerstone of his contentions that the federal government was plotting to lock up those who opposed the coming global government. Comments and articles on the topic appeared in "alternative press" publications like *The Phoenix Liberator*, a newsletter that blurred the lines between political paranoia and the paranormal. *The Phoenix Liberator* featured articles which, supposedly, had been psychically channeled from "Gyeorgos Ceres Hatonn," who described himself as "Commander in Chief, Earth Project Transition, Pleiades Sector Flight command, Intergalactic Federation Fleet-Ashtar Command" and served as the "Earth Representative to the Cosmic Council and Intergalactic Federation Council on Earth Transition … a fourth dimensional Project Commander in charge of Earth Transition."[8] Despite these otherworldly origins, Hatonn often addressed topics that were resolutely earthly and political in nature.

In July 1992, Hatonn presented a conversation with an informant who claimed

2. New World Orders

> I ... had a friend and drinking buddy who was "career army." He was assigned duties with the California Specialized Training Institute which was based at Camp San Luis. He was discouraged and disgusted to learn that certain portions of his army were training to fight a new war against a very unusual enemy, **the citizens of the United States of America!** A plan called **"Rex 84" from the Federal Emergency Management Agency** (FEMA) *would suspend the Constitution and install martial law!*[9] [emphasis in original].

This story, based on existing plans, would surface repeatedly in conspiracy literature during the 1990s. The 1994 film *America Under Siege*, written, produced, and directed by militia activist Linda Thompson, contained the following narration over footage of trains carrying tanks through the American countryside and the building at the Amtrak repair facility in Beech Grove, Indiana—a facility which Thompson claimed was actually a detention center to which the forces of the New World Order would condemn patriotic Americans:

> Are these tanks part of operation garden plot? To be used to round us up for the slave labor camps, along with the black helicopters and federal law enforcement that look like active duty military stationed in our roadways as they were in Waco? Welcome to the New World Order. Expect no mercy.[10]

At the time that Hatonn was writing and Thompson was filming, the documentation for Garden Plot was classified. These documents would, eventually, reach the public in the early years of the twenty-first century as the federal government revamped its domestic security operations in the wake of the terror attacks of September 11, 2001.

Defense department documents about operation Garden Plot have been declassified and released to the public following the reorganization of disaster-preparedness operations that took place after the terror attacks of September 11, 2001. A 1978 iteration of the Garden Plot program outline four instances in which forces might be activated:

a. Aid state authorities at the request of the state.
b. Enforce the laws of the United States in any state or territory.
c. Protect the civil rights of citizens within a state.
d. Protect Federal property and functions.

And in a more expansive explanation of the circumstances in which Garden Plot might be activated, the report stated that "sudden and unexpected civil disturbances or other emergencies endangering life or Federal property or disrupting the normal processes of government which require that immediate military action be taken to protect life or Federal property Or to prevent disruption of Federal activities."[11] As the *Miami Herald* article reported, the definitions of and required conditions for the federal government or military to take these actions are quite vague.

The 1978 version of the Garden Plot plan described the instigating event as "the President is advised by the highest officials of the state, that the situation cannot be controlled with the resources available."[12] Regardless of the reason for military forces being called into service, the bulk of Garden Plot consists of carefully designed procedures to be followed to ensure that the

Operation Garden Plot was a collection of plans and operational orders for the imposition of military support for civilian government in the event of "civil disturbance."

2. New World Orders 53

APPENDIX 3 (COMMAND RELATIONSHIPS FOR EMPLOYMENT) TO ANNEX H (COMMAND RELATIONSHIPS) TO DEPARTMENT OF THE ARMY CIVIL DISTURBANCE PLAN

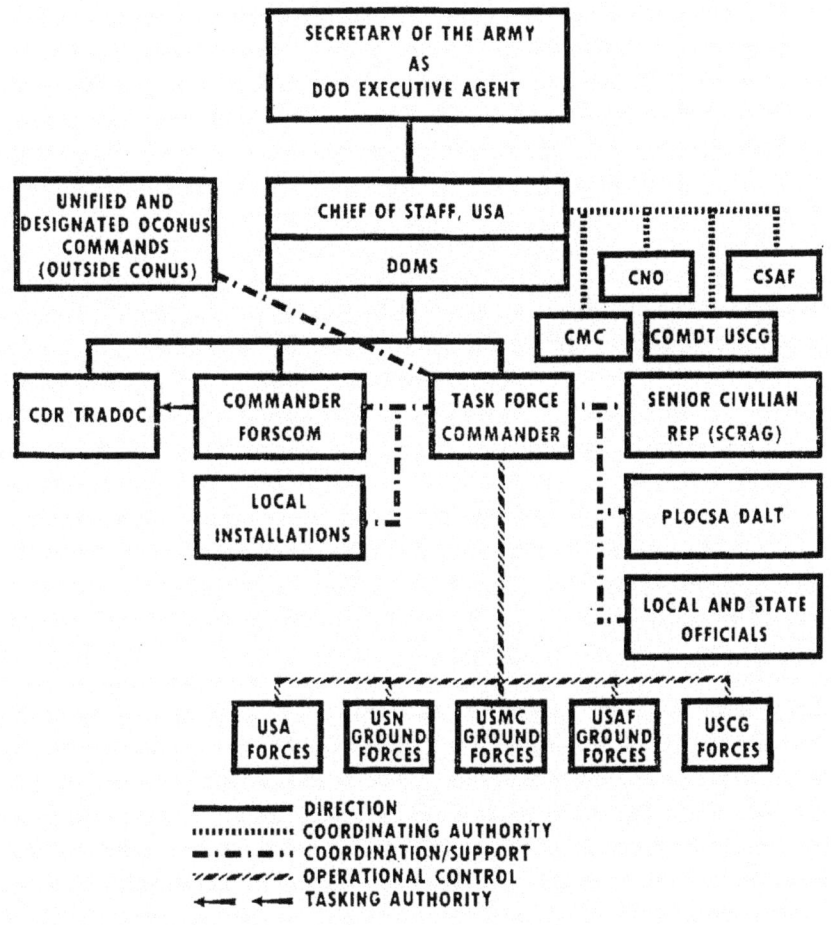

H-3-1

While Garden Plot was certainly headed by military officials, this organizational chart illustrates how civilian officials would have been integrated into the emergency plans.

division of authority between civilian and military elements is properly maintained. For example, in setting out the various jurisdictions and areas of responsibility in the event of a severe civil disturbance, Garden Plot clearly states "the Attorney General is the chief civilian official in charge of coordinating all Federal Government activities relating to civil disturbances."[13] While this may have been a distinction without a difference to those dissidents who may be the target of military action, it does establish that Garden Plot did not set out to establish martial law in the strictest legal sense of the term.

The various military departments responsible for designing Garden Plot—generally the Army and Air Force—would periodically update the plans to account for changes in policy and procedure. Small, but substantive, changes to the 1991 iteration of Garden Plot were made in 1996. These changes are to the guidelines or the authorization of deadly force, with criteria for the use of deadly force becoming more stringent. For example:

- "Self defense to avoid death or serious injury" is amended to read "Self defense against a hostile person or force to avoid imminent death or serious bodily injury posed by the hostile force."
- "Prevention of the destruction of public utilities or similar property vital to public health or safety" is changed to "Prevention of the destruction of public utilities or similar critical infrastructure vital to public health or safety, damage to which would imperil life.
- The permission to use deadly force in the "detention or prevention of the escape of persons who have committed or attempted to commit" serious crimes is amended with the caveat that such force is permitted "only if escape of the persons would pose and imminent danger of death or serious physical injury to military or law enforcement personnel or to any other person."[14]

While the documentation supporting Garden Plot does not make mention of the deadly 1992 Ruby Ridge standoff or the 1993 Branch Davidian compound disaster in Waco, Texas, these additional restrictions on deadly force seem to address what many in the conspiracy culture have seen as a failure of government restraint in those situations. Along with the revelation of REX 84 and Garden Plot's existence, these violent and, ultimately, deadly incidents galvanized the right wing conspiratorial community in the early 1990s.

During the late 1980s and early 1990s, Federal law enforcement officials had been investigating white supremacist organizations in the American west. Randy Weaver, who had been associated with such groups, was caught in a sting operation selling a short-barreled shotgun to federal law enforcement officers. When Weaver refused to act as an informant for the Justice Department, he was indicted. When he missed a 1991 court hearing, law enforcement began plans to arrest Weaver. Weaver and his family had moved to a cabin in the hills of Idaho, adopting a survivalist lifestyle. Knowing the Weavers had a number of firearms, the U.S. Marshals and FBI used caution. Caution, however, was not encouraging Weaver to surrender to law enforcement, despite the fact that the agents had already killed his 14-year-old son. As *New York Times* writer Clyde Habermas wrote,

> On the fly, Federal Bureau of Investigation officials loosened their rules of engagement for their agents. An order to shoot any armed man on sight was now in effect. When Mr. Weaver came into view, an F.B.I. sniper, Lon Horiuchi, fired and wounded him in the arm. As the family scrambled, another round hit Vicki Weaver in the head, killing her as she held her 10-month-old girl. That bullet kept going, wounding Kevin Harris, a young man staying with the Weavers.[15]

A few days after this, Weaver surrendered. Although placed on trial, he was acquitted on most charges. The federal government would, eventually, award more than $3 million in damages to Weaver and his surviving children.

As Weaver stood trial, a federal siege of the Branch Davidian compound near Waco, Texas, began to unravel. For 51 days, the Bureau of Alcohol, Tobacco, and Firearms had been mired in a standoff with the religious group that was suspected of federal firearms law violations. During a shootout at the beginning of the siege, four agents and six residents of the compound had been killed. The final federal assault led to a fire (of disputed origin) in which 75 of 84 people inside the compound died. Congress would subject both the Ruby Ridge and Waco incidents to investigation. For many (particularly on the political right) who were already suspicious of the actions of the Bill Clinton administration, inconsistent explanations from Attorney General Janet Reno about her reasoning behind the final assault added to their concerns. Reno had "told TV reporters shortly after the fiery conclusion to the siege that she had authorized the FBI assault because 'we had reports that [children] had been sexually abused, that babies had actually been beaten.'" However, "the FBI quickly corrected her, saying that it never had evidence of child abuse during the 51-day standoff—a point she eventually conceded." At her subsequent testimony to Congress, Reno claimed that she had ordered the raid because of "an escalating threat in April 1993 from armed groups converging on the Branch Davidians compound from around the country. But she could cite only one example, the so-called Unorganized Militia of the United States, which she said was en route to Waco during the standoff 'either to help Koresh or to attack him.'" The "Unorganized Militia of the United States" consisted mostly of Indianapolis attorney and activist Linda Thompson, along with a van full of supporters.[16] The unclear communication did not go unnoticed by Congress, with a Congressional investigation concluding that "every agency involved with the Weaver case was careless at some level in the way it handled information." Later, FBI director Louis Freeh, in testifying about Ruby Ridge, "admitted to 'a series of terribly flawed law enforcement operations with tragic consequences.'"[17]

A perception grew that the government as well as the media had manipulated public perception in both the Ruby Ridge and Waco incidents. That view was, unsurprisingly, shared by those involved in the situation. In his book, *Them: Adventures with Extremists*, journalist Jon Ronson recounts a conversation with Jack McLamb, who had been present at the Ruby Ridge siege. According to McLamb, "the first thing Randy Weaver yelled though the cabin walls at him, the very first thing he yelled to the outside world, having been under siege for a week ... was, "*Why is the radio calling me a white supremacist when those are not my views?*"[18] (emphasis in original). The Weavers were, to the contrary, white *separatists*, a slight distinction and one often lost in reporting. Moreover, David Thibodeau, one of the few to survive the catastrophe at Waco and the only one who was not sentenced to prison, believed that media representation had contributed to the deaths at the Branch Davidian compound, asserting that "journalists by and large vigorously set about demonizing us, creating climate in which federal agencies and their political masters were allowed, even encouraged, to wipe us out. Conjured into a bunch of maniacal words by the press, we were dehumanized and made ripe for murder."[19]

Ruby Ridge and Waco were, said Clyde Haberman, "a one-two punch, as some put it. It gave antigovernment militias and assorted extremists ample proof, as if they needed more, that the federal authorities were inherently a force for evil."[20] When viewed in connection with the acknowledged reality of plans like REX 84 and Garden Plot, these events reinforced the beliefs of those who harbored suspicions of the federal government rounding up and imprisoning or eliminating those who did want to be part of the cultural and political mainstream. Concerns about the growing "patriot movement" and their armed militias—as expressed by Janet Reno—led to increased media scrutiny on the phenomena which, in turn, led to fears on the extremist right about the same media manipulation they perceived at work at Ruby Ridge and Waco. Timothy McVeigh, convicted of carrying out the deadly bombing of Oklahoma City's Murrah Federal Building in 1995, cited those two incidents as part of the motivation for his actions, saying, "What the U.S. government did at Waco and Ruby Ridge was dirty ... and I gave dirty back to them at Oklahoma City."[21] When investigators and the media connected McVeigh and his co-conspirator Terry Nichols to several militia groups, some militia activists suspected that the entire incident had been manufactured to discredit and bring suspicion on the militias. One story was that McVeigh was a sleeper agent for the secret government and that in 1993 he was ordered "to prepare a strike team to do a domestic bombing event" due to the fact that "after Waco, the patriot, militia and survivalist movements all grew in strength and some of the government people saw this as one of the largest threats to ever face the nation."[22]

Some within the patriot movement believed incidents like Ruby Ridge, Waco, the Oklahoma City bombings, and later terror events were "false flag" attacks carried out by the government as an excuse to extend its power. In 2012, writer Dave Hodges outlined his belief that the theatre shootings in Aurora, Colorado, were, in fact, a government plan undertaken to force additional gun control laws on the American people (including the possibility of a United Nations treaty that would suppressed the Second Amendment. Linking together a string of tragedies, Hodges warns,

> JFK, RFK, 9/11, Oklahoma City, Ruby Ridge, Waco; We won't get fooled again! … Members of the Obama administration are on record of having said that the only way that the Obama presidency survives into a second term is if the country will unite behind an Obama candidacy following a series of terrorist events which will culminate in a second term…. [Such as] the possible carrying out of this event as well as a series of possible false flag events coming in the future (e.g., in Chicago and at the London Olympics).[23]

The deaths at Ruby Ridge and Waco would have a resonance in the conspiracy community, particularly among the conspiracists of the right. These events were evidence, in their minds, that they were not paranoid to think that the federal government would use deadly force to eliminate those whose political or religious beliefs were outside some accepted norm.

By 1995, when the Oklahoma City bombing took place, the pieces of the late twentieth century global domination conspiracy narrative were in place. Previous conspiracies had targeted specific groups such as the communists, the freemasons, the Jews, the Catholics, "insiders" like the Rockefellers or the members of the Council on Foreign Relations. By the 1990s, however, *all* of these groups and many more had been combined in a broader super-conspiracy. As conspiracy-oriented radio talk show host Alex Jones told Jon Ronson, "The Bilderbergers … are the Roman Senate. It's a pyramid. They're way up there. Below them you've got the IMF, the World Bank, the United Nations, then you've got us down here, the cattle, the human resources."[24] Members of the patriot community perceived vast and seemingly diverse forces arrayed against them. They wished to keep the people of the United States free of both an overbearing federal government as well as international entanglements and, of course, firmly within the realm of a strict interpretation of the U.S. Constitution. Ruby Ridge and Waco, however, demonstrated that the federal government would use any means at its disposal to prevent that.

One distinguishing characteristic of conspiracy narrative and culture in the 1990s was the role of issuing strong calls for people to take action. One example of this is a pamphlet entitled "Operation Vampire Killer 2000: American Police Action Plan for Stopping World Government Rule." Written in 1992 by conspiracy theorist Jack McLamb (who would later be present at the Ruby Ridge standoff), this is a guide for law enforcement to help them resist "internationalists" who seek to subjugate the United States and " promote an active program that will defend America from those at work forming an oligarchy of Imperialism against this nation of free people." It calls upon "the People's Protectors (the Police, Guardsmen and Military)" to assist "their countrymen in the private sector" against the threat of a "New Age/New World Order Government Plan":

> Many of our nation's INTERNAL PROTECTORS know of the well laid plan which will culminate in the year 2000, to usher the United States, along with the rest of the nations of the world, into a "utopian" global community allegedly under the control of a "philanthropic" United Nations. A great many of our fellow Officers and National Guardsmen are taking a stand against this plan because they realize that their fellow Americans were never allowed to know of this plan nor given the opportunity to vote on such a change in their government…. These elitists and their families have made most of their massive fortunes off the American people, and have dedicated entire lifetimes to using public funds to subjugate the People to the will of their new world ARISTOCRACY [capitalization in original].

While some of the military and law enforcement personnel in the United States are vaguely aware of this danger

> few realize that the actual behind the scenes plan is for an oligarchy of the world's richest families to place ½ the masses of the earth in servitude under their complete control, administered from behind the false front of the United Nations. To facilitate management capabilities, the plan calls for the elimination of the other 2.5 billion people through war, disease, abortion and famine by the year 2000. As we can plainly see, their plan for "Population Control" (reduction) is well established and under way.

"Operation Vampire Killer 2000" attributed very specific goals to the New World Order. As we have seen, however, the notion of a sinister foreign force subverting the sovereignty of the United States and the liberty of its people is well-worn. The New World Order or the United Nations have not just taken the place of the Roman Catholic Church or the freemasons. Rather, the global conspiracy that emerged in the 1980s and 1990s subsumed nearly all of the previous concerns, blending them together in a melange of fear and paranoia. Like other anti–NWO tracts of the time, "Operation Vampire Killer 2000" largely consists of quotations, many of them provided with little context. Two examples used in OVK2000 (that also emerge repeatedly within the wider genre) come from President George H.W. Bush in the wake of the

Cold War. In 1991, Bush said, "My vision of a NEW WORLD ORDER foresees a United Nations with a revitalized peacekeeping function." And in 1992, "It is the SACRED principles enshrined in the UN Charter to which we will henceforth pledge our allegiance." The author of OVK2000 opined that these statements "ought to FRY THE GRITS OF EVERY LAWMAN AND TRUE AMERICAN THAT READS THIS QUOTE. Brother and sister Officers, how many of you are going to take a "sacred" oath of allegiance to the U.N. World Government?"[25] (capitalization in original).

While the dire predictions of "Operation Vampire Killer 2000" regarding world government and the subjugation of American sovereignty have not come to pass, the fears the document embodied persisted into the twenty-first century. In 2009, U.S. Army veteran Stewart Rhodes founded an organization called "Oath Keepers." Described by the Southern Poverty Law Center as "a particularly worrisome example of the Patriot revival,"[26] the group identifies its membership and mission as "a non-partisan association of current and formerly serving military, police, and first responders who pledge to fulfill the oath all military and police take to "defend the Constitution against all enemies, foreign and domestic."[27] Just like Operation Vampire Killer 2000, the Oath Keepers see a special role for the military and police in preventing disaster.

The Oath Keepers represent one of the most recent iterations of the various strands of conspiracy narrative we have seen in this chapter. The Oath Keepers website includes a paged entitled "Declaration of Orders We Will Not Obey"—a listing of potential triggers for resistance to the federal government. As their website states, "Such orders would be acts of war against the American people by their own government, and thus acts of treason. We will not make war against our own people. We will not commit treason. We will defend the Republic." While the Oath Keepers website does not explicitly call for armed insurrection against the government, its use of the phrase "acts of war" is certainly freighted with meaning. The list of offending orders reflects many of the same fears as conspiracy narratives of the 1980s and 1990s. For example, "We will NOT obey any order to blockade American cities, thus turning them into giant concentration camps" and "We will NOT obey any order to force American citizens into any form of detention camps under any pretext" (emphases in original) certainly evoke the specter of REX-84 and Operation Market Garden. Similarly, this inappropriate order—"we will NOT obey orders to assist or support the use of any foreign troops on U.S. soil against the American people to 'keep the peace' or to 'maintain control' during any emergency, or under any other pretext. We will consider such use of foreign troops against our people to be an invasion and an act of war" (emphasis in original)—evokes fears of UN armies marching on the United States, detaining patriots. This is, again, reminiscent of conspiracy theories of the 1990s, particularly discussions of the so-called "quadrant sign code." This was a conspiracy theory that focused on state or federal Department of Transportation stickers placed on the back of road signs. While various transportation departments claimed the stickers were for benign purposes, Jim Keith, drawing on the work of Michigan researcher Harold R. Green, Jr., explains that "these stickers are widely alleged to incorporate a secret code that will be used during a New World Order takeover in directing foreign troops who do not understand English to their destinations in the U.S." Green believed he had deciphered a system in which the positioning of these stickers in particular "quadrants" of signs indicated where invading military convoys would turn as they transported loyal American patriots to detention camps.[28] The Oath Keepers, while deeply immersed in at least some of the conspiratorial trappings prevalent in the 1990s, avoid ephemera like this and present slightly more logical justifications for their fears and suspicions. They do not mention REX84 or Operation Market Garden. They do not present evidence of "FEMA concentration camps" in suburban Indianapolis. Rather, they present these threats (such as that of detention centers) as something grounded in historical precedent:

> Mass, forced internment into concentration camps was a hallmark of every fascist and communist dictatorship in the 20th Century. Such internment [sic] was unfortunately even used against American citizens of Japanese descent during World War II. Whenever a government interns its own people, it treats them like an occupied enemy population. Oppressive governments often use the internment of women and children to break the will of the men fighting for their liberty—as was done to the Boers, to the Jewish resisters in the Warsaw Ghetto, and to the Chechens, for example.[29]

Those examples are much easier, rhetorically, to defend than decades-old civil unrest scenarios such as REX84. That plan, Market Garden, grainy photographs of the Amtrak train yard in suburban Indianapolis, and the other hallmarks of right wing conspiracism are still out there, living on smaller scale websites, recirculating anecdotes and theories from the 1990s. The Oath Keepers are a fresh face of conspiracy theory on the Internet (as well as in the "real" world), appealing to newer populist movements within American politics but still retaining the fears and suspicions of decades past. Indeed, it is difficult to know the extent to which followers of or advocates for the Oath Keepers are aware of the longevity and persistence of these ideas. Rarely do conspiracy-oriented websites or books set out the long history of such theories. For new readers, novitiates in the conspiratorial cloister, such claims are new and relevant.

This supposition of imminent danger is a defining characteristic of 1990s conspiracy literature. In the examples that follow, we will examine two of the key figures in the conspiracy culture of the 1990s, Bill Cooper and David Icke. Their work exemplifies the long tradition that undergirded this culture as well as the manner in which the conspiracy culture of the end of the twentieth and the beginning of the twenty-first century absorbed and integrated a vast and diverse collection of ideas.

William Cooper

Milton William "Bill" Cooper was a key figure in the UFO and conspiracy communities from the late 1980s until his death in 2001. A critical aspect of his significance was the manner in which his ideas blended the worlds of UFO belief, global conspiracy, and fears of powerful, ancient secret societies. He played an important role in politicizing the paranormal during the 1990s. Cooper emerged into the UFO scene in the 1980s presenting himself as a whistleblower, alleging that he had scene secret information that verified a number of political and extraterrestrial conspiracy theories. Cooper alleged that he had seen top secret information about extraterrestrial contact, the John F. Kennedy assassination, and other conspiracies as an enlisted man in the U.S. Navy in the early 1970s.

This entree onto the UFO and conspiracy scene was entitled "The Secret Government: The Origin, Identity, and Purpose of MJ-12." Cooper attempted to put together the pieces of various extraterrestrial-themed conspiracies and—presumably—make some sort of name for himself. In his introduction, he states that "some of this information was derived from sources that I cannot divulge for obvious reasons." Cooper claimed that his conclusions were "the only scenario that has been able to cohesively bind all the diverse elements which have been driving researchers to tears in their quest for answers."[30] The explicitly UFOlogical aspects of Cooper's career will be a part of the story in the next chapter, but his attempts to "cohesively bind" different conspiracy narratives together would lead to his crucial role as a nexus point connecting ufology, political conspiracy, and the deep historical and esoteric conspiracy theories.

"The Secret Government," Cooper's one of first publicly released articles on the supposed UFO cover-up, clearly presented a political conspiracy angle in addition to speculation about the origin and intentions of the alien visitors by discussing the hidden cabal at the heart of the American political structure that sought to monopolize power. When the political, social, and cultural situation was right, this "secret government" would suspend the Constitution and declare martial law. The secret alien army of implanted humans and all dissidents, which translates into anyone they choose, will be rounded up and placed in the one-mile-square concentration camps which already exist.... Anyone who resists will be taken or killed. This entire operation was rehearsed by the government and military in 1984 under the code name REX-84A and it went off without a hitch. When these events have transpired, the SECRET GOVERNMENT and/or ALIEN takeover will be complete. Your freedom will never be returned and you will live in slavery for the remainder of your life. You had better wake up and you had better do it now![31]

Thus, with Cooper's writing came one of the first and the one of the most lasting connections between the paranormal and political conspiracy theories and paranoia. Cooper promoted a vision of the government (whether the elected government, the "secret government," or elements of each) that had extensive plans for rounding up, imprisoning, and possibly executing millions of Americans deemed to be dangerous. Cooper's prophecies invoked the specter of pure totalitarian oppression.

Cooper's connections between the world of UFO and more prosaic political conspiracy narratives encompassed other topics. In 1990, Cooper uploaded to a BBS (Bulletin Board System) a collection of writing which would become known as "The Release of the Cooper Material." Cooper claimed that it had been uploaded to his personal network and was "obviously written by someone who has access to the same Top Secret information to which I also had access." He urged readers to use caution, for "the information could be true or could only be partly true." This document addressed myriad topics of interest UFO conspiracy buffs but also drifted into the more political realm:

> The coming currency call-in is related to drug money laundering.... The ban on assault weapons will soon be extended to every gun. A declaration of martial law, with the resulting major security upgrade to deal with the alien crisis, will be much easier when these things occur. The drug situation started out as a social experiment back in the 1800s. There was a question of whether people could be controlled by the use of drugs and to what extent.... The experiment ran its course, and yielded little in terms of the controlling effects that were desired. The side benefit, however, was billions of dollars in profits from the selling of drugs. The drug situation has assisted the funding of the aliens in building their underground civilization. Much of this money has gone into helping them in their efforts to establish bases underground. In exchange, the United States got technology a promise that the aliens would not go to war with the United States or other countries of the world.[32]

Here we have a panoramic view of 1980s and 1990s conspiracy narrative with topics such as an illicit drug economy being a government plot, taken out of its plausible context of money laundering and influencing international politics and places it in the more paranoid milieu of social control experimentation and connecting back into the larger issue of extraterrestrial visitation and collusion between the aliens and the U.S. government.

These sorts of connections would be a hallmark of Cooper's writing, blending paranormal and political paranoia and conspiracies so thoroughly that it became difficult to determine where one aspect ended and the other began.

Cooper would stick to his ufological guns into 1991, publishing *Behold a Pale Horse*. The book is a compilation of Cooper's writings, slightly rewritten from online postings, as well as newspaper clippings, copies of correspondence and declassified government documents. He also included a copy of the *Protocols of the Elders of Zion*, but other conspiracy researchers claimed that its supposed indictment of a Jewish plot for global domination was disinformation, designed to throw people off the trail of the real threat. What was that threat?

While *Behold a Pale Horse* offers a précis of Cooper's views in the early 1990s, the key document for understanding Cooper's point of view in later years is simply called "MAJESTYTWELVE." Cooper states that this was the name of "a set of Top Secret documents" he saw while in the U.S. Navy. MAJESTYTWELVE is an account of how numerous aspects of popular culture, conspiracy culture, religion, and other aspects of life are connected to a shadowy group of elites who have existed since the dawn of recorded history, outlining their "plan for the destruction of the united States of America and the formation of a socialist totalitarian world government." The title referred to the "planned placement of ultimate power in a body of wise men who are destined to rule the world as the disciples of a Messiah front man. This Messiah will serve as a buffer between the wise men and the sheople [sic]." What has changed from Cooper's previous writings is that the extraterrestrial invasion angle is so altered as to be nearly absent. He issues a *mea culpa* for this—possibly the only mistake to which Cooper ever admitted[33]—saying, "For many years I sincerely believed that an extraterrestrial threat existed and that it was the most important driving force behind world events. I was wrong and for that I most deeply and humbly apologize." Prominent UFO researchers were, he claimed, "socialist change agents" who were " Illuminati, Marxist, CIA, or KGB ... agents operating in furtherance of propagandizing the American People."[34]

This conspiracy, and the "socialist change agents" that comprise it, are made up of the "highest adepts of the combined total of the so-called fraternal orders and secret societies. They are bound together by blood oaths, a secret religion, and the promise of an elite status within regional government, or the world supra government." This Illuminati is a quite varied group but they share, according to Cooper, a common spirituality, their religious beliefs encompassing "the Kabbalah, the Luciferian Philosophy, and the worship of the Sun." The Illuminati is a threat not only to the United States but to every sovereign nation, for "they are not bound by any oath or allegiance save their own. They are loyal to no government or People save their own. And they are Citizens of no country save their already in place secret world government." To bolster his assertion that this cabal of fiends is truly antithetical the wellbeing of humanity, Cooper advises that anyone who wishes to more fully understand the degree of penetration achieved by the Illuminati should watch the film *They Live*, a 1988 horror flick which starred professional wrestler Rowdy Roddy Piper as a man attempting to expose the secret takeover of the world by a race of reptilian aliens disguised as humans. At the highest levels, the leadership of "Freemasonry, Theosophical Society, Anthroposophic Society, Fraternitis Rosae Crucae, Knights Templar, Sovereign and Military Order of the Knights of Malta" and other secret societies are, according to Cooper, part of this Illuminati. Understanding the depth of the philosophy taught by the Illuminati and the "mystery schools" that preceded it is impossible "without many years of study and a complete knowledge of their 'symbolic' language." But Cooper helpfully offers a simple summary: "Illuminism is COMMUNISM" (capitalization in original).[35]

The manner in which Cooper combines a wide variety of organizations and secret societies into one overarching enemy echoes the work of Edith Starr Miller's *Occult Theocrasy*. Like Miller, Cooper sees Communism (and socialism, and any left-leaning political stance) as a threat. Like Miller, he sees these different, and often disparate, groups as part of a larger plot doing back to ancient times and connected to present day people and institutions by threads that stretch for millennia.

MAJESTYTWELVE continues with long discussions of the "illuminati" roots of *Star Trek* and the impossibility that humanity has achieved manned space flight. Cooper also "exposes" preeminent 1990s late night radio host Art Bell as an agent of the Illuminati, arguing that Bell's programs "dish up nightly servings of ridiculous, outrageous, and fantastic conspiracy fantasies." While Bell does, from time to time, discuss "legitimate, real and dangerous conspiracies" his inclusion of "incredulous fantasy with fact serves to debunk all conspiracies." Cooper asserts that Bell's approach—interviewing serious conspiracy researchers while, at the same time giving airtime to dozens of nightly callers with a variety of outlandish ideas—"effectively implants the idea that anyone who believes in any conspiracy is a whacked out nutcase that should be locked up in a mental institution." Bell, according to Cooper, "is a most effective change agent operating on behalf of our enemies." As he does throughout MAJESTYTWELVE, Cooper downplays to the point of absence his own role in promulgating outlandish conspiracy theories, particularly in the area of extraterrestrial visitation and alien abduction.

Cooper presents the entire question of extraterrestrial visitation as a ruse, promulgated not only by ufology but by popular culture in general. Science fiction television programs films such as *Star Trek* and *Star Wars* serve to acculturate Americans to the possibilities of interstellar travel and non-human life. *Star Wars*, in particular, was for Cooper an exercise in propaganda aimed at the American people. The following selection, while long, is a one of the most compact examples of Cooper's method of extracting some manner of esoteric value from nearly any piece of popular culture:

> In Star Wars Luke Skywalker (Apollo, Horus, Osiris), the SON of a widow (initiate) goes in search of himself (Secret, lost Word, or Great Work). Jedi Knight Darth Vader (Osiris, Sun Father, Apollo, Doctrine, Lucifer, Master of the FORCE (magic) who has gone over to the Darkside [sic] (religion, nationalism, superstition) separates the Princess (the title signifies BECOMING) Lea [sic] (Isis-Moon-Church) from the Doctrine (illumination).
>
> Luke falls in love with Lea [sic] and begins a sexless, but spiritual relationship with the Princess. This mystical union produces the child HORUS (falcon headed God) which, in the movie, is personified in the illumination of Luke transforming him into an Adept or Priest (Jedi Knight-Sun Son-Adept-Reincarnated Osiris-Apollo-God-Doctrine). He embarks upon a Quest in the Millenium [sic] (saviors always return at the millenium [sic]) Falcon (Horus as savior) to rescue Princess Lea which results in a confrontation with Vader who imparts knowledge (Intelligence-Fire) resulting in Luke finding the Holy Grail (Bloodline, Identity, Lost Word, Obelisk, Penis, Creative Force, apotheosis). With this knowledge he succeeds in reuniting (uniting in marriage) the Force (doctrine) with Princess Lea [sic] (Church) which reestablishes the Order of Jedi Knights (Congregation—full body of Adepts or Priests—sixth root race—evolved and matured mankind-God Race, Horus) producing chaos, rebellion, and the establishment of the New Dawn on the horizon (Horus Risen), the New Age, the New Atlantis, a New World Order, the socialist utopian world.[36]

As is typical with Cooper's interpretations of culture and esoterica, it is not entirely original. Few, if any, have denied that there is a mythic element to *Star Wars*. Indeed, the "hero's journey" or monomyth as discussed by Joseph Campbell has long been applied to *Star Wars*. Similarly, Cooper's attempts to apply esoteric symbols, such as Apollo, Osiris, and others to *Star Wars* (and nearly everything else) is largely appropriated from writers such as Manly Palmer Hall, whose *Secret Teachings of All Ages* was first published in 1928 and set out a system of secret, symbolic meanings which, he asserted, dated back to the dawn of time. "Symbolism," Hall wrote, "is the language of the Mysteries; in fact it is the language not only of mysticism and philosophy but of all Nature."[37] Just as Cooper appropriated much of his discussion of secret societies from Edith Starr Miller, Manly P. Hall was the source of a great deal of his "research" into the so-called "mystery schools."

Much of Cooper's significance, however, rested upon his connection of the paranormal and esoteric aspects of conspiracy theory to the far more prosaic realms of right wing extremism in the 1990s such as his involvement in the Militia movement and other related fields such as the so-called tax protest movement. He closes MAJESTYTWELVE with this call to action for his readers:

> Seek out and join a lawful Militia or form one in your area. If you wish to remain Free you will have to fight for it ... not because we want to fight, or you want to fight, but because the traitors will give us no choice in the matter. There will be either a revolution (the Marxist's choice) or there will be a serious attempt to restore Constitutional Republican government under Law (the Patriots [sic] choice). In any event there WILL BE WAR between the Citizens of the united States of America and the Marxist minions of the subversive corporate United States' new world odor [sic] [capitalization in original].[38]

Here, we see small typographical hints of Cooper's political views. The use of "united States" rather than "United States" indicates what Cooper and other right-wing thinkers viewed as the "real" composition of the country—a collection of small state republics rather than the "corporate" U.S. which allegedly emerged after the Civil War, when the Fourteenth amendment designated people as citizens of the United States first, and of the individual states only incidentally. It also illustrates his vision of the inevitability of armed conflict between the "militias" and the federal government. These positions on statehood, the Constitution, and taxation, like his views on esoteric symbolism, secret societies, and extraterrestrials were not wholly original ideas. They had been circulating in conspiratorial communities for decades. Those who came to conspiracism though Cooper's writings, however, would get no hint of this. Cooper did not cite those who addressed these topics before him. Rather, he relies upon those writer's citations and, often, their out-of-context quotations.

Cooper's views of state sovereignty and the illegitimate nature of the federal income tax was an issue with which he became closely associated at the end of his life, as Cooper and his wife were under investigation throughout the late 1990s for failure to file income tax returns. Cooper argued—as have others who question the authority of the federal government to collect income tax—that the federal government only has power to tax within its lawful jurisdiction and that "the United States has no jurisdiction or venue within the territorial boundaries of the State of Arizona except over land that was ceded to the United States by the by the State Legislature." In the summer of 1998, Cooper, after meeting with a U.S. Marshall about the charges issued a series of public statements on his website and through his shortwave radio program *The Hour of the Time*. Cooper stated that despite the threat of arrest, he and his wife Annie would not appear in court to answer a summons, saying, "We will not appear as we are not the legal fictions[39] named in the summons, the Court has no jurisdiction or authority over us as Citizens of Arizona, and we will not allow an unconstitutional arrest to occur. We will stand and fight their Gestapo with all the means at our disposal any assault which may be mounted upon our property or upon us."[40] Cooper's declarations were doom-laden and paranoid. On his radio broadcast, he announced:

> Our children will remain with us. They are not shields, as our enemies will claim, any more than children have been shields for families which have been attacked by despotism throughout history. Allowing our children to disappear into the immoral and destructive government child care and foster home industry run by the mind controlling bogus Psychology profession only to be abused and sexually assaulted for many years is a fate worse than death, and we simply will not allow such a thing to happen to our precious little girls.[41]

The references to mind control echo other extreme interpretations of long-deactivated government psychological experimentation that was part and parcel of conspiracy narrative in the mid– to late 1990s. On his web site, Cooper placed this notice:

> WARNING !! Any attempt by the federal government or anyone else to execute the unconstitutional and unlawful arrest warrants issued by Judge Irwin will be met with armed resistance. Any person who attempts to kidnap our children will be shot upon discovery.
> We are formed as the Constitutional and Lawful unorganized Militia of the State of Arizona and the united States of America.... By invading the Sovereign jurisdiction of the State of Arizona to attack the Citizens of the State of Arizona the United States has declared war upon the Citizens of the several States of the Union
> Therefore a STATE OF WAR exists between the Citizens of the Union States and the corporate United States [capitalization, spacing, and punctuation as in original].[42]

Not wanting to precipitate an incident which might turn into another Ruby Ridge or Waco, federal law enforcement agencies took their time in executing arrest warrants on Cooper. On November 6, 2001, however, Apache County, Arizona, sheriff's deputies attempted to serve a warrant on Cooper related to local assault charges. During the confrontation, Cooper shot a deputy in the head and was, in turn, killed when the law enforcement officers returned fire. In a *Los Angeles Times* story drawn from wire service reports, Cooper's death was summarized as the coda to years of anti-government activism, citing his long-pending tax evasion charges and quoting a representative from the U.S. Marshall's service who said Cooper "had vowed that he would not be taken alive."[43]

Cooper's death triggered a wave of suspicion within the conspiracy community. Much of this suspicion centered on Cooper's "prediction" on his June 28, 2001, broadcast that there would likely be some sort of manufactured terrorist attack on the United States than that Osama Bin Laden would be implicated in it. This summary by a conspiracy-oriented website over a dozen years later is typical of reactions to Cooper's death: "Many believe that Cooper was killed ... because of the things he says here: disclosing highly sensitive information & particularly forewarning listeners to disregard any connection to Osama Bin Laden should a future attack on US soil occur."[44]

This angle was played up in the 2005 documentary *The Hour of Our Time: The Legacy of William Cooper*. This film, nearly hagiographic in its treatment of Cooper, presents a fairly streamlined version of Cooper's work, concentrating on his political conspiracies and painting Cooper and his associates as hard working seekers after the truth. The opening narration positions him as a latter day prophet:

> If you listened to shortwave radio throughout the 1990s, you were bound to invariably come across the sound of a captivating voice in the wilderness. That authoritative and self-assured voice for five nights a week would educate us, enlighten us, and most importantly, warn us of things to come…. That voice spoke to us of matters esoteric and exoteric, political and supernatural, scientific and lawful.

It featured interview footage of Cooper that was, seemingly, chosen to address specific claims made against him. For example, his use of the *Protocols of the Elders of Zion* had led to Cooper being labeled as Anti-Semitic. In the film, Cooper presents his summary of the nature of the forces which targeted American liberty:

> I get people who still come to me all the time and say, "Bill you're all wrong, it's the Jews, the Jews are subverting the world." Man, it's not the Jews, it's not the Catholics, it's not the blacks. It's these men who belong to the ancient mystery schools, who meet in secret to decide the fate of the world. They belong to all different races and all different nationalities and different religions to the public's point of view. But in secret, it's a different story.

As presented by this documentary, the circumstances surrounding Cooper's 2001 death, recounted by his fellow militia members and his radio co-host, comes across as some combination of a misunderstanding and a determined assassination. Their image of a man who was simply minding his own business runs counter to the warnings and declarations of war Cooper put on his website. In summing up Cooper's legacy, one associate claimed that "probably due to the life and circumstances of research he was involved in and what he was exposing, I have no doubt he is in a much better place." Cooper's activities—largely repurposing and restating obscure ideas from decades before—ensure a heavenly reward.

Even from beyond the grave, Bill Cooper remains a notable presence within the online conspiracy community. Neophyte conspiracists come across his writings and ask their elders what it might all mean, such as this poster ("broctune") on the heavily trafficked *Above Top Secret* internet forum in 2013:

> William Cooper was a little before my time, but I've really enjoyed listening to some of his stuff on youtube [sic]. To some of you a little older that may have heard him during his life, was he legit? What did you think of him? Any ideas about the controversy surrounding his death?[45]

One poster responded:

> Cooper predicted 9/11 and he predicted that Bin Ladin [sic] would be framed.
> For that he was shot 5 times in the back by Federal Agents delivering a warrant.
> And then they let his body sit and bake in the hot sun for half a day before he was declared dead.
> Emergency services were never called.
> He could have been alive after being shot 5 times in the back, but we won't know that because he was left until the murder scene could be investigated.
> He was a true patriot, a great man, and an even better American.
> God bless him.[46]

There are, of course, a number of factual errors in this post (for instance, Cooper was shot by county deputies, not federal agents) but, more than a decade on from his death, Cooper was as much myth as man. In death, he himself has become a conspiracy theory, undergoing an kind of apotheosis. This has helped ensure that his views, very much bound to the historical context of the times in which they were conceived, continue to undergo resurrection and revision, giving Cooper's theories and interpretations a continued currency as well as a sheen of credibility that would not exist if he had died of natural causes or was still living.

3

They Came from Outer Space

Fearful and suspicious narratives of "global control" are one of the foundations of conspiracy theory in the late twentieth and early twentieth centuries. Their themes, prominent figures, and style have influenced conspiracy narratives in a variety of sub-genres. Another major component of the modern conspiracy landscape is the persistent question of whether or not intelligent extraterrestrial beings exist and if the strange lights, craft, and other anomalies seen in the sky since the 1940s are proof that they are visiting the earth. Examinations of the UFO phenomenon and the culture that has grown up around it is just as complex and multi-layered as those of political or economic conspiracy theories, if not more so. Ufology[1] is not necessarily connected with a conspiratorial mind set and, particularly in the earliest decades of the phenomenon, devotees approached the subject from the viewpoints of science or journalism. Some approaches to ufology and ufologists have done groundbreaking work without delving into paranoid conspiracies. Scholars in fields such as sociology, religious studies, and history have focused on topics within ufology that are nearly devoid of conspiratorial content. Conspiracy theory, however, has long been a significant factor in the aspects of ufology that have received the most public attention and scrutiny. Especially since the 1980s, ufological conspiracies have occupied some of the same thematic territory as political and economic conspiracy theories.

Just as the theories of global domination and tyranny will surface over and over in subsequent chapters, ufological conspiracies play a similarly vital role. Conspiracy narratives about flying saucers and those who control them tie into theories about the hollow earth and mysterious underground military facilities. Aliens have shouldered partial blame for mind control projects and conspiracy theorists have linked extraterrestrial experimentation with cattle mutilations and the ubiquitous black helicopter sightings of the 1980s and 1990s. Accusations that elements of the defense and intelligence establishments have concealed important information about UFOs raises the same concerns about governmental power and secrecy as political conspiracy theories while narratives that focus on illegal secret alliances between the American government and alien species simply extend fears of international cabals and the "one world government" and cast item in interstellar, rather than international terms. There are also conspiracy theorists who view the UFO conspiracies as a disinformation tool, one of the levers that will bring about world government, as the United Nations convinces the people that the planet must unite to defeat interplanetary, *Independence Day*–style conquerors. The increasingly paranoid conception of alien incursion in the last decades of the twentieth century is deeply intertwined with the wholly terrestrial conspiracy theories discussed in the last chapter.

The history of UFO belief and the ufological subculture is, in some ways, briefer and more compact than that of conspiratorial thinking or the organization and collation of conspiracy theories. While a full history of the UFO phenomenon and the varied personalities, organizations, and belief systems is beyond the scope of this study, a brief sketch of the basic shape and development of ufology will cast the conspiratorial aspects of the movement into sharper relief and provide context for the overtly conspiracy-oriented aspects of the movement I examine in this chapter.

A Brief History of Flying Saucers

The June 26, 1947, edition of the Chicago *Sun* may have contained the first use of the phrase "flying saucer." Two days before, pilot Kenneth Arnold had seen nine strange objects flying at what were apparently supersonic speeds near Mount Rainier. Arnold's sighting was not the only one—throughout the summer of 1947 sightings occurred around the United States. These included a strange report, retracted quickly, that the Army Air Force had retrieved the wreckage of such a craft in New Mexico and many more prosaic sightings of strange lights and bizarre craft in the skies. The age of the UFO had begun.

News reports soon speculated that the craft could be from another planet in our solar system. Give the popularity of science fiction magazines and books during the 1930s and 1940s, the notion of people from outer space was not beyond most Americans' imaginations. Superman, after all, was an alien. Beginning in the 1950s, group of flying saucer believers known as Contactees claimed to have met and conversed with beings from other worlds and conveyed messages from their friends from other planets. These were largely concerned with social injustice and fear of nuclear weapons as well as the tense relationship between Earth's superpowers. While many Contactees were, within a few years of reaching popularity, exposed as frauds (especially their photographs of flying saucers which were, in fact, hubcaps, window shades, and the like) their stories contained elements that would persist in ufology for decades.[2]

By the 1950s, organizations ranging from the local to the global emerged seeking to "solve" the mystery of these mysterious craft. One of the longest lasting and most prominent was the National Investigations Committee for Aerial Phenomena (NICAP). The group emerged as a reaction to the more outlandish claims and theories of flying saucer enthusiasts, particularly the Contactees. UFO researcher and historian Jerome Clark asserts that NICAP appealed to "many middle-class Americans and others interested in UFOs" who were "repelled by ufology's fringe aspects." NICAP "served as a sober forum for UFO reporting, inquiry, investigation, and speculation."[3] The United States Air Force also undertook efforts (such as Project Blue Book, which existed from 1952 to 1970) to collect and scrutinize flying saucer sighting reports with an eye toward detecting potential national security threats. Their efforts, like those of civilian organizations NICAP and APRO (Aerial Phenomena Research Organization) failed to produce any sort of consensus on the origin or intentions of these alleged craft.

The UFO question reached a turning point in the late 1960s. From 1966 to 1968 the U.S. Air Force funded the University of Colorado UFO Project (usually referred to as the Condon Committee after its director, the physicist Edward Condon). The study examined hundreds of UFO sighting reports from sources ranging from the Air Force's Blue Book files as well as those collected by civilian organizations like NICAP and APRO. At the end of the two year study, the committee's report—released in mass-market paperback—concluded that "nothing has come from the study of UFOs in the past 21 years that has added to scientific knowledge. Careful consideration of the record as it is available to us leads us to conclude that further extensive study of UFOs probably cannot be justified in the expectation that science will be advanced thereby."[4]

For the scientific community, the case was largely closed. The mainstream press would often cite the Condon report when high profile UFO cases appeared in the news. The Air Force, in response to the report, closed Project Blue Book in 1970. As James W. Moseley, a fixture in the UFO world from the 1950s until his death in 2012, recalled, "public interest in UFOs evaporated almost overnight.... NICAP ... had defined itself in terms of government cover-up and demands for disclosure and and objective investigation....

People reasoned that it had gotten what it wanted, the answers were in, and that was that."[5] Ufology would persist however, with its public profile becoming defined in the 1980s and 1990s by three factors: so-called alien abductions, the rise of the "Roswell Incident" as a key event, and an increasing blurring of the lines between political conspiracy theory and the world of the paranormal. Large national groups such as MUFON (Mutual UFO Network) would continue to carry the torch of "scientific" collection and analysis of sighting data and the social justice–style messages of the Contactees would persist through "new age" style channelers bringing messages from beyond. Cover-ups and cabals would become the dominant theme of ufology. Conspiracy and cover-up were nothing new for the world of flying saucers.

"The Silence Group": UFO Cover-Ups in the 1950s and 1960s

During the 1950s and 1960s, groups like the National Investigation Committee on Aerial Phenomenon (NICAP) and the Aerial Phenomenon Research Organization (APRO) took a media-savvy approach to saucer research, working to solve the mystery of the saucers while, at the same time, calling into question aspects of the American government and the scientific establishment—placing themselves in a context that, from our perspective, is certainly related to the notion of conspiracy theory. NICAP head Donald Keyhoe appeared on numerous television and radio shows and, to many of the public, was the person most associated with the call for further investigation of the saucers.[6] Keyhoe and APRO founder Corel Lorenzen both wrote several books that documented hundreds of saucer sightings from around the world. These books and the newsletters published by NICAP and APRO reached thousand of saucer believers in the United States.

While NICAP and APRO both held that careful scientific investigation would solve the mystery of the saucers, significant differences existed between them, centered on the proper role of the government in the saucer issue. Corel Lorenzen's APRO denied that the government or military had any secret knowledge of the flying saucers. Donald Keyhoe, however, insisted that a cover-up existed at the highest levels of the government and military. This insistence that the government actively hid information that could solve the saucer issue sparked public debate about the Government's policy towards the flying saucer issue and would eventually lead the University of Colorado UFO study. Keyhoe's suspicions about the cover-up represented a significant effort to break down the walls of Cold War military-scientific-government collusion. APRO and Corel Lorenzen's approach, though different from Keyhoe's, also made strong statements about the relationship between government and science. For Lorenzen, the scientific truth of flying saucers lay outside of governmental control. The truth behind the saucers, however, would remain hidden unless investigators pushed the mainstream scientific community to consider the possibility of life on other planets. In the minds of APRO members and leadership, many scientists were trapped in a limited paradigm that did not allow them to acknowledge the possibility of life on other planets.

Keyhoe's writings, from their very beginning, demonstrate his assumption that the government of the United States concealed information about flying saucers from the eyes of the public. While he did claim a cover-up existed, he was careful to not attribute malicious motives to the conspirators. In the foreword to 1955's *The Flying Saucer Conspiracy*, he said,

> In revealing this censorship, I am not attacking the Air Force as a whole. Most of the officers and officials I have encountered are simply obeying orders. Nor do I attribute unpatriotic motives to the "silence group" members who originate these orders. Undoubtedly they are actuated by a high motive—the need, as they see it, to protect the public from possible hysteria.... If the public is not informed of the facts, fear of the unknown may prevail.

Despite its noble motives, Keyhoe considered the cover-up dangerous to the United States. Continual denial, Keyhoe wrote, "only heightens the possibility of hysteria."[7] Thus, with this reasoning, Keyhoe both acknowledged appropriate motives on the part of the conspirators and argued that continued secrecy would do more harm than good. Openness on the part of the government would not cause hysteria—rather openness would reassure Americans that their government was, in fact, in control of the situation. In Keyhoe's conception of the conspiracy, the suppression of information of UFOs was the work of a small cabal within the otherwise upstanding government and military establishment.

At the heart of Keyhoe's claims throughout the 1950s was the assumption that Air Force officials had standing orders (Air Force Regulation 200-2) that restricted the kinds of information on saucers that officials could release to the public, and that only "hoaxes, practical jokes, and erroneous UFO reports ... be given to the public." Keyhoe considered "this hidden order ... a revelation in its apparent distrust of the American people."[8] The cover-up, he claimed, took the form not only of these denials of saucer sightings but of outright censorship. One incident that *The Flying Saucer Conspiracy* detailed was that of NICAP member Frank Edwards. Edwards was a prominent radio and print journalist who worked as a news commentator for the American

Federation of Labor. During the summer of 1954, Edwards had persuaded AFL president George Meany to let him broadcast a nationwide special on the existence of AFR 200-2 and report on some extraordinary sightings that began in Wilmington, Delaware, and had spread across the country. Keyhoe and Edwards both felt that this report would force the USAF to reveal the hidden details about the saucers. Then, a few days before the broadcast, Edwards called Keyhoe and informed him that George Meany had ordered Edwards to scrap all mention of saucers and told him that there would be a censor in the studio prepared to end the broadcast if Edwards failed to comply. Edwards resigned rather than go on the air with those conditions.[9] Edwards discussed this, and other instances of censorship, in his first book *Flying Saucers—Serious Business*. In a chapter entitled "Muzzles for Americans?" Edwards acknowledged that the government might have had good reasons for saucer censorship. But he also charged that such censorship was not confined to the realm of UFOs—that any "falsification was all right if the results were good." Edwards then went even farther, equating the event with "the old Nazi line that it's all right to lie to the public if it is for their own good. Whether it was justified would be decided by those who did the lying, of course."[10]

Keyhoe, who certainly opposed saucer censorship, never went so far as to compare the government to the Nazis. He did, however, present the perceived government cover-up of saucer information was dangerous. Frank Edwards was on the NICAP board and Keyhoe featured him prominently in all of his books throughout the '50s and '60s. Thus, Edwards's views on government censorship could not have varied too much from the NICAP party line. Establishing a political, conspiratorial framework for UFO secrecy would, in later years, serve to give Keyhoe and NICAP a visible, high profile adversary, making their quest more accessible to the public. AFR 200-2 has since been declassified and, like many of the supposedly shadowy government documents conspiracy theorists purport to be smoking guns, there is room for misinterpretation of the text. The Air Force guideline on releasing information about UFO sightings to the public did entail restrictions on what press officers could reveal about the mysterious phenomenon. For example, information on sightings would only be released "if it has been *positively identified as a familiar or known object*" (emphasis in original). Inexplicable incidents could reported as being "under investigation," the implication being that—eventually—an earthly explanation would emerge.[11] The U.S. Air Force was focused on the management of information about flying saucers to as great, if not a greater degree, than on the investigation of the phenomenon. At its most basic, this was one of the charges of the saucer conspiracists of the 1950s and 1960s. For a variety of reasons—such as the potential national security implications of strange things in the skies or the perceived need to maintain an authoritative image—the Air Force and other government agencies downplayed the anomalous nature of some UFO sightings.

Keyhoe experienced what he considered to be similar censorship to Frank Edwards when he appeared on an Armstrong Circle Theatre television program about UFOs in 1958. Here, Keyhoe was upset that he only received seven minutes of airtime (the Air Force received 25) and was required to clear his comments with the producers and the USAF before he was allowed on the air. Keyhoe's script went through three revisions before producers cleared it for broadcast. The program, entitled "UFOs: Enigma of the Skies," was broadcast January 22, 1958. A few minutes into his segment, Keyhoe deviated from the approved script:

> And now I'm going to reveal something that has never been disclosed before. For the last six months, we have been working with a Congressional committee investigating official secrecy about UFOs. If all the evidence we have given this committee is made public in open hearings, it will absolutely prove that the UFOs are real machines under intelligent control.[12]

The show's producer silenced Keyhoe's microphone before he finished his first sentence. This incident led many to believe that CBS and the Air Force were attempting to silence Keyhoe. It followed that the government was trying to hide something; perhaps Keyhoe was right about government saucer secrecy and NICAP membership rose significantly after this appearance.[13] Government secrecy was rapidly becoming a fact of life in the America of the 1950s. Though most Americans had little knowledge of the inner workings of the CIA, such as its operations in Central America or the Middle East, the government made clear the need for covert means to ensure national security and the defensive value of secrecy. The Rosenberg trial, Senator McCarthy's HUAC hearings, the launch of Sputnik, and U-2 spy plane crash and subsequent capture of Francis Gary Powers convinced many Americans that the stakes in the Cold War were high, and that government agencies' extraordinary measures to ensure security were justified. Conversely, however, the self-destruction of McCarthy's anti-communist crusade raised doubts in American's minds about whether the government was going too far to protect its secrets from the menace of an international communist conspiracy. Thus, Keyhoe had two obstacles to overcome. First, he had to convince the public that a flying saucer cover-up existed. Second, he had to persuade those people that the cover-up was wrong and that NICAP was the best organization to end that cover-up.

By 1960, with the release of *Flying Saucers: Top Secret*, Keyhoe had fur-

3. They Came from Outer Space

ther refined his cover-up theory. During the late 1950s, he became convinced that the Air Force was getting its orders to continue the cover-up from a source higher up the executive branch. Keyhoe recounted a conversation with fellow NICAP investigator Henry Brennard in which he revealed the identity of these uber-conspirators:

"I'm convinced it's the CIA that sets the policy. I suppose they think people should be kept from worrying, until it's certain there's nothing to worry about."

"Sure—Big Papa," growled Brennard. "Personally, I don't want anybody—or any government agency—deciding what's safe for me to know."[14]

It is, perhaps, telling that Keyhoe would focus his attention on the CIA rather than the military. He had, in general, confined his criticism to *elements* of the Air Force. A wholesale condemnation of the CIA was a shift. As an entity that was solely a creation of the Cold War, Keyhole grounds this new iteration of the cover-up in the new national security state dictated by the American government's policy of containment. To Keyhoe and followers of NICAP it may have seemed that a policy of containment was behind the saucer secrecy. The government "contained" evidence of the saucers, compartmentalizing it, and hiding it from the American people. While this might not have been a conscious feeling, the concept of "Containment," first expressed in the Truman Doctrine, had begun to permeate nearly every aspects of American society to some degree. Suburban homes contained housewives, suburbs contained houses and families, the goal being to create strong American communities that could withstand the assaults of international communism. Along with physical containment went intellectual and political containment. Leftist ideologies or suspicion of American leadership, goals or values could brand one an un-American radical.[15]

Keyhoe believed that scientific information existed that held unimaginable consequences for the human race and that this information languished in some government vault. The Cold War military-intelligence complex, in its fervor to protect the citizens of the United States, had gone too far. That barrier between government and the people, as well intentioned as it might have been, was what NICAP saw as the enemy. The conversation between Keyhoe and Brennard is reminiscent of Orwell's *1984*, published in 1949. Keyhoe used the parallel between that book's Big Brother and Brennard's reference to "Big Papa" to convince his readers that, if UFO secrecy continued, the U.S. might become like the England of *1984*.

Keyhoe's use of the term "Silence Group" and his broader conception of a powerful force opposing the revelation of UFO information soon spread to other parts of the ufological world, including that of the Contactees. George Adamski was the earliest of the Contactees and his 1950s books established that particular genre of UFO writing. The political aspects of their testimonies were broad, dealing with global issues of war and peace and justice and, until the 1960s, conspiratorial thinking did not play a role in traditional Contactee tales. The focus of Adamski's iteration of a "Silence Group" was distinct from Keyhoe's in that—like Contactee narratives more generally—its scope was global. Adamski's Silence Group was centered in Zurich: "What happened to the money-changers Christ drove out of the temple? It seems as though they have gathered over the centuries in Zurich.... The invisible reins of financial influence extend from Zurich to puppet organizations in every nation."[16] Adamski's identification of the entity seeking to stifle him as being international and financial in nature, moved ufology's conspiratorial needle closer to what we would see in the 1980s and 1990s as being connected to multinational cabals and threats of a tyrannical world government.

The Men in Black

The increasingly conspiratorial mindset of Donald Keyhoe and his NICAP group was not unique in the world of UFOs during the 1950s and 1960s. Suspicions arose that the Air Force (or other shadowy organizations) were not content with merely withholding information. Rather, some began to fear an active campaign of intimidation toward those who got near the truth of the UFOs. The Men in Black phenomenon has its roots in the 1950s and Albert K. Bender, founder and head of the International Flying Saucer Bureau. Founded in April 1952, the IFSB was one of the earliest of the many, many saucer investigation organizations to appear and vanish in the 1950s and 1960s.[17] The most significant thing the International Flying Saucer Bureau ever did was end. In the October 1953 issue of their newsletter, *Space Review*, Bender authored two items that would establish an enduring ufological trope. A "Late Bulletin" informed IFSB members that

> a source, which the IFSB considers very reliable, has informed us that the investigation of the flying saucer mystery and solution is approaching its final stages. The same source to whom we had referred data, which had come into our possession, suggested that it was not the proper method and time to publish this data in *Space Review*.

This bombshell announcement was followed by a "Statement of Importance":

> The mystery of the flying saucers is no longer a mystery. The source is already known, but any information about this is being withheld by orders from a higher source. We would like to print the full story in *Space Review*, but because of the

nature of the information we are sorry that we have been advised in the negative. We advise those engages in saucer work to please be very cautious[18]

Space Review sputtered to its end running stories about conventional rocketry and space exploration and probably would have been largely forgotten if not for Gray Barker. Born in in Braxton County, West Virginia, in 1925, Barker began investigating potentially paranormal events in 1952. He would go on to establish a number of UFO zines and serve as a publisher of many UFO books. Take as a whole, his work made a significant contribution to a number of mythic elements including the Men in Black. In his 1956 book *They Knew Too Much About Flying Saucers* Barker dramatized (and likely, to a degree, fictionalized) his involvement in the IFSB. Over the course of the book, Bender relates that after he learned the truth about "the mystery of the flying saucers," three men visited him and made him promise "on his honor as an American" that he would not divulge what he knew.[19]

They Knew Too Much About Flying Saucers posited several possibilities for the identity of these mysterious men, from Air Force officers to denizens of the inner earth. Bender wrote his own book on the incident in 1961 in which he revealed that the Men in Black were themselves malevolent aliens from the planet Kazik. The idea of mysterious men dressed in black, intimidating UFO witnesses into silence would be a persistent one in ufology over the subsequent decades, appearing in witness reports with increasing regularity. Over time, the various paranormal or extraterrestrial explanations for the Men in Black faded away and the assumption that they were some manner of government UFO knowledge suppression unit became commonly accepted with ufology and within the wider culture, with films like the Men in Black series reinforcing that idea. During the 1970s, 1980s and 1990s, UFO conspiracy theorists would incorporate the Men in Black into their increasingly complex and paranoid visions.

The 1980s and 1990s

Despite the decline of the 1950s-era "Contactees" alleged encounters between humans and extraterrestrial beings continued to appear in the UFO press. One of the most significant of these incidents emerged in John Fuller's 1966 book *The Interrupted Journey*.[20] This book told the story of Betty and Barney Hill. This New Hampshire couple, under hypnosis, reported that they had been taken aboard a spacecraft and had been "treated well by the occupants, rather as humans might treat experimental animals." The beings on the craft performed various procedures on the Hills, including collecting fingernail trimmings and "skin shavings."[21] Many UFO writers and researchers consider this encounter by Betty and Barney Hill to be the first instance of what would come to be known as the classic "abduction" case.

This so-called abduction phenomenon came to dominate the UFO scene from the 1970s through the 1990s. By the early 1990s, a number of largely self-appointed "experts" on the abduction phenomenon had emerged, publishing books and appearing at UFO believer conventions to share the results of their research. This research often relied on experiencer testimony garnered from hypnosis. Some experts came from academia, lending some prestige and respectability to what was an increasingly dark and frightening manifestation of UFO lore; Harvard psychologist John Mack and Temple University historian David M. Jacobs were among the most prominent. These abduction tales became the most visible manifestation of the UFO and extraterrestrial subculture, drawing far more attention than run of the mill reports of strange lights in the sky.

In 1987, novelist Whitley Strieber published *Communion: A True Story*, a book that became to 1980s abduction lore what Betty and Barney Hill's story had been to the 1960s and 1970s. Accompanied by a haunting cover illustration of the classic "gray"-style alien, *Communion* recount a series of Strieber's experiences at an isolated cabin in upstate New York, as well as an account of his attempts, through hypnotic regression sessions, to understand those experiences. He does not refers to his abductors as aliens, choosing the friendlier term "visitors" and presents these events as part of an important journey of discovery: "Something is here, be it a message from the stars or from the booming labyrinth of the mind ... or from both.... And we will all go down the labyrinth, to meet whatever awaits us there."[22] Strieber would become a leading figure in the UFO subculture, writing many more books about his experiences and the phenomenon in general and being a frequent radio and television show guest.

During the 1990s, researchers devoted an increasing amount of attention to what the purpose of these abductions might be. Different abduction researchers presented different conclusions about the meanings of these experiences and their implications for humankind. David Jacobs, in his 1998 book *The Threat: Revealing the Secret Alien Agenda* claims that the beings (often referred to as "Grays") are involved in a complex program of genetic manipulation with a view toward creating creatures which are a hybrid between the aliens and humans. This will lead, eventually, to a "new order" which will feature "insectlike aliens in control, followed by other aliens, hybrids, abductees, and, finally, nonabductees." Jacobs closed *The Threat* on a pessimistic note:

We know the alarming dimensions of the alien agenda and its goals. I could never have imagined it would turn out this way. I desperately wish it not to be true. I do not think about the future with much hope. When I was a child, I had a future with much hope. When I was a child, I had a future to look forward to. Now I fear for the future of my own children.[23]

Jacobs's frightening vision for the meaning of these supposed abductions was not unique. A wide variety of other sources similar scenarios that explained the UFO phenomenon in general and abductions in particular.

Despite the ominous nature of many abduction researchers' conclusions, the "conspiratorial" aspect of the abduction phenomenon was restricted to a supposed plan by the aliens to create a race of hybrids or some similar plot. During the 1980s and 1990s UFO-oriented conspiracy theorists would integrate alleged alien abductions into an expanded and more fully developed iteration of conspiracy theories that had circulated since the early days of flying saucer enthusiasm, such as allegations that the U.S. government (particularly the Air Force and Central Intelligence Agency) had misled the public about their investigations into the true nature of UFOs.

Expressions like "Cosmic Watergate" (coined and used extensively, but by no means exclusively, by UFO writer and lecturer Stanton Friedman) indicated a shift in the emphasis of this supposed cover-up. In the wake of the Watergate investigation and hearings that brought down the Nixon administration, as well as the numerous Congressional committee hearings on the inappropriate use of intelligence and law enforcement assets already discussed. Within the UFO community, politicized rhetoric such as the phrase "Cosmic Watergate" signaled a move toward a conspiratorial style of thinking that was closer to the realm of John F. Kennedy assassination theories, paranoia about the Federal Reserve system or fears about the New World Order than ufology had previously employed. Indeed, these political conspiracy theories would woven into the fabric of the field during this time.

This rise of a more political, traditional conspiracy theory approach to ufology developed throughout the 1980s. At the same time, the crash of an alleged alien craft at Roswell Army Air Field in July 1947 began to emerge into the public sphere in 1980 with the publication of *The Roswell Incident* by Charles Berlitz and William Moore. Stanton Friedman, the first civilian UFO researcher to investigate the happenings at Roswell, did uncredited research for this book and later co-wrote his own account, *Crash at Corona*. The assumption of a government cover-up of information ranging from the mere crash of an alien craft to the recovery of the bodies of its otherworldly crew, some of whom may still have been alive. Although the Roswell Incident had been part of American UFO lore since the 1980s (and rumors of a New

Mexico crash had circulated in ufological circles with little fanfare since the 1950s), the late 1980s and 1990s saw a surge of interest in the story and the idea that the government had recovered, and concealed, the crashed saucer was the dominant UFO conspiracy narrative of the 1990s. The story penetrated the popular media (particularly through television series such as The X-Files and Dark Skies) to such a degree that the Roswell Incident, rather than Kenneth Arnold's much more humble and relatively low-key saucer sighting a few weeks earlier, became synonymous with the dawn of the flying saucer era.

It was not surprising, in the increasing conspiratorial decade of the 1970s, as the press revealed troubling government cover-ups with unprecedented regularity, that Roswell would re-emerge. In July 1947, based on a press release from Roswell Army Air Force Field, the headline of the Roswell *Daily Record* announced, "RAAF Captures Flying Saucer on Ranch in Roswell Region." Within hours, they retracted this story and "the Air Force told the world that all the confusion was due to an errant weather balloon." That error, of course, could not really have been an error. As UFO and conspiracy researcher Richard Dolan sarcastically summarized the correction by saying, "Sorry, folks. Intelligence experts at the 509th Bomb Group couldn't tell the difference between a flying saucer and an ordinary balloon."[24] Thanks, Dolan says, to the tireless efforts of researchers who interviewed witnesses and pored over records, the truth about the flying saucer crash would "frighten the Air force into creating not one but two bogus reports in the 1990s." Dolan asserts that the reports were "so dense and unreadable—and most importantly so *weak*— that they are tantamount to proof something important did crash" (emphasis in original). Exactly what crashed has been the most pressing issue facing Roswell conspiracists in the decades since the incident resurfaced in the public sphere. Numerous explanations have arisen, ranging from Japanese "Fugo" balloons to the suspicion that what became known as the Roswell Incident actually involved illegal U.S. experimentation on Japanese prisoners of war.[25]

The development of the Roswell Incident and the shifts and changes to theories that have occurred over the years is a massive subject that, like the John F. Kennedy assassination, is the subject of numerous books that occupy the entire spectrum of belief on various aspects of the event. For our purposes, Roswell will appear here and there, hovering like a specter over a wide variety of conspiratorial narratives, not only those involving UFOs. Along with the supposed recovery of an alien craft, technology and bodies at Roswell, other related allegations of massive government cover-ups with regard to UFOs gained ground in the 1980s that connected Roswell with abductions, a vast government cover-up, and other topics explored throughout this book.

Many of these theories and narratives were rooted in a number of documents that (their supporters claimed) proved the existence of a secret group of government, defense, and intelligence experts tasked with managing the cover-up of extraterrestrial contact and preparing possible defenses against the beings that controlled them. The so-called MJ-12 papers, in the form of an alleged briefing document, were anonymously delivered on a roll of undeveloped 35mm film to UFO researchers William L. Moore, Stanton Friedman, and Jamie Shandera in 1984. The document seemed to indicate that a secret government control group (Majestic 12) dedicated to investigating and, ultimately, concealing information about the extraterrestrial presence on our earth came into being during the late 1940s in the wake of the Roswell Inci-

President Truman presents a Medal of Merit to Secretary of Defense James Forrestal in the Oval Office, January 27, 1948 (National Archives and Records Administration, Office of Presidential Libraries, Harry S. Truman Library). According to the conspiratorial UFO lore that emerged in the 1980s, Truman established MJ-12, of which Forrestal was a member until he either committed suicide because he could not handle "the truth" of the alien presence or was murdered because he threatened to go public with the truth about the flying saucers.

S E C R E T

DL 65C-

Dallas notes that within the last six weeks, there has been local publicity regarding "OPERATION MAJESTIC-12" with at least two appearances on a local radio talk show, discussing the MAJESTIC-12 OPERATION, the individuals involved, and the Government's attempt to keep it all secret. It is unknown if this is all part of a publicity campaign.

███████ from OSI, advises that "OPERATION BLUE BOOK," mentioned in the document on page 4 did exist.

Dallas realizes that the purported document is over 35 years old, but does not know if it has been properly declassified.

REQUEST OF THE BUREAU

The Bureau is requested to discern if the document is still classified. Dallas will hold any investigation in abeyance until further direction from FBIHQ.

S E C R E T

2*

Above and opposite page: As the MJ-12/Majestic 12 documents increased in prominence, the FBI initiated an investigation, which found that the papers were not legitimate government documents.

dent and other, less sensational sightings of supposed extraterrestrial craft. The MJ-12 papers have been the subject of an enormous amount of scrutiny, with the FBI undertaking an investigation into the documents in 1988, finding that they were "fake."[26] Despite this, some UFO researchers have maintained that a Majestic 12 group existed, although it might not have been connected to a UFO cover-up.[27]

```
TOP SECRET / MAJIC
    EYES ONLY
    * TOP SECRET *
    ***************

EYES ONLY                                          COPY ONE OF ONE.

On 24 June, 1947, a civilian pilot flying over the Cascade
Mountains in the State of Washington observed nine
disc-shaped aircraft traveling in formation at a high rate
of speed. Although this was not the first known sighting
of such objects, it was the first to gain widespread attention
in the public media. Hundreds of reports of sightings of
similar objects followed. Many of these came from highly
credible military and civilian sources. These reports res-
ulted in independent efforts by several different elements
of the military to ascertain the nature and purpose of these
objects in the interests of national defense. A number of
witnesses were interviewed and there were several successful
attempts to utilize aircraft in efforts to pursue reported
discs in flight. Public reaction bordered on near hysteria
at times.

In spite of these efforts, little of substance was learned
about the objects until a local rancher reported that one
had crashed in a remote region of New Mexico located approx-
imately seventy-five miles northwest of Roswell Army Air
Base (now Walker Field).

On 07 July, 1947, a secret operation was begun to assure
recovery of the wreckage of this object for scientific study.
During the course of this operation, aerial reconnaissance
discovered that four small human-like beings had apparently
ejected from the craft at some point before it exploded.
These had fallen to earth about two miles east of the wreckage
site. All four were dead and badly decomposed due to action
by predators and exposure to the elements during the approx-
imately one week time period which had elapsed before their
discovery. A special scientific team took charge of removing
these bodies for study. (See Attachment "C".) The wreckage
of the craft was also removed to several different locations.
(See Attachment "B".) Civilian and military witnesses in
the area were debriefed, and news reporters were given the
effective cover story that the object had been a misguided
weather research balloon.

            * TOP SECRET *
            ***************
EYES ONLY TOP SECRET / MAJIC        T52-EXEMPT (E)
          EYES ONLY
```

The first mention of this group, however, sheds light on the degree to which elements of the military and intelligence communities manipulated UFO believers and researchers during the 1980s, undermining the foundations of some conspiracy theories while providing fuel for new ones. The phrase "MJ TWELVE" appeared in 1980 in a document associated with something called Project Aquarius ("THE RESULTS OF PROJECT AQUARIUS IS [sic] STILL CLASSIFIED TOP SECRET WITH NO DISSEMINATION OUTSIDE OFFICIAL INTELLIGENCE CHANNELS AND WITH RESTRICTED ACCESS TO 'MJ TWELVE'").[28] This, in turn, was part of an elaborate Air Force disinformation and counterintelligence operation against an Albuquerque, New Mexico, man named Paul Bennewitz. Bennewitz operated Thunder Scientific Labs and had done work for the Air Force's nearby base at Kirtland. After becoming involved in the case of an alleged UFO abduction victim, he became convinced that the Air Force was covering up important information about extraterrestrial beings and vehicles. Bennewitz believed that he had detected signals from these craft but according to researcher Greg Bishop, he had probably stumbled upon top secret Air Force experiments. The Air Force Office of Special Investigations (AFOSI) along with UFO researcher Bill Moore engaged in a complex campaign of disinformation, convincing Bennewitz that he was, in fact, in contact with extraterrestrials. Eventually, Bennewitz suffered from significant psychological trauma from the entire affair. Bennewitz, for example, began work on a weapon that he believed would be effective in fighting any alien incursion.[29] Bill Moore, in 1989, gave a talk at the Mutual UFO Network symposium which he revealed his role in the Bennewitz affair and other connections with government and military intelligence operatives.

Moore said that he "found himself face-to-face with an opportunity to learn more about what our government knows about UFOs" and in 1980 was introduced to "a well-placed individual within the intelligence community who claimed to be directly connected to a high-level government project dealing with UFOs." This group claimed to be "uncomfortable" with the ongoing UFO cover-up and wanted to help Moore with his research. In Moore's words, "I knew I was being recruited, but at that point I had no idea for what." Moore's part of the bargain was to keep his intelligence community handlers in the loop by supplying information about on-going UFO investigations (Moore, at the time, was an investigator for APRO, a major UFO organization). His 1989 speech focused on his role in what would become known as the Bennewitz Affair. Bennewitz, who had become obsessed with the UFO activity he had witnessed in the Kirtland AFB area, was "the subject of considerable interest on the part of not one but several government agencies …

they were actively trying to defuse him by pumping him as much disinformation as he could possible absorb." Soon, Benewitz's stories—bolstered by the disinformation provided by his government contacts—"contained virtually all the elements found in the current crop of rumors circulated around the UFO community."[30]

In a 1992 interview, Moore outlined the elements of the disinformation that Bennewitz had encountered. It included "the whole story of Government/alien involvement, treaties with aliens, underground bases, a plot to take over the planet, implants, two difference races of alliances, one hostile and one friendly, etc." This was all a fabrication of "counter-intelligence people for the purpose of discrediting Bennewitz."[31] Those ideas would be developed and solidified at UFO conferences and, increasingly, on Bulletin Board Systems (BBS) such as Paranet Information Services, which would be home to a number of documents that helped establish the parameters of conspiratorial ufology in the late 1980s and early 1990s. The core ideas in these documents could be traced back to Bennewitz and the disinformation fed to him. One of the earliest and most influential of these documents was a 1987 statement by John Lear.

John Lear, trading on his reputation as an award-winning pilot and son of LearJet inventor William Lear issued a statement on December 29, 1987. Uploaded initially to the Paranet BBS, it has circulated on the internet ever since. While acknowledging that "John is who he says he is, and has numerous contacts in sensitive positions that could conceivably allow him access to information of this type," Paranet's owners presented the information "to encourage debate" rather than expressing agreement with its contents. In this statement Lear revealed that the truth about the MJ-12 group was far more frightening and important than the mere study of UFOs and the maintenance of secrecy about these extraterrestrial visitations. President Truman had established MJ-12, Lear wrote, in the aftermath of the Roswell Incident. In 1964, the first communications and meetings took place between the aliens and the Americans; between 1969 and 1971, they had entered into a series of agreements with the aliens. In exchange for alien technology, MJ-12 "agreed to 'ignore' the abductions that were going on and suppress information on the cattle mutilations. The EBE's assured MJ-12 that the abductions (usually lasting about 2 hours) were merely the ongoing monitoring of developing civilizations." Lear explained that there were several goals for these abductions, including the "impregnation of human females and early termination of pregnancies to secure the crossbreed infant" and "termination of some people so that they could function as living sources for biological material and substances."

Apart from general body horror imagery, the Lear statement raised the issue of mind control as one of the EBE's undertakings, claiming that he part of the alien agenda was "the insertion of a 3mm spherical device through the nasal cavity of the abductee into the brain. The device is used for the biological monitoring, tracking, and control of the abductee." The ultimate goal of these implants was "implementation of Posthypnotic Suggestion to carry out a specific activity during a specific time period, the actuation of which will occur within the next 2 to 5 years," echoing conspiracy theories about the extent and purpose of government mind control experimentation during the Cold War era.

Lear goes on to tie this new MJ-12/EBE alliance to the use of secret bases such as Groom Lake/Area 51 and the alleged base near Dulce, New Mexico, including a full-blown battle at Dulce between humans (who had discovered that the EBEs were duplicitous and abducting many more people than they reported) and the EBEs at the underground Dulce base:

> In 1979 there was an altercation of sorts at the Dulce laboratory. A special armed forces unit was called in to try and free a number of our people trapped in the facility, who had become aware of what was really going on. According to one source, 66 of the soldiers were killed and our people were not freed.[32]

The story of Dulce base was, of course, part of the information supplied to Paul Bennewitz who, according to Moore, "was meeting with everybody who was anybody and telling that story to anyone who would listen," including John Lear and Bill Cooper. It was, Moore claimed, "the kind of paranoia that they wanted to hear."[33] In the years that followed, other documents of dubious provenance flooded the UFO scene.

William Cooper's writings provided support for even Lear's most outlandish claims. As discussed in Chapter 2, Cooper initially burst onto the conspiratorial scene as part of the dark stories and suspicions surrounding the UFO phenomenon. In late 1988, Cooper began posting several files to UFO-oriented bulletin board systems. The first one, "TOP SECRET/MAJIC EXECUTIVE CORRESPONDENCE BRIEFING SESSION," consisted of explanations of the secret projects (with their cryptonyms) that covered ongoing relationship between elements of the U.S. government and the alien beings with whom they had established contact. These project summaries were presented in clipped, concise language that reinforced the notion that it came from an official source:

> (TS/ORCON) PROJECT SIGMA: (PROWORD: AQUARIUS) Originally established as part of Project SIGN in 1954. Became a separate project in 1976. Its mission was to establish communication with Aliens. This Project met with positive success ... in 1959, the United States established primative [sic] com-

munications with the Aliens. On April 25, 1964, a USAF intelligence officer met with Aliens at Holloman AFB, New Mexico. The contact lasted for approximately three hours. After several attempted methods of communicating the intelligence officer managed to exchange basic information with the Aliens (Atch 7). This Project is continuing at a site in New Mexico.

This echoes material from the Lear document and also connects with then-current theories about the underground base at Dulce ("a site in New Mexico"). Within the developing conspiratorial narrative, it seemed that Lear's 1987 statement had opened the floodgates, emboldening others who had access to similar secret information. This new information, in turn, seemed to reinforce Lear's claims as well as informing the on-going debate about the MJ-12 papers and quiet talk about underground bases in the American west that had been circulating since the early 1980s. Based on the statements of William Moore and the research of Greg Bishop and others, however, the story becomes more complex, with the source of the many of these stories being traceable to the disinformation campaign run against Paul Bennewitz.

Shortly after the release of the "TOP SECRET/MAJIC" briefing document, Cooper issued "Reasons for Going Public" in which he introduced himself as a Navy veteran who was, in the early 1970s, attached to the staff of the commander in chief of the Pacific Fleet and responsible for intelligence briefings. While there, Cooper claims he encountered material, from a variety of sources, which corroborated other UFO-related material that was emerging into the public domain:

> I saw and read GRUDG [sic]/BLUE BOOK REPORT NO. 13. I saw and read the MAJESTY document which contained the Aquarius information. I was present at a briefing where much more information was discussed and some of it has become cloudy over the years but has come back to me when I saw information on that subject. About 50% of the information comes from my sources who will remain un-named. About 60% of the information is backed up by research and information available to you all however the information is not generaly [sic] shared. It is out there in various places and on various boards. Due to the potential monetary value of the information I believe that it probably never will be shared.[34]

Typically, Cooper co-opted work that had already existed, while claiming special knowledge—he would, in time, employ similar methods when dealing with conspiracy theories about the government or secret societies. The GRUDGE/BLUE BOOK REPORT Cooper mentions had been introduced into the UFO wild by William S. English, who claimed he had seen the document (which, unsurprisingly, bolster's the John Lear-style alien/government collaboration conspiracy theory), similarly "MAJESTY" is a reference to MJ-12. Beyond those two connections, the vague discussion of un-named sources adds a frisson of intrigue and would open the door for Cooper to introduce his more political bent to the alien invasion conspiracy.

Cooper would continue to produce lengthy documents and post them as well as distributing other material which claimed mysterious figures had uploaded to his own BBS. Often, he would explain that, while not all the material in the documents could be corroborated, much of it verified what he learned in the 1970s. One such piece of material was the so-called O.H. KRILL document.

The saga of O.H. KRILL and the document that bears his/her/its name is one of the most complex to emerge in the 1980s. O.H. (standing for Original Hostage), Krill was allegedly an alien held by the United States government. Bill Cooper uploaded the document to several networks with the observation that "the KRILL papers ... have stirred up a small hornets [sic] nest of speculation" and that despite questions about their origins and veracity, "much of it is correct and agrees with the information that I have already released."[35] The document itself is a contains many revelations (which "had a basis in fact") including the knowledge that "we live in a multi-dimensional world that is overlapped and visited by entities from other dimensions. Many of these entities are hostile. Many are not hostile." and that the alien presence would become widely known and acknowledged by the general population "within five to ten years." The Krill document tied together many strands of UFO and conspiracy belief, including MJ-12, Roswell, alien abductions, black helicopters, cattle and livestock mutilations, and the Men in Black. It described a multi-layered conspiracy, more devious and convoluted than UFO researchers may have suspected:

> The Greys [sic] Trojan Horse-style manipulation and lying which allied MJ-12 forces with them four decades ago; the government's disinformation of the subject of UFOs in order to perpetuate the agreement with the Greys free of public scrutiny; the lies to the abductees; the Greys on-going abduction of people and mutilation of animals in order to harvest enzymes, blood and other tissues for their own survival needs; and a genetic blend of the Grey race and a tall Nordic race to enable Grey interface with humans to be done with greater ease.[36]

Cooper's endorsement of the KRILL document would be one of the factors which led to his exit from the UFO field. The document's similarities to previously-released material such as John Lear's statement could be attributed to the fact that they shared the same author—John Lear. By the early 1990s, it was widely accepted in the UFO community that Lear, along with UFO researcher John Grace had put together the KRILL as a hoax. Cooper, by claiming he had seen similar information decades before, fell into the trap. As a writer calling him/herself "I. M. Feddup" wrote in an attack on

Cooper entitled "Behold a Stale Horse," Cooper did not take news of the hoax well:

> Mr. Cooper, as usual, made an ass of himself in an interview discussing the subject of O.H. Krill. The origin of the O.H. Krill document is well known in the UFO community It was originally put together by UFO researcher John Grace.... One evening during a television interview of Mr. Cooper, Lear overhead Mr. Cooper use the O.H Krill name and mention the fact that he had first seen this document while working for the Office of Naval Intelligence in the early 1970's. As Mr. Lear has related, he immediately pulled Mr. Cooper aside and quietly told him, "Bill, O.H. Krill is a joke! John Grace and I used Krill ... because of a woman who allegedly channeled an entity named CRYLLL. Grace just pulled the O.H. out of thin air!" Mr. Cooper instantly unleashed his hostile self and in his usual denial of reality, replied that Lear was mistaken, insisting that he had seen it in 1972 while working for Naval Intelligence.[37]

In a 2008 interview, John Lear recalled the incident, acknowledging that he and Grace had assembled the Krill document, but denying that it was a hoax, saying, "We weren't trying to shy anybody on. We weren't trying to put any false information out. It was just what we thought the state of the art was then." Lear recalls the television interview where Cooper "said he'd seen them in the Navy 20 years prior! When, you know, John Grace and I had dreamed them up like two months prior to that." Lear said he took Cooper aside during a break in the interview and asked, "What in the hell are you talking about? John Grace and I wrote that Krill paper" and recalls that Cooper replied, "Well that may be, but I saw them in the Navy." Lear says this was the beginning of the end of his association with Cooper, who was falling victim to what Lear called "UFO disease ... where you get so popular in the UFO field and you don't have anything new to say, you make it up."[38] By 1990, prominent publications like *UFO Magazine* were openly denouncing Cooper and his claims. Don Ecker of *UFO Magazine* began to investigate Cooper's claims that he had seen information corroborating that of Lear and others while part of a Naval Intelligence briefing team. In an 1990 issue of the magazine, Ecker presented this conclusion:

> During this investigation *UFO Magazine* has found that much of Cooper's material is entirely fabricated, lifted from others' work, or facts he's selected and twisted to support his own story. Several times Cooper has told those who have disagreed with him or questioned his information, "I will crucify you..." At what point will someone allow a demagogue to intimidate him or her into silence? At what point will truth be the final casualty in a war of words with liars?[39]

Cooper segued out of the UFO field, denouncing its major players as disinformation agents claiming, in fact, that he saw the very names of those who had criticized him listed as intelligence assets in those fabled 1972 briefing documents. As he moved into the world of more overtly political conspiracy thought, he would only occasionally admit that he had fallen prey to this supposed disinformation.[40] Lear and others who had promoted paranoid conspiracies of an alien/government conspiracy faded from the scene as well as researchers declared the line between fact and fiction to be almost irreparably blurred by hoaxes, speculation, and active government disinformation such as that revealed by William Moore in his 1989 address to MUFON. The conspiracy theories that emerged in Lear's statement, drawn from the Bennewitz incident, and expanded upon in the work of Cooper and others would, however, persist. The early 1990s were a heyday for lore about the underground base at Dulce as well as elaborations on stories of connection between aliens and terrestrial governments. Jason Bishop III, in a document simply called "The Dulce Base," retold the basic story with added details. He shifted the dates to remove human-alien contact from its post-war context and presented it as a story with deep historical roots:

> Centuries ago, Surface People (some say the Illuminati) entered into a pact with an "Alien Nation" (hidden within the Earth). The U.S. Government, in 1933, agreed to trade Animals and Humans in exchange for High Tech Knowledge, and allow them to use (undisturbed) UNDERGROUND BASES, in the Western USA. A Special Group was formed to deal with the Alien Beings. In the 1940's, "Alien Life Forms (ALF)" began shifting their focus of operations, from Central and South America, to the USA.[41]

Similarly, "Commander X," a collective pen name for a number of conspiracy writers (such as Jim Keith),[42] published *Underground Alien Bases* in 1990, which combined the alien-invasion stories of Paul Bennewitz with tales of an inhabited hollow earth (see Chapter 5) and more prosaic political and economic conspiracy theories. He linked the underground base at Dulce to powerful corporations such as Bechtel ("a supersecret international corporate octopus … some say the firm is really a 'shadow government'—a working arm of the CIA"). Bechtel, and other entities, are part of of "an interconnected control system" linking "the Tri-Lateralist plans, the C.F.R. [Council on Foreign Relations], the Orders of 'Illuminism' (Cult of the All-Seeing Eye)" with other groups.[43] These connections between a supposed alien agenda and the political machinations of humans would continue to grow throughout the decade.

Flying Saucers and the New World Order

The conspiratorial worlds of ufological and political conspiracy theory are deeply intertwined. While some of these connections are obvious, such as the ominous tales of illegal, secret treaties between the United States and malevolent alien beings. This recurring meme combines the traditional ufological conspiracy of the government establishment knowing more about the UFO phenomenon than the general public and blends it with conspiratorial notions of the American government actively working to subjugate and enslave its citizens. There is, clearly, an overlap between those two conspiracy narratives. A significant strand of conspiratorial thought involving the question of an extraterrestrial presence visiting the earth emerged in the 1990s that positioned the major ufological conspiracy theories of he time as a tool of disinformation deployed to bring the New World Order into power. There are several examples of conspiracy theorists and writers who have taken this approach. Here we will examine the work of two men who were familiar figures in the conspiracy world of the 1990s—Bill Cooper and Jim Keith.

The ufological world cast Bill Cooper into the outer darkness within a few years of his entry into the field. He then shifted more fully to politically-oriented conspiracy theories, particularly those claiming that a totalitarian world government threatened to end American sovereignty. The UFO phenomenon, however, would remain part of the narrative to which he clung and that he tirelessly promoted until the end of his life in 2001.

The essence of Cooper's connection of ufology to his conspiratorial worldview was that the UFO movement—as well as the community of investigators and devotees the movement had produced—was a mechanism for disinformation. He did, at times, acknowledge that he had played a role in promoting the UFO movement and its ideals, and he did so repentantly, saying that "for many years" he had "sincerely believed that an extraterrestrial threat existed and that it was the most important driving force behind world events. I was wrong and for that I most deeply and humbly apologize."[44] In his 1991 book *Behold a Pale Horse*—published after numerous gaffes had begun to force his exit from the field—saw Cooper begin to hedge his bets on the impending alien invasion. This contained an "updated" version of "The Secret Government," Cooper's summary of the John Lear-style conspiracy theory of humanity being subjugated by aliens and their human co-conspirators. In closing "The Secret Government," Cooper tells the reader,

> If the documentation that I viewed while I was in Naval Intelligence is true, then what you have just read is probably closer to the truth than anything ever written. If extraterrestrials are a hoax, then what you just read is exactly what the Illuminati wants you to believe. I can assure you beyond any shadow of a doubt that even if aliens are not real, the technology IS REAL.[45]

By the mid- to late 1990s, Cooper had shifted from affirming and promoting the claims of the Krill Document or John Lear and began to focus on a global socialist or communist (Cooper often used the terms interchangeably) conspiracy to end American freedom, saying, "The plan for the creation of a socialist world government is protected by an artificial extraterrestrial threat from space. The entire UFO phenomenon and the uFOOLogy [sic][46] movement has been created to further the protection and activation of the plan." The push for a global government would, Cooper argued, be made successful through the powers-that-be (generally the "Illuminati" or an analogue) engineering an extraterrestrial invasion as an impetus for the nations of the world to band together for humanity's defense.

Cooper provided some evidence that so-called "elites" (or at least prominent political, social and cultural figures) had proposed such a scenario. One example is that of educator John Dewey, who in a 1917 speech on international cooperation during the First World War said the following:

> Some one remarked that the best way to unite all the nations on this globe would be an attack from some other planet. In the face of such an alien enemy, people would respond with a sense of their unity of interest and purpose. We have the next thing to that at the present time. Before a common menace, North and South America, the Occident, and Orient have done an unheard of thing, a wonderful thing, a thing which, it may well be, future history will point to as the most significant thing in these days of wonderful happenings. They have joined forces amply and intimately in a common cause with one another and with the European nations which were most directly threatened.... Nations from every continent have formed what for the time being is nothing less than a world state, an immense cooperative action in behalf of civilization.[47]

Cooper introduces this quotation, of which he only uses the opening two sentences, by saying, "The plan to create an artificial extraterrestrial threat to the Earth was first mentioned by the Marxist, John Dewey." Dewey, however, said nothing about creating a threat and, in fact, explains that the then-current geopolitical situation accomplished much the same thing result. Nevertheless, Cooper uses this to explain that many of the signal events in the "history" of the UFO field had been hoaxes designed to prepare the earth's population to accept a global government in the face of an extraterrestrial threat. The Orson Wells "War of the Worlds" broadcast, for example, was a psychological conditioning operation since "the public believed the *War Of The Worlds* was real." The program was successful in "setting the stage for the implementation of an alien threat scenario."[48] The Roswell Incident, Cooper argued, was another in this series of hoaxes designed to prepare the public to accept an extraterrestrial threat:

> The natural guilt harbored by the men of the 509th Atomic Bomb Wing after the bombing of Hiroshima and Nagasaki made them eager conspirators in orchestrating the faked crash of an extraterrestrial craft and discovery of shaved

and surgically altered monkeys near Roswell, New Mexico, in 1947. The artificial extraterrestrial threat was thus implanted in the mind of the public.[49]

The Roswell Incident, however, was not widely known—even in ufological circles—until the publication of the Berlitz/Moore book in 1981. This explanation of the Roswell Incident, little discussed by Cooper outside of the MAJESTYTWELVE document, illustrates the degree to which Cooper was willing to bend the established ufological chronology to establish a narrative that suited his position that UFO belief—particularly belief in a hostile alien invasion scenario—was a tool of the New World Order.

On Cooper's website and on his radio program, every prominent ufologist was a target—they were disinformation agents, servants of the New World Order. UFO promoters like William English, whose story Cooper promoted just a few years earlier, are viciously denounced as either dupes or con artists. One example is William English, whose claims in the early 1990s corroborated much of Lear/Cooper/Krill style of dark and paranoid conspiracy. Interviewed by UFO researcher Jacques Vallee, Cooper described English as a persecuted hero:

> There is a man named Bill English who is in hiding near Albuquerque, and who has seen the same things I did. He is afraid for his life. They have already tried to kill him twice. The government blew up a van in which he was riding with two other fellows. They died, and he's lucky to have escaped.[50]

Cooper's tone had changed by 1999, responding on his radio program to an attack on him by English, who had left the UFO field for a time. English had returned, with an open letter to the UFO community in which he castigated Cooper for his supposed frauds and accused him of becoming involved in the militia movement only because he'd been driven out of ufology. English claimed that he had left ufology due to "people like Cooper and the damage they were doing to a field that I felt deserved better than what they were giving it." Cooper replied that "William S. English left the so-called ufoology field, if there is such a thing, because he was laughed out, ladies and gentlemen. So many people have proven him a liar that he ran for cover and until recently has not emerged." Cooper, of course, did not acknowledge that at one time he had accepted English's claims. On his radio program, and in this installment in particular, Cooper would often be less than humble about his brief sojourn in the world of alien invasions, claiming that he "popped the ufoology bubble" when he "exposed" it as part of a plot to usher in a totalitarian, "socialist" world government.[51]

Cooper's transition from the UFO world to the more terrestrial political conspiracy world—as well as the blending of these two worlds—shows him to be, in some ways, a chameleon. Interestingly, as we saw in Chapter 2, many of his core views did not change. From his alien paranoia to his government and secret society paranoia, Cooper is consistent in what the end point of the conspiracy will be: the subjugation of humanity under a socialist or communist world government. "The New World Order," he wrote, "cannot, and will not, allow our Constitution to continue to exist. The New World Order will be a totalitarian socialist system. We will be slaves shackled to a cashless system of economic control."[52]

Cooper was far from along in suspecting that the UFO movement might be a tool of disinformation. William Moore's role in cooperating with the Air Force and that operation's effect on Paul Bennewitz certainly illustrates the reality of such interactions. Prolific conspiracy writer, researcher, and underground zine publisher Jim Keith, in his 1999 book *Saucers of the Illuminati*, connects the UFO question to the larger questions of political conspiracy. Unlike Cooper, however, Jim Keith does not settle on one particular conspiratorial conclusion. Rather, he examines concrete events such as the Bennewitz affair, asserting "it is obvious that the government is attempting to defuse UFO investigations by overwhelming them with incendiary disinformation and by having informants report on the activities of groups and individuals."[53] Complicating this assertion, however, is the role his own pseudonymous writings as "Commander X" played in promoting some of that disinformation both as Commander X and in his various zines. Conspiracy writer Kenn Thomas, in his Forward to the 2004 reprint of *Saucers of the Illuminati*, writes that Keith "didn't necessarily believe any of it, but he believed in the importance of having it all discussed."[54] Jim Keith's work is, however, far more exploratory and less dogmatic about the ultimate goal of those seeking to deceive researchers, acknowledging that something strange is occurring, related to the phenomenon, considering that "encounters with aliens" or interaction with "spiritual or non-material entities" connected to a "crossover dimension ... where reality slides in and out of thought and imagination and possibility."[55] While Keith does not make a stand on any one explanation of the UFO phenomenon, he shares Cooper's suspicions about the roots of UFO experiences and believes that

> the evidence ... suggests that our vision has been purposely obscured by what we have been led to believe about the UFO experience, and it is probably not directly being done by insectoid extraterrestrials.... The most sensible, yet least voiced explanation is that some UFO encounters are being staged for an ultimate—and ulterior purpose. Is it within the real of possibility that there is a group working behind the scenes to convince us that we are being invaded by space aliens?[56]

While Bill Cooper asserted that UFOs were merely exclusively government craft or holographic projections designed to deceive witnesses and perpetuate the mythology of alien invasion and conquest, Keith's opinions were much less rigid. Both, however, saw deep and undeniable connections between the flying saucer mystery and earthly political conspiracy.

Despite the admitted hoaxes, disinformation campaigns, and dearth of evidence, Conspiracy theories surrounding extraterrestrial visitation and UFO sightings did not end with the 1990s. New iterations, such as the Exopolitics movement, emerged. This trend blended the notion of friendly, helpful aliens promoted during the 1950s with a 1990s-inspired conspiratorial streak which contended that the government (or other powerful forces) sought to keep the technology and knowledge provided by the aliens secret from the public for their own benefit. Exopolitics, however, is only one of the ways in which alien-oriented conspiracies continued to play an important role in the development of conspiracy culture. Nearly every other aspect of conspiracy culture discussed in the pages that follow ends up, somehow, connected to the question of extraterrestrial life and its supposed presence on earth. From Nazi flying saucers, to "aliens" being connected to belowground civilizations, the alien question is one that surfaces time and again in the modern conspiracy world.

4

Mind Control

Richard Condon's 1959 novel *The Manchurian Candidate*, and its subsequent 1962 film adaption, remains one of the signal touchstones of popular culture paranoia. Its basic notions of brainwashed assassins and mind controlled sleeper agents have been part of the conspiratorial lexicon for decades. In the late 1950s when the novel first appeared, the basic idea of brainwashing was well-established within the context of the Cold War. Books and magazine articles had appeared since the early 1950s that positioned this technique firmly within the grasp of America's communist enemies. The American fascination with mind control, however, was not limited to lurid political thrillers, nor would it be limited to the decade of the 1950s.

The topic of "mind control," perhaps more than any other within the realm of conspiracy narrative, marries outrageous, often truly terrifying and disturbing claims with historical documentation that are nearly as disturbing. There is a well-established record of elements within the United States government (as well as associated private contractors) engaging in research and experimentation with the goal of developing methods to some level of control over individuals' actions. Further, the considerable amount of real or perceived cover-up of these experiments have fueled conspiratorial tales since the 1970s. Its historical roots, however, extend back further. The history of the U.S. government's mind control experiments has its roots in Cold War paranoia about the scientific capabilities of the Soviet Union and its Communist compatriots. In particular, interrogation methods supposedly used by China and North Korea on American prisoners during the Korean war indicated to some observers that our foes on the other side of the Iron Curtain had developed new and frightening methods of psychologically breaking down and rebuilding their subjects. At the very least, they were ahead of us. This would prompt elements of the U.S. military and intelligence communities to engage in their own experimentation in order to narrow that gap.

The range of the intelligence and defense establishment's scientific (and other decidedly less scientific) investigations extended beyond psychological experimentation. While some were quite prosaic, such as space-based weapons systems, others, such as the exploration of psychic ability and its potential applications for intelligence operations, have more sinister implications. One example of this is the military and intelligence communities' explorations of the potential of the human mind extended to its supposed paranormal capabilities as well, particularly in the form of the supposed phenomenon known as "remote viewing." Remote viewing refers to a systematic application of psychic abilities for the purposes of espionage. During the 1980s and 1990s reports surfaced illustrating that the U.S. Defense Department experimented with psychic spying. What began as an abandoned attempt to close a perceived "psi-gap" with the Soviet Union transitioned into the civilian world as various remote viewing operatives commercialized these so-called "protocols," offering to allow the general public to learn the psychic secrets of the elite.

On one end of the spectrum of mind control conspiracy theories are tales of sinister forces targeting individuals and turning them into mind controlled slaves. At the other extreme, opposite of this bespoke, personal mental manipulation are arguments that our entire culture is being manipulated through mind control on a massive scale. While the mass media, pharmaceutical industry, or other entities are common culprits the motives behind their manipulation vary widely. Some are remarkably prosaic: a desire for increased profits or domination of a particular market leads a corporation to use techniques such as subliminal advertising, to covertly influence buyers' decisions. Others mind control culprits are more exotic, using technologies such as extremely low frequency (or ELF) waves to manipulate entire populations to accept or reject those policies or politicians that the shadowy manipulators found desirable or undesirable.

Mind control conspiracy narratives—particularly those involving governmental agencies manipulating individuals, often ruining their lives in the process—excel in their lurid extravagance. Personal accounts which describe horrific psychological and, often, physical tortures usually involve prominent political and media figures, involving them in transgressive activities that reinforce the public's darkest suspicions of their leaders. As one reviewer of Cathy O'Brien's *TRANCE Formation of America* wrote, "considering the sordid reputation our government officials have, as spelled out in many other conspiracy books, I truly want to believe at least some" of the stories about politicians like Bill Clinton, Dick Cheney, or Henry Kissinger.[1]

Paranoia surrounding mind control and subsequent attempts by the U.S. government to gain access to this supposed treasure trove of scientific technique had its origins in the Cold War. In particular, the Korean War was a significant factor in influencing elements of the defense and intelligence communities. In particular, the notion of brainwashing, popularized by the media with regard to the rise of Communism in China and the treatment of American prisoners of war energized many into believing that highly specific control of the human mind was not only possible but, in fact, had been attained by America's enemies. Concern over the susceptibility of the mind was wide spread during the era. Allison Graham observes that

> psychology occupied a central place in Cold War anxieties about scientific techniques that could be used for political purposes, and hypnosis was often center stage in the fears people expressed. Hypnosis turned up in descriptions of Communist projects to take over American minds, in accounts of American marketing "persuaders" working their subtle influence in public spaces, and in government sponsored projects such as the Central Intelligence Agency's (CIA) MK-ULTRA program.[2]

The broad array of concerns related to mind control during the Cold War would persist in the literature of the conspiracy culture through the late twentieth century and into the twenty-first. This fear of mind control techniques and technologies was reflected in alien abduction and invasion scenarios in the 1980s and 1990s with John Lear, among others, discussing mind control devices implanted in abductees. Indeed, artifacts supposedly extracted from the bodies of these abductees sparked debates over whether the implants were alien in origin or part of a government mind control plot.

It is not often the case that a word or term's origin can be pinpointed with any degree of accuracy. The concepts and terminology underlying "brainwashing," however, are firmly rooted in an identifiable historical context. On September 24, 1950, as the Korean War raged, the *Miami News* published an article entitled "'Brain-Washing' Tactics Force Chinese into Ranks of Communist Party." Its author was Edward Hunter, a journalist who was later revealed to have ties to the CIA and who would, in time, be the editor of *Tactics*, a journal devoted to psychological warfare.[3] Initially, Edward Hunter discussed brainwashing and mind control in the context of the mass control that the Communist Party exercise over the peoples of China and North Korea. It was a system for political indoctrination, not too dissimilar in its effects to what the Soviet Union or Nazi Germany had accomplished during the 1930s. As scholar Timothy Melley observes, "If this system was innovative, what made it so was the scale of the operation and ruthlessness of its proponents, who aimed for nothing less than the mental transformation of an entire continent."[4]

While "brainwashing" was initially discussed in terms of a ruthless, broadband propaganda strategy designed to engender love and support of the new Communist regimes in East Asia, it would later be used in relation to Chinese and North Koreans coercing American POWs into confessing war crimes and other illegalities committed by American troops against Koreans and Chinese. American writers' treatment of brainwashing shifted from a broad-based effort to manipulate whole populations to "a secret program for human enslavement." Timothy Melley argues that this shift was necessary due to those confessions made by U.S. military officers. Investigators were able to use the concept of brainwashing as a partial explanation for how otherwise solid and upright Americans had, apparently, readily confessed to such crimes. "If American POWs looked weak," Melley explains, "it was because they had been subjected to a mind-control weapon of extraordinary power."[5]

Edward Hunter, the journalist who first introduced the term, wrote two books that brought these ideas of mind control to the American masses in the 1950s. The first, *Brain-Washing in Red China*, was published in 1951 and—as its title suggests—focused on the mass propaganda facets of brainwashing as a means through which the Communist Party asserted and maintained control of China. His second book, *Brainwashing: The Story of Men Who Defied It*, focused much more heavily on the use of brainwashing and other mind manipulation techniques to affect individuals. Hunter addresses brainwashing and mind control in a manner that is thoroughly integrated with American Cold War politics:

> The war against men's minds has for its primary objective the creation of what is euphemistically called this "new Soviet man." The intent is to change a mind radically so that its owner becomes a living puppet—a human robot—within the atrocity being visible from the outside. The aim is to create a mechanism in flesh and blood, with new belies and new thought processes inserted into a captive body ... slave race that, unlike the salves of olden times, can be trusted never to revolt, always to be amenable to orders, like an insect to its instincts. The extent is to atomize humanity.[6]

Thus, as Hunter explains, brainwashing is part and parcel of the stander subversive communist tool kit. It was something, moreover, that American soldiers had no defense for, no preparation. Hunter calls for widespread education about the dangers of communist brainwashing. "Facts," he pronounces, "can demolish the entire face communist paradise. Nothing should be allowed to interfere with the task of getting those facts across to the people who need and can use them."[7]

Hunter, as mentioned above, has been identified as an asset of the CIA on a number of occasions and some scholars, such as Dick Anthony, have argued that his discussion and framing of brainwashing served the interests of the Central Intelligence Agency, asserting that "the brainwashing paradigm was developed originally by the American CIA as a propaganda device to explain why a few Korean POWs appeared to convert to communism while imprisoned." Anthony claims that Hunter's books and articles (as well as his testimony before Congress on the dangers of communist brainwashing) and novels such as Richard Condon's *The Manchurian Candidate* were not their original ideas but were "developed by many covert operatives within the CIA."[8] Anthony's research is particularly focused on the ways in which what he views as the misapplication of flawed brainwashing theory to "cults" has resulted in the persecution of minority religious groups. His observations on the origins of the notion of brainwashing and subsequent theories of "mind control" are illustrative of the long history of the American intelligence community's interest in directing the wider conversation about brainwashing and mind control technology. Particularly in Hunt's work there is a strong suggestion that the United States—being made up, largely, of decent people who would never think of something as dastardly as brainwashing—is far behind its communist enemies in this horrifying but useful field. Taking into account the revelations of CIA mind control and manipulation programs that would emerge in the 1970s, the works of Hunt and Condon begin to look like carefully planned spadework, preparing the American people to be as amenable as possible to American efforts to combat the brainwashing science of the communist forces. Their actions, of course, would be carried out in secret. Secrets, however, have a way of getting out.

The emergence of information about psychological experimentation by the American intelligence community was part and parcel of the changing political culture of the 1970s. The events and forces that weakened the American public's faith in the government of the United States, along with reports by journalists, spurred Congress to conduct its own investigations into a wide array of possibly illegal actions by a number of executive branch agencies including the FBI and CIA. Some of the impact of these investigations, conducted by the Church Committee and the Rockefeller Commission were discussed in Chapter 2. Also coming to light, however, were a number of psychological experiments involving techniques and tools chillingly similar to those decried in the brainwashing panic of the 1950s.

Unfortunately for the Church Committee and subsequent investigatory committees, then-CIA director Richard Helms authorized the destruction of the bulk of the agency's records on psychological experimentation in 1973, which comprised a number of projects under the umbrella cryptonym of Project MKULTRA.[9] His reasoning was partially based on the fact that a number of private contractors—including universities in the United States and Canada were involved in the research, Sidney Gottlieb, head of the CIA's

Technical Services Division requested that the records be eliminated. DCI Richard Helms, testifying before the Church Committee defended the destruction of these records, claiming that Gottlieb

> said that he was retiring ... and he thought it would be a good idea if these files were destroyed. And I also believe part of the reason for our thinking this was advisable was there had been relationships with outsiders in government agencies and other organizations and that these would be sensitive in this kind of thing but that since the program was over and finished and done with, we thought we would just get rid of the files as well, so that anybody who assisted us in the past would not be subject to follow-up or questions, embarrassment, if you will.[10]

It is important to bear in mind the CIA's actions (and Helms's testimony) when examining the more lurid and unsupported (often unsupportable) claims and stories revolving around the broad topic of mind control. For every alleged operation, experiment, or other action for which there is no supporting documentation, conspiracists and those who believe their claims may respond with the following explanations and defenses. First is the explanation that, for claims of events that occurred before 1973, the records that *would* confirm the truth of those claims had been destroyed as part of Helms's cover-up. For events that occur after 1973 (or, indeed, after the CIA and other entities had officially abandoned such experiments), there is the explanation that the CIA had illegally destroyed records before; indeed, that the entire modus operandi of the intelligence world is deliberate deception and obfuscation. Why should we believe anything they say? While many records had been destroyed in 1973, however others survived. The existence of this testimony and its essence—if not always its precise content—would serve as the foundation of a number of mind control oriented conspiracy narratives.

In 1977, the successor to the Church Committee, the Senate Select Committee on Intelligence reopened an investigation into the program. Committee chair Senator Daniel Inouye (D–HI) opened the hearings with a statement that made clear the current disposition of such programs:

> It should be made clear from the outset that in general, we are focusing on events that happened over 12 or as long as 25 years ago. It should be emphasized that the programs that are of greatest concern have stopped and that we are reviewing these past events in order to better understand what statutes and other guidelines might be necessary to prevent the recurrence of such abuses in the future. We also need to know and understand what is now being done by the CIA in the field of behavioral research to be certain that no current abuses are occurring.[11]

CIA Director Admiral Stansfield Turner explained that the newly uncovered MKULTRA files had been misplaced and only found by accident. Turner testified that "the Agency failed to uncover these particular documents in 1973 in the process of attempting to destroy them; it similarly failed to locate them in 1975 in response to the Church Committee hearings." Despite this, Turner was "convinced that there was no attempt to conceal this material during the earlier searches."[12] The comments of Inouye and Turner, as with Helms's comments years earlier, could fuel suspicion of a cover-up. One consistent theme within conspiracy theories that, in general, shadowy organizations possess amazing, almost supernatural capabilities, seeming nearly omnipotent and omniscient. From a conspiracy theorist's point of view, it is unlikely that the CIA—which had masterminded this bizarre array of psychological experiments—would be subject to such a mundane bureaucratic mishap such as this.

One of the key pieces of information that emerged during these hearings that opene the door to further investigation, was a July 26, 1963, inspector general report regarding MKULTRA which was addressed to the Director of Central Intelligence. This was part of a larger inspection of the Technical Services Division, under whose aegis MKULTRA operated. This is an eye-opening document which notes the history of the project (it had been initiated by DCI Allan Dulles in 1953) and succinctly states the basic goals of the project. MKULTRA was "concerned with the research and development of chemical, biological, and radiological materials capable of employment in clandestine operations to control human behavior." It also discussed the complexity and scope of the program revealing that in addition to MKULTRA—the "research and development" portion of the project—there was MKDELTA, the "system for control of the operational employment of such materials." This was not merely a speculative exercise—administrative mechanisms were in place to put whatever was learned into practice.[13]

The inspector general, J. S. Earman, notes in his introductory summation "the concepts involved in manipulating human behavior are found by many people both within and outside the Agency to be distasteful and unethical." But regardless of this distaste, "there is considerable evidence that opposition intelligence services are active and highly proficient in this field." If, as Dick Anthony argues, stories of communist proficiency at brainwashing were element of a propaganda ploy then this ploy was effect at high levels of the CIA. The inspector general concludes "that the structure and operational controls over this activity need strengthening; improvements are needed in the administration of research projects; and some of the testing of substances under simulated operational conditions was judged to involve excessive risk to the Agency."[14]

Along with this insight into the leeriness with which some aspects of

4. Mind Control 105

the CIA had toward experiments into behavioral control, the inspector general's report also provides crucial insight into the degree of secrecy and security used by the Agency. The investigation was more difficult than most because

> there are just two individuals in TSD [Technical Services Division] who have full substantive knowledge of the program and most of that knowledge is unrecorded. Both are highly skilled, highly motivated, professionally competent individuals. Part of their competence lies in their command of intelligence tradecraft. In protecting the sensitive nature of the American intelligence capability to manipulate human behavior, they apply "need to know" doctrine to their professional associates and to their clerical assistants to a maximum degree. Confidence in their competence and discretion has been a vital feature of the management of MKULTRA.[15]

High levels of security, however, do not guarantee positive outcomes. The report stated that "as of 1960 no effective knockout pill, truth serum, aphrodisiac, or recruitment pill was known to exist" and described MKDELTA (the operational use of chemical or pharmaceutical means to coerce or interrogate) as "inherently a high-risk, low-yield field of operations." Further, some CIA operatives feared "over-reliance on and misuse of drugs in lieu of perfecting classic espionage techniques."[16] One of the key insights one takes away from reading the 1963 inspector general's report is that there was marked disagreement over whether or not the CIA should be investigating these things and, in cases where they did, whether or not it the results were useful for intelligence work. Crucially, this was a closely held, very secretive project. Despite that, there is a fairly solid historical through-line illustrating the origins, development, and supposed termination of such programs.

MKULTRA was an umbrella designation covering nearly 150 different programs but not all of them are fully documented due to the destruction of so many records. It is important to reiterate that these gaps in the record are crucial to the proliferation of conspiracy theories and narratives surrounding the topic of mind control. The secrecy inherent in intelligence operations and the legally questionable destruction of records that Richard Helms ordered continue to fuel speculation. Thus "Project Monarch," an alleged MKULTRA program which does not appear in any government records, is discussed in the literature of the conspiracy culture alongside other exotic-sounding cryptonyms as MKNAOMI (the use of biological warfare materials in intelligence work), Project ARTICHOKE (the immediate precursor to MKULTRA) or Project CHATTER (a late 1940s U.S. Navy investigation into the uses of various drugs, such as mescaline, in interrogation). These projects are solidly part of the historical record while Monarch, as we will see, is not.

As with most aspects of conspiracy culture, the real and the unreal (or, more charitably, the undocumented or unverifiable) often blend together.

One significant source that conspiracy researchers often cite when discussing MKULTRA programs is *CIA v. Sims*, a 1985 U.S. Supreme Court case in which the court ruled on a whether or not the Central Intelligence Agency had acted properly in exempting some information on MKULTRA for reasons of national security. This case illustrates one of the significant aspects of MKULTRA that complicates research into the extent of the experimentation: the vast array of entities to whom the CIA had subcontracted MKULTRA work. There was no secret CIA lab where the entirety of MKULTRA took place. Rather, throughout the United States and Canada universities and other research institutions carried out various aspects of experimentation. The culpability of higher education and the scientific establishment has been one of the most thoroughly studied aspects of MKULTRA, placing it within the context of other medical and scientific experimentation carried out upon the unwitting or unwilling. The plaintiffs, John C. Sims and Sidney M. Wolfe, sought the release of "grant proposals and contracts awarded under the MKULTRA program and the names of the institutions and individuals that had performed research." The CIA released some of the names to Sims and Wolfe, but withheld others, citing statutory law which allows the Agency to deny Freedom of Information Act requests to protect the identify of assets.

The Supreme Court had to determine, in part, whether or not MKULTRA researchers constituted actual "intelligence assets." In *Sims*, the court ruled that the definition of "intelligence asset" was, in fact, remarkably broad and did include scientific researchers—a group that the plaintiffs had asserted was not properly considered so. The "legislative history" of the National Security Act of 1947, the court ruled

> indicates that Congress was well aware that the Agency would call on a wide range and variety of sources to provide intelligence. Moreover, the record developed in this case confirms the obvious importance of scientists and other researchers as American intelligence sources.

The CIA, the majority decided, acted within the proper scope of its powers in refusing to release some names of researchers because "Even a small chance that some court will order disclosure of a source's identity could well impart intelligence gathering and cause sources to 'close up like a clam.'" While the decision of the court was unanimous, Justices Thurgood Marshall and William Brennan authored a concurring opinion in which they expressed concern that the Court's "wholesale" adoption of the CIA's definition of "intelligence source" was an error that undermined the purpose of the Freedom of Information Act.[17]

Many aspects of MKULTRA, as illustrated in official reports and court transcripts, were carried out in controlled laboratory environments. The 1963 inspector general's report, however, reinforces that crucial portions of these experiments were far from sterile and controlled:

> The final phase of testing of MKULTRA materials involves their application to unwitting subjects in normal life settings. It was noted earlier that the capabilities of MKULTRA substances to produce disabling or discrediting effects or to increase the effectiveness of interrogation of hostile subjects cannot be established solely through testing of volunteer populations.[18]

It is this type of operation that surfaces in personal claims and accounts of mind control in conspiracy literature: victims in many different walks of life who are subjected to horrific abuse.

Cases and Connections: Mind Control Adventures of the Rich and Famous

Particularly significant to the development of the mind control mythos in American conspiracy culture is the emergence of two specific kinds of paranoid writing on the subject. The most prominent of these are first-person memoirs written (or co-written) by those who allege that they are victims of government mind control programs. Several of these have become prominent enough within the conspiracy community that researchers and writers often repeat their claims uncritically. Books such as *TRANCE Formation of America* by Cathy O'Brien and *Thanks for the Memories: The Truth has Set me Free!* by Brice Taylor give a human face to the supposed depredations of government mind manipulators and the political and intelligence community actors who take advantage of this technology. They also provide lurid accounts of troublingly brutal sexual violence committed by prominent political and media figures. Often these figures—particularly those in the entertainment fields—are ones who would be considered by most Americans to be benign, even beloved. Men like Bob Hope, Boxcar Willie, and others do not readily spring to mind when pondering the most depraved figures in twentieth century American entertainment. These purported autobiographies combine elements of traditional, straightforward conspiracy whistleblowing with transgressive sexuality, what one could quite legitimately label "conspiracy porn."

These revelations, which began to emerge in the mid–1990s gave rise to a groundswell of more-or-less similar claims. Taking root chiefly—but not exclusively—on the fledgling World Wide Web, were sites and forums that provided a haven for alleged mind control victims and survivors to tell their stories of government harassment, control, and manipulation. Their stories ranged from the heartbreaking to the absurd and, as with the autobiographies of figures like O'Brien and Taylor, one suspects that some manner of abuse or harm had come to the claimants at some point in their lives. Here we see the effects of conspiracy thinking in brutally real terms, as the alleged victims tell stories of lives ripped apart by what they believe to be government mind control programs and the ongoing effort of these programs to cover-up their crimes.

The outpouring of thousands of pages of declassified information through Congressional investigations and Freedom of Information Act requests bolstered their claims. Such as flood of information and evidence that the government had undertaken horrific crimes against its unwitting and unwilling citizens *must*, they cried, give credence to their claims of ongoing harassment and experimentation. After all, the argument goes, no one really *believes* the CIA when they say they no longer engage in these types of experimentation since the CIA lies as a matter of course. A wide variety of conspiracy theorists, like David Icke, latched on to these personal mind control testimonies, folding them into their own theories and using them as supporting evidence for cover-ups far beyond even what their originators had believed.

In addition to claims of individual mind control there are broader discussions of the ways in which the government as well as its corporate minions (or controllers, depending on the conspiracy theory) use the mass media as a means to control whole populations. Subliminal messaging and other technological means of manipulating the vast majority of Americans have the potential to direct the outcome of elections, affect the economy, or any number of myriad other goals and outcomes. From our mobile electronics to the artificial sweeteners we put in our coffee, our hidden controllers have a plan for us and the thoughts we mistakenly believe to be our own. These mind control conspiracies also have strong connections to many of the other conspiracy theories which would come into vogue during the 1990s and early twenty-first century. Mind control theories would tie into questions and concerns ranging from alien abductions to the New World Order and fears of a totalitarian global government. These stories would feed on the anxieties and secrecy surrounding escaped Nazi war criminals who might be hidden by the United States government and blur into the realms of out of control scientific experimentation and innovation. Conspiracy narratives centered around mind control would be one of the cornerstones of the paranoid culture that emerged in the 1990s, offering a personal angle and emotional quality that many other conspiracy theories often lack.

Cathy O'Brien, Brice Taylor, and "Project Monarch"

Since in the 1990s, several accounts have emerged that claim to tell the story of supposed "mind controlled slaves" who escaped various degrees of violence and exploitation. These mind controlled slaves are, supposedly, used not only to satisfy the perverted whims of the rich and powerful but also as high level operatives in games of political cat and mouse. Perhaps none of these tales were as notorious as that told by Cathy O'Brien in a book entitled *TRANCE Formation* [sic] *of America*. The book was first published in 1995 and co-written with O'Brien's husband Mark Phillips, who claims that he used hypnosis to help O'Brien recover her memories as a mind-controlled slave. While, he claims, he may "lack the official published academic credentials," Phillips claims that he is "recognized internationally by mental health and law enforcement as an authority on the secret science concerning external control of the mind."[19] Phillips's contribution to *TRANCE Formation of America* consists of a brief history of his alleged involvement with the Central Intelligence Agency and his introduction to the world of mind control.

Phillips describes a horseback riding accident in his childhood that left his mother with permanent disabilities, along with his own issues with a persistent stutter. According to Phillips, "my curiosity peaked [sic] about the brain and the resultant invisible mind and had set the course for my life's interest."[20] Phillips describes becoming involved with a variety of intelligence and defense contractors during the 1970s and 1980s. He enters into a business relationship with Alex Houston, an entertainer and ventriloquist on the Nashville country music scene who appeared on stage and in variety programs such as *The Porter Wagoner Show*. In the course of this relationship, Phillips claims that he learned that Houston was involved in "the CIA, drugs, money laundering, child prostitution, and the big one … slavery."[21] Phillips learns (from an unnamed source within the intelligence world) that Houston is the "controller" of the mind-controlled Cathy O'Brien and her similarly controlled young daughter Kelly and he resolves to rescue them from their captivity. Using a set of "trigger words"—a technique he learned as part of his studies of the mind as well as his exposure to secret government projects—Phillips convinces O'Brien and her daughter to escape with him to Alaska where he uses his knowledge of hypnosis to deprogram the pair.

O'Brien then takes over the story in the second part of the book, crafting a violent and disturbing autobiography. It is a sprawling narrative that covers events from the 1960s to the 1990s. O'Brien names dozens of political figures ranging from household names (Bill Clinton, George H.W. Bush) to much more obscure figures (such as Guy Vander Jagt, U.S. House member from

Michigan and chair of the Republican National Committee) and weaves them into a tale of pedophilia and other violent sexual crimes told against a backdrop of political intrigue. O'Brien recounts a childhood filled with physical, emotional, and sexual abuse. She graphically describes her father—Earl O'Brien—and other relatives being involved in a child pornography production and trafficking ring in western Michigan during the 1960s. This abuse involves Roman Catholic churches and clergy in the area as well, painting a picture of entire communities in collusion with the abuse of O'Brien and her siblings. When, O'Brien claims, her father and others in the ring were investigated by authorities, he was offered immunity from prosecution on child pornography charges. The price for this immunity was an arrangement with the Central Intelligence Agency and the Defense Intelligence Agency which required him to subject his children to mind control experimentation.

O'Brien claims that this arrangement was part of Project Monarch. This was a program which she and Phillips asserted was one of the many projects under the MKULTRA umbrella. However, as Michael Barkun reports, "scholarly and journalistic treatments of MKULTRA and related projects make no mention of a Project Monarch."[22] In a subsequent book, O'Brien and Phillips do acknowledge that the historical provenance of the Monarch project is uncertain, saying that "'Project Monarch' was reportedly one of over 125 long-term research genetic mind control sub-program [sic] of MK Ultra focused on multi-generational abuse base families, aside from being considered an urban myth since it has it to be declassified or available through US Freedom of Information Act."[23] Despite the historical cloudiness of the Monarch project, it would become a mainstay of mind control conspiracy literature. Many of the MKULTRA programs for which documentation exists clearly show that mind control and other experimentation took place at universities or other research centers under controlled circumstances, O'Brien claims that Monarch's methodology was to train parents (such as Earl O'Brien) to use sexual and physical abuse to "splinter" children's personalities. O'Brien and Phillips explain that Multiple Personality Disorder (MPD) and Post Traumatic Stress Disorder (PTSD) are key components of mind control, that when a mind is fractured, proper trained mind controllers can use specially designed code words to access different parts of the fragmented mind. Thus O'Brien and other mind controlled slaves would have a part of their mind designed for sex work, a part designed for espionage, and so on.

O'Brien and Phillips spend the bulk of *TRANCE Formation of America* implicating public figures from the local level (at the time the "childhood" portion of the book takes place, future President Gerald Ford represented parts of western Michigan in the House of Representatives) to George H. W.

4. Mind Control

President Gerald Ford and Secretary of State Henry Kissinger, seated, in the Roosevelt Room of the White House, Washington, D.C., August 9, 1974 (Library of Congress Prints and Photographs Division Washington, D.C.). Ford and Kissinger, along with numerous other political and cultural figures, featured prominently in the mind control tales of Cathy O'Brien and Bryce Taylor.

Bush and Bill Clinton. O'Brien was "assigned" to West Virginia senator Robert Byrd and later became a "Presidential Model" mind controlled slave, able to use her abilities of total recall and photographic memory—one of the alleged effects of the MPD-based mind control training—to transmit information with complete clarity. This total recall and fidelity also allows O'Brien to claim that the dialogue presented in *TRANCE Formation* is not an approximation but the actual words spoken decades ago. O'Brien's role was to serve as a messenger between various members of the government. Her perfect recall allowed her to memorize and transmit hundreds of pages of information between U.S. presidents and other politicians or foreign leaders. *TRANCE Formation of America* also connects the American intelligence and political figures with the trade in cocaine and other illicit drugs, human trafficking, and other crimes. In between assignments for the powerful and well placed, O'Brien and her fellow mind controlled slaves were subjected to routine tortures including being turned loose in woods and being hunted like animals by political figures such as Dick Cheney. O'Brien claims that Cheney called this "a most dangerous game" and that it was designed "to condition military personnel in survival and combat maneuvers. Yet it was used on me and other slaves known to me as a means of further conditioning the mind to the realization there was 'no place to hide,' as well as traumatize the victim for ensuing programming."[24] (O'Brien does not give any indication that this plot device of human hunting, minus the mind control trappings, was pioneered by Richard Connell in his 1924 short story "The Most Dangerous Game.") The bulk of the book veers between lurid descriptions of abuse, such as Cheney's hunting adventures and long-winded discussions of how cocaine was trafficked by country music stars and CIA operatives. While O'Brien was far from the first conspiracy writer to allege connections between the U.S. government and the drug trade, her innovation was to connect talk of government sponsored drug trade to mind control conspiracies as well as wider, global cover-ups as well.

Entertainment figures also play a significant role in O'Brien's story. O'Brien claims that the country music industry, centered around Nashville, Tennessee, and Branson, Missouri, was at the heart of mind control and drug trafficking conspiracies during the 1990s. Along with ventriloquist Alex Houston, O'Brien alleges that other country music figures such as Lee Greenwood and Boxcar Willie were involved with CIA operations. The entire basis of Boxcar Willie's popularity, O'Brien claims, was due to "an ad campaign of high tech hypnotically persuasive produced television commercials." O'Brien also cites Boxcar Willie as one of those who routinely abused that her daughter Kelly.[25] O'Brien also cited women in the country music business, such as Loretta Lynn and the Mandrell sisters, as victims of mind control conspiracies. Women, in general, are portrayed as victims in *TRANCE Formation of America*. O'Brien and her daughter were victimized by men (O'Brien's father, entertainers, and various politicians). Their rescue, as well, was due to the actions of Mark Phillips. When women are not victims in this story, they are merely pawns of powerful men, working to prevent O'Brien and her daughter from escaping their mind control hell or, like her mother, docile bystanders, complicit in their victimization. One exception to this strict assignment of gender roles is O'Brien's portrayal of Hillary Clinton—shown as a violent, dominant lesbian.

In addition to telling the story of Cathy and her daughters lives in and escape from mind control slavery, O'Brien and Phillips have a broader goal of education. Mind control and manipulation are not ends in themselves. Rather, they are "little known tool[s] that 'our' United States Government is covertly, illegally, and un-constitutionally [sic] using to implement the New World Order (One World Government)" and to "expose the world domination motivations of those in control of our government, commonly referred to as the Shadow Government."²⁶ This characterization of government mind control operations and their connection to the New World Order illustrates one of the hallmarks of conspiracy theory—atemporality, a sense that historical chronology is not a necessary part of these narratives. Historical context, then, is lost. There are numerous examples of documentation of these programs over the decades. These programs—and the revelation of them—existed in specific historical and political contexts—that of the Cold War and intelligence agency's attempt to close a perceived "brainwashing gap" with the Soviet Union. Despite this well-defined historical placement, O'Brien and others who have contributed to this conspiratorial genre have consistently disconnected it from its Cold War moorings and bolted it onto fears of global government and the diminution of national sovereignty. In addition to the drug trade, O'Brien also dies education into the wider conspiracy through her discussion "Global Education 2000," an outcome-based educational program which O'Brien claimed was part of the global mind control conspiracy. O'Brien also blends the mind control conspiracies with other conspiracy notions, asserting that the imagery of demons and evil spirits as well as extraterrestrial visitation prominent theories was—at least in her case:

> Under MK-Ultra Project Monarch trauma-based mind control, I lost control over my own free will thoughts—I could not think to question, reason, or consciously comprehend—I could only do exactly what I was driven to do. Those who controlled my mind, and ultimately my actions claimed to be "aliens," "demons," and "gods." But it was my experience that [they were] perpe-TRAITORS [sic] of the New World Order.²⁷

In O'Brien's account, political and cultural figures—regardless of political ideology or party affiliation—collude to subjugate humanity under a totalitarian world government. O'Brien describes a world in which major institutions at levels reaching from small towns to the highest reaches of global politics are involved in a horrific array of abuses. From her parish priest to Saudi royalty, Cathy O'Brien and, eventually, her young daughter are continually used and exploited by figures of both moral and political authority.

TRANCE Formation of America is a convoluted book, made especially awkward due to the story of O'Brien's rescue from MKULTRA being positioned at the beginning of the book rather than then end. Readers are presented with the tale of Cathy O'Brien's mind control odyssey in reverse, with her rescue and recovery described before she is given the opportunity to tell her story. Despite the largely unsupported and unsupportable nature of her allegations, O'Brien's story—promoted not only through the book but through speaking engagements at conspiracy conventions—became the cornerstone of a wave of mind control-oriented conspiracy theories throughout the 1990s and into the twenty-first century. It also forged strong links between conspiracy theories about a New World Order and stories of Satanic Ritual Abuse such as those that surfaced with the McMartin Preschool case in the 1980s.[28]

Cathy O'Brien and Mark Phillips would experience a resurgence of prominence with the 2014 publication of *ACCESS DENIED for Reasons of National Security: Documented Journey from CIA Mind Control Slave to U.S. Government Whistleblower*. The book is an expanded discussion of O'Brien's emergence from her alleged mind control as well as the trials and tribulations of attempting to obtain custody of her daughter Kelly from Wayne Cox, who O'Brien claims was part of the Monarch mind control program. While, as in *TRANCE Formation of America*, O'Brien asserts that the dialogue presented is accurate (due to the perfect recall she possesses as a result of her mind control conditioning), it is stilted and detailed in a manner that is dissimilar to the manner in which most people actually speak. From the opening sentence, *ACCESS DENIED* is flowery and pretentious: "This true life's recorded account of extraordinary proportions began unfolding, like some kind of hyper Origami, near Nashville Tennessee on a cold winter morning February 8th 1988."[29] And, while *TRANCE Formation* certainly portrayed O'Brien and Phillips in a manner that was noble and heroic as they struggled mightily against the forces of darkness, *ACCESS DENIED* pushes their characterizations further. O'Brien's first-person narration veers from motherly concern over the fate of her daughter to prose that seems more suited to a romance novel than a conspiracy expose. Following an intimate moment, O'Brien observes "circumstances were intense, yet life's conditions could not reach the realistic spiritual high that comes with being free to live true-to-soul in harmony with love. Unconditional love celebrated through unconditional sex helped balance the intensity of our lives."[30] Mark Phillips portrays himself as an adventure heron, brandishing weapons at Federal employees while uttering quips and threats with absurd amounts of machismo.

ACCESS DENIED also benefits from a great deal of hindsight. Although the book is presented as an account of events in the early 1990s, it portrays O'Brien and Phillips as having a greater deal of insight into crucial to elements of conspiracy culture of the time that would, in fact, emerge later. The O'Brien and Phillips attempt to updated their story is, perhaps, best described as a "retcon." Drawn from comic book fandom, a retcon is an effort to fit new events into the historical fabric of a series or narrative. One example in *ACCESS DENIED* is the invocation of journalist Danny Casolaro. In the early 1990s, Casolaro was in the process of investigating an array of alleged cover-ups and conspiracies ranging from a controversy involving the computer company Inslaw and their PROMIS software package to the Iran-Contra cover-up. He referred to these collectively as "the octopus." In 1991, Casolaro was found dead in a motel room in West Virginia. While his death was ruled a suicide, his family as well as conspiracy writers have insisted that foul play was involved.

O'Brien and Phillips imply that their efforts to gain custody of Kelly in the face of government resistance was on Casolaro's radar, part of his ongoing investigations. Phillips, after allegedly talking to Casolaro, tells O'Brien:

> One tentacle of the Octopus extends to Byrd and Senate Appropriations; another into CIA cocaine ops and mind control. When Danny's story breaks, it will expose your case and Kelly's. Inslaw also ties in with Iran-Contra, BCCI, and the October Surprise, among others.... Casolaro says "The Octopus" is the biggest story to ever break in this country. He believes it could re-establish Constitutional values of truth and justice by exposing high-level criminals.... Pretty exciting stuff.[31]

Unfortunately, Casolaro's death would occur before he had the chance to reveal O'Brien's story to the world. While the inclusion of Casolaro and The Octopus in their narrative certainly connects some dots—which as we've seen, is a crucial activity for conspiracy writers—it does not match up well with the chronology of Casolaro's revelations. While he had written a few articles introducing the concepts he was investigating, at the time of his death, Casolaro's research was very much ongoing, The wide array of conspiracies Phillips describes to O'Brien were not as clearly known as his explanations suggested and would not become so until after Casolaro's death. To place such a conversation in the context of the couple's adventures is—again, like many conspiracy narratives—almost too obvious a connection to make.[32]

TRANCE Formation of America and the O'Brien/Phillips narrative served as a launching pad for similar stories and fueled the connections between government mind control conspiracies. It was not, however, accepted uncritically, even within the fringe and conspiracy communities. Jeff Rense, a radio host whose show, since the mid-1990s, has focused on a variety of political and paranormal conspiracy theories, has been vocal in his doubts about O'Brien's story and her credibility. The guest on the April 20, 1997, edition of his program was "Gurudas," the pen name of conspiracy writer named Ron Garman. Gurudas was a regular guest who addressed a wide range of conspiracy theories, usually centered on the New World Order and fears of global tyranny. On the April 20 program, the conversation turned to mind control and, in particular, the type of "trauma-based" mind control carried out through organized, centrally directed programs of torture and abuse of young children. When asked what evidence of these efforts existed, Gurudas cited Cathy O'Brien and *TRANCE Formation of America*. Rense expressed a surprising degree of skepticism about the story:

> I must say that that book is one of the most unbelievable—and I am using the word advisedly—I have ever put my hands or eyes on. Now we have to again assume that some of that book is false. you cannot take a book like that and accept it one hundred percent. No journalist, no investigative researcher, nobody worth his intellectual salt could do that.

He then asked Gurudas where he "personally [drew] the line of reality and fraud in that book" and challenged his guest's acceptance of O'Brien's claims. Rense, however, does place the outrageous and probably fallacious nature of *TRANCE Formation of America* within a wider conspiratorial framework, further asking Gurudas, "How do we know ... that she might not have been implanted with a lot of these memories so she would go on the stump and make these outrageous charges?" Thus, the false conspiracy is a component of a wider disinformation effort, presumably to discredit any legitimate "mind control victims" that may come forward. The bizarre and unsupportable nature of O'Brien's claims is indeed evidence of a conspiracy but *not* the conspiracy that O'Brien is alleging.

Reese's comments on this program are not too far out of the ordinary within the wider culture of conspiracy. Government agencies undertaking organized disinformation efforts as well as their attempts to infiltrate subversive organizations have a history stretching back to the 1960s and 1970s, including operations such as COINTELPRO, which attempted to monitor and influence anti-war organizations and civil rights groups, as well as terrorist organizations such as the Ku Klux Klan. During the 1980s and 1990s, the efforts of the Air Force Office of Special Investigations to use UFO investigators as informants and sowers of disinformation (see Chapter 3) taught many on the paranoid fringes to be wary of those who tell stories that, while they adhere to the basic narrative frameworks of alleged conspiracies are, in fact, *too* outrageous.

O'Brien's allegations were unproven and, in large part, not provable. But, as Gurudas insisted, what was publicly known about MKULTRA and its related projects as well as the widely acknowledged propensity of the intelligence and defense establishment to hide its alleged evils lent a degree of credibility to O'Brien's story. Even if details of her story were inaccurate, he asserted, the danger of this supposed mind control program was great. Addressing the audience, Gurudas issued a warning: "If any of you are thinking of giving up children for adoption I think you should not do that in this country. There's just too much going on behind the scenes. I mean they have an extremely developed system in many hospitals and adoption agencies where they grab these children and into these torture centers they go."[33] This was a view shared by Bill Cooper, who cited similar concerns in one of his statements on his family's legal battle with the IRS.

Jaye C. Beldo echoed Rense's skepticism of O'Brien's claims in his review of *TRANCE Formation*, observing that "Cathy is, at times, really no different from some of the questionable UFO abductees making extravagant claims of being transported to other solar systems and back again. Obviously something happened to her of a traumatic nature.... You can hear the trauma in her voice." Despite the possibility of these damaging experiences, Beldo also argues that "how she has chosen, whether unconsciously or not, to manifest the effects of the trauma deserves some responsible scrutiny from the reader." Beldo, while not dismissing the potential that O'Brien suffered very real, literal abuse, suggests that the most productive way to view her claims is as "an elaborate albeit disturbing metaphor of the effects of sexual abuse on young children and how it manifests later on in their lives. Cathy's work may very well provide us with a useful perspective on how trauma can embody itself, how it can be projected upon political figures."[34]

As with radio host Jeff Rense, other figures in the conspiracy culture that were, broadly speaking, amenable to accepting conspiracy claim at face value were taken aback by O'Brien's claims. One was Jim Keith, a writer we will be encountering several times throughout this book. Keith's 1998 book *Mind Control, World Control: An Encyclopedia of Mind Control* is a wide-ranging work that devotes an entire chapter to Cathy O'Brien and the mystery of Project Monarch. Keith picks apart the writing style, grammar, and factual inconsistencies of the book but concludes that the greatest flaw in the book is that there is no actual evidence of Project Monarch:

> The single most telling detail suggesting that MONARCH is a hoax or a product of delusion is that the term itself does not appear in any intelligence agency document, or in the statements of any bonafide intelligence agent that I am aware of. Nor do any of the other MONARCH buzzphrases that are so handily tossed about by "experts" on the subject. There is no corroboration of MONARCH terms in any verified intelligence agency documents that I am aware of, nor by any actual defectors from the intelligence community, of which there are many.[35]

As Keith explains, there is not exactly a shortage of information about government mind control programs in the public domain. O'Brien and Phillips's book was the first mention of an MKULTRA subproject called "Monarch."

Among the number of alleged mind controlled sex slaves that have shared their suspicions and accusations over the past twenty years, O'Brien remains a fixture, telling her story at conferences as well as on podcasts and radio interviews. While her evidence remains insufficient to fully prove her claims, the very real specter of MKULTRA provides a link to reality that is tangible enough for radio hosts and listeners. Talk show host Richie Allen, who interviewed O'Brien on his show in March 2015, assures his listeners that "What makes O'Brien's allegations seem believable to some, is the fact that mind control programs like MK-ULTRA have been exposed, and that the aims of such experiments included some unthinkable practices including torture, mind-altering drugs, sexual abuse, and hypnotism." This is not too far afield from the response Gurudas gave to Jeff Rense in 1997. As is typical of conspiracy narratives, stories are endlessly recycled, as are the arguments that circulate around them.[36]

Cathy O'Brien's story served as a template for other claims of "trauma-based mind control" that would surface during the late 1990s and into the twenty-first century. While few were as detailed as O'Brien's, Susan Ford (writing as Brice Taylor) takes up the story of the supposed Monarch project and wove her own story of mind control in her 1999 book *Thanks for the Memories.... The Truth Has Set Me Free!* (which included the lurid subtitle *The Memoirs of Bob Hope's and Henry Kissinger's Mind-Controlled Slave*). Taylor's book echoes O'Brien's story. She describes how she was subjected to violent trauma for the purposes of turning her into a mind controlled slave, becoming a "Presidential sex toy and personal computer."[37] Taylor claimed to be a victim of the same Project Monarch that O'Brien did and, again like Cathy O'Brien, she claimed to have been extensively and brutally abused and tortured from infancy in an effort to fracture her mind to the point that multiple personality disorder was introduced. In both O'Brien's and Taylor's accounts, the use of trauma-induced multiple personality disorder is a key step in the process of gaining control of victims' minds. The descriptions of the trauma in Taylor and O'Brien's stories bear close resemblance to the tales of satanic cult abuses during the 1980s. Taylor's account, for instance, even features a church with secret tunnels connecting it to other facilities reminiscent of similar tunnels under the infamous McMartin preschool story.

Taylor begins her story with a challenge, an attempt to guilt the reader into believing her story, asking, "Who with conscience could read the following autobiographical account and, in the name of freedom, justice and love, brush aside the misuse of power, human slavery, and mind control described in this book?"[38] Like *TRANCE Formation of America*, *Thanks for the Memories* benefits from its author's supposedly trauma-perfected memory. As Taylor explains, "Having been programmed to have a perfect photographic memory greatly aided me toward this enhanced, often meticulously detailed account. The training my controllers gave me backfired on them."[39] Like O'Brien, Taylor was subjected to sexual abuse and violence from an early age, initially by her father (who she claims was also a mind control victim). She claims to have been trained at a variety of military and NASA facilities and to have been a sex slave and "mind file" computer for figures such as Lyndon B. Johnson and Henry Kissinger. Unlike O'Brien's tale, Taylor goes into much more detail on the connections between government mind control operations and the goals of organizations such as the Freemasons.

Taylor's story, like O'Brien's, moves its focus beyond the basics of mind control to broader conspiracy theories. As a mind control subject, Brice Taylor claimed to have filled a role as a sex/espionage agent serving within the government and beyond to an overarching cabal of only a handful of individuals, who he overheard referred to as "The Council." "This Council's goal was "to control not only our government, but foreign governments as well" with an ultimate goal of "a one world government, where you and I are to work in varying levels—as controlled slaves or, as they say, 'worker bees.'"[40] Taylor's mentions of The Council also integrate other, more specific individuals, institutions, and concepts that surface consistently in mind control conspiracy theories. One of these is the Tavistock Institute.

The Tavistock Institute of Human Relations was founded in 1947 is a British think tank which initially sought to "to find ways to apply psychoanalytic and open systems concepts to group and organizational life."[41] Since then, they have published papers with titles like 1947s "Frontiers in Group Dynamics" and the 1953 study "Working-Through Industrial Conflict: The Service Department at the Glacier Metal Company."[42] Tavistock works with both private and public clients and, while there is nothing in its publicity literature that suggests a powerful role for this organization, it has figured prominently in many manifestations of mind control conspiracy theories. Brice Taylor connects Tavistock to Nazi Germany and occult organizations such as the Order of the Golden Dawn.[43] These allegations, like many about the Institute give it a position of vital importance to both mind control and wider ranging conspiracy theories. Conspiracy researcher and writer John Coleman, for example, has placed the Tavistock Institute at the center of a global conspiracy to destroy the United States:

> The Tavistock Institute for Human Relations has had a profound effect on the moral, spiritual, cultural, political and economic policies of the United States of America and Great Britain. It has been in the front line of the attack on the U.S. Constitution and State constitutions. No group did more to propagandize the U.S. to participate in the WWI at a time when the majority of the American people were opposed to it.[44]

Despite the fact that Coleman attributes to the institute actions that occurred before it existed throughout several publications he maintains that it is a crucial element of a global conspiracy.

Brice Taylor's *Thanks for the Memories*, like Cathy O'Brien's *TRANCE Formation of America*, is a combination of information that emerged in the public record during the 1970s and 1980s, details of Satanic Ritual Abuse allegations, and suggestions of an overarching conspiracy that crossed political and national lines. In both of these stories, the victims were conditioned from birth and even before birth, with their very existence part of a larger plan. In these conspiracy tales, dark forces, which loom in the background have total control over their subjects and often these forces are some blend of governmental and non-governmental institutions. There is also the implication that these programs imparted extraordinary powers to those who were victimized by the mind controllers. O'Brien and Taylor had perfect recall, serving as walking databanks of information for the global manipulators who used their services. While the conspiracy theories presented in the books of O'Brien and Taylor dovetail well into the broader New World Order stories of global control Taylor's book also ventures into what we may call a meta-conspiracy theory. As noted, there are number of similarities between *TRANCE Formation of America* and *Thanks for the Memories* and, given the similar nature of their narratives, it is not surprising that O'Brien, Phillips, and Taylor would all meet at some point. In *Thanks for the Memories*, Taylor tells the story of meeting O'Brien and Phillips and, for a time, financially supporting them. Taylor allowed Mark Phillips to attempt to "deprogram" her, to free her of her supposed mind controlled status. According to Taylor, "one and one-half years, forty-two journals, and $50,000+ traveling and living expenses later, Mark Phillips informed me that nothing have ever happened to me ... nothing what-so-ever!" Taylor then reported that O'Brien told her she "should be happy that nothing happened and that your children have not been abused!" Taylor broke contact with O'Brien and Phillips, believing Phillips to be "some kind of 'containment agent' who is being directed though his 'handlers' whose motivations ultimately serve the New World Order."[45]

This split between Taylor and O'Brien/Phillips spilled over into debates on Internet websites devoted to mind control and other conspiracy-inspired topics. One writer, Ray Bilger, agrees with Taylor's assessment:

> The Elite's choice of Mark Phillips for this extremely important assignment was an excellent decision, as he does his job very well. He may himself be a mind control victim. Cathy's life seems to be better, but she is not free from the mind controlling, she just has a new handler named Mark!
>
> Think about their whole story seriously for a moment. Don't you think that if the Elite Controllers wanted Mark and Cathy dead, that they would be dead by tonight? These Controllers kill presidents if they want to, but somehow they can't seem to kill a couple who are openly speaking to the public, and who stay in public hotels?[46]

Thus, in the eyes of some, Phillips and O'Brien move from being the victims of a mind control conspiracy to being tools of this conspiracy. In their 2014 book *ACCESS DENIED*, O'Brien and Phillips fired back at Taylor's allegations as part of their "recollection" of the events following O'Brien's rescue from her mind control. Phillips reported that Taylor was "role-playing a mind control victim.... She is either deliberately perpetrating fraud or is indeed a victim of false memories from her therapists. To counter Taylor's claims that she had financially supported the couple, they wrote that her "contribution to household expenses rarely covered the rent and utilities" and that her "personal wealth was extravagant, yet the gourmet foods she stored in our refrigerator were off limits to us. When her constant additions to her wardrobe overfilled her closets, there was plenty of room in ours."[47] The book goes on to portray Brice Taylor/Susan Ford as a conniving villain and criminal mastermind rather than a fellow victim. As O'Brien and Taylor discuss whether or not people who are mind controlled are culpable for any crimes they commit, O'Brien writes that Taylor smiled as she said, "Mind control is the perfect defense for any crime." O'Brien comes to believe that Taylor sought to steal a friend's fictional book on mind control and promote it as "her reality so she can use mind control as a defense against any crime."[48]

By the end of the 1990s, stories such as those told Cathy O'Brien and Brice Taylor had become a mainstay of the conspiracy community. Imitators arose and mind control tropes began to penetrate many different aspects of that world. Project Monarch would become a consistently referenced element of MKULTRA mind control programs despite the absence of documentation outside the conspiracy world. The lurid and scandalous nature of the Monarch stories, along with their highly emotive and personal nature, would ensure their survival.

One example of the connections between the Project Monarch stories, and O'Brien's claims, in particular, is David Icke's use of *TRANCE Formation of America*. Icke excerpted a portion of the book to introduce his reptilian conspiracy theory to his followers. Icke wrote,

> Cathy believes that holographic projections were used to give the appearance to her of people transforming into "lizard-like" aliens. This relates to the theme in some UFO and extraterrestrial research of a race known as "Reptillians" operating on the planet. What if it was not a hologram that Cathy saw? What if these reptile-like extraterrestrials can manifest in human form? I know it sounds fantastic, but with each month that passes I am more convinced by the weight of evidence that this is the case. I will expand on this in my next book.[49]

It also connects to Bill Cooper's theories that extraterrestrial imagery could be used to deceive humans into believing the earth had been invaded by aliens as a prelude to world government imposing its will on the people. O'Brien's interpretation of these events takes a back seat to the vision of Icke, or other conspiracy theorists. Her story would, like many conspiratorial narratives, would take flight and be woven into a variety of paranoid claims.

The Proliferation of Mind Control Narratives

The reports that surfaced during investigations into the various MKULTRA programs during the 1970s illustrate that much of the experimentation was technological and chemical in nature as opposed to the brute trauma oriented techniques outlined in the Project Monarch-oriented mind control stories. Conspiracy writer Alex Constantine's *Psychic Dictatorship in the U.S.A.* succinctly states what could be a summary of the technology-based mind control fears of conspiracy culture in the 1990s:

> For the past fifty years a pathological sciences has evolved in the netherworld of the national security elite. Like a buxom siren, the science of mind control beckons technocrat with Machiavellian ambitions into assuming the position of a petty god. He dreams of cybernetic control of whole populations.

Constantine addresses "electromagnetic and biotelemetric mind control experimentation" ranging from the CIA use of cult organizations as a cover for drug running and drug sales to the role Nazi scientists played in developing NutraSweet—an artificial sweetener, yes, but also a drug with harmful effects on the brain of those who consume it. Like Cathy O'Brien and Brice Taylor, Constantine positions himself as a victim of these mind control efforts as well as playing a role in exposing the conspiracy. Constantine claims that the CIA "attempted for six years to subvert my radio broadcasts and magazine articles by assaulting me with 'non-lethal' weapons … an apartment constantly filled with infra-sound and pulsed microwaves."[50] This strand of mind control narrative, involving technological and chemical effects aimed at the victims' minds in order to not only to control their victims but also to harass and harm them as well. Often, Constantine alleges, elements of the U.S. government uses technology such as those "pulsed microwaves" to remotely control the actions of unwitting subjects, enabling those government elements to commit unlawful acts with impunity, claiming that "electromagnetically controlled 'offensive behavior' has lurked behind a long line of murders and suicides throughout the western hemisphere."[51]

Some conspiracy writers and researchers contend that the efforts of MKULTRA have continued in much more subtle yet wide-reaching ways than pulsed microwaves and trauma-based personality manipulation. Alex

4. Mind Control 123

Ansary, for example, alleges that television, radio, popular film, and other elements of media are being used—sometimes wittingly, sometimes not—as tools of a government that wants a public that unquestioningly accepts its policies. The public will not fight back against corruption and evil because "our minds are already pre conditioned to accept living in a police state economy and society because we read it in the paper, saw it praised on the news and talk shows, or saw it in a movie." Pushing back against these evils, however, is difficult because "the indoctrination through these mediums warns us that views other than those presented by them are unimportant and too be condemned. This Administration and media monopoly has a carefully crafted dehumanization program to anyone that dissents the official version of events."[52] Just because one is not a Cathy O'Brien–style mind control slave does not necessarily mean you are free to think as you please. Mind control permeates the media sphere, surrounding us and drawing us into a web of manipulation.

The MPD-driven, trauma-based mind control stories like O'Brien's and Taylor's would play a large role in conspiracy culture during the early decades of the twenty-first century as would tales of more technologically driven mind control processes, such as those described by Alex Constantine. As Michael Barkun observes, "similar stories have circulated sufficiently to call into being a community of self-described victims, who allege that as a result of torture, abuse, or implanted electronic devices, they were enslaved by a government that had taken possession of their minds."[53] One online venue for these claims was the Mind Control Forum.[54] The Mind Control Forum emerged in 1995 (the year *TRANCE Formation of America* was published) and served as a collection site and online support group for those who believed they had been victimized by a variety of covert mind control technologies. Writing in 1998, the founder of the Forum, Ed Light described the efforts of the Mind Control Forum this way:

> Since it's [sic] inception in the winter of 1995, the Mind Control Forum has had the blessing of many contributors. It now has over 60 victims' personal stories.... Although it has been grueling keeping up with the many contributions coming in, due to my continual electro-shocking, it's awesome to realize that the site has become a major player in the abolition of covert human rights abuses of the human mind.... In a time in which American elites are taking over the world under the guise of economic progress, may "Big Brother" lose and pay all human rights abuse victims and non-consensual [sic] experimentees [sic] back for their time and suffering. If not, the book 1984 will become a reality.[55]

Light positions the Mind Control Forum as a force for change, using the testimony of alleged mind control subjects, victims, and survivors as a wedge to push for public action against the forces arrayed against them. As has become typical of much mind control narrative, Light assumes a global takeover by "American elites" is at the heart of the mind control conspiracy, however he does not provide an explicit connection between these mind control projects and any plans for worldwide domination as O'Brien, Taylor, or other conspiracy theorists might.

Light alleges that his mind control wrought difficulties had existed for a very long time, with "a secret mind-control project permanently disabl[ing him] in 1979." Light had been unable to seek any work since that time due to constant "mind-bending experiments." Light could pinpoint the moment the technological harassment began because as he was driving "there was a popping noise next to my van's steering column, inside the turn signal mechanism. The turn signal would no longer stay on by itself for left turns." Light is not certain why he has been targeted for this "mind-bending" experimentation, but he does have a few suspicions, including:

> 1. I tried to get conscientious objector status in the draft in 1965, settling for 4F (physical disqualification). 2. I planned to build a trucking company that would support Peace and Freedom Party candidates. 3. My mother was a left-wing activist. 4. My uncle had top security clearance at General Electric, presumably working on defense projects, and so they must have investigated his whole family.[56]

Light's claims certainly bear many marks of a paranoid personality but he was hardly alone. By the time the Mind Control Forum site ceased active development in 2012, hundreds of self-identified victims had voluntarily told their stories many of them, apparently, using their real names and providing email addresses through which they hope to communicate with fellow sufferers.

Light's story of damaged turn signals might seem paranoid even within the context of conspiracy theory but, in general, the testimony of these self-reported mind control and harassment victims is far removed from Cathy O'Brien's and Brice Taylor's accounts in terms of the scope and scale of the abuses. The O'Brien and Taylor stories were deeply horrifying for a number of reasons, including the excessive degree of violence (sexual and otherwise) presented in them. They also provided long lasting and significant because of the wide array of political and media figures they portrayed as utterly depraved and almost comically evil. It is important, also, to remember that stories like those of Cathy O'Brien make significant inroads into the conspiracy culture and become long-lasting tropes or touchstones because of large amount of promotion undertaken by the authors. O'Brien and Mark Phillips do numerous speaking engagements and radio or podcast appearances; they are actively marketing their story.

4. Mind Control

The victim statements at the Mind Control Forum, while informed by the star-studded accounts provided by O'Brien and Phillips, are often much more low key. Rarely are these sufferers involved in the machinations of the wealthy, powerful, or famous. They are victimized by forces that are often nameless and faceless, torturing them with little rhyme or reason. The Mind Control Forum or small-scale newsletters or magazines are these alleged victims' only outlet for telling their stories.

The stories that alleged mind control victims tell on this website are often deeply sad. Like Jaye Beldo suspected in the case of Brice Taylor or Cathy O'Brien, there is often a strong suggestion that the tellers of these tales have undergone some type of trauma, that they suffer from some physical or psychological issues that desperately need to be addressed in a professional and clinical setting. It is important to examine these testimonies not in a way that is voyeuristic but rather as a means to comprehend the degree to which conspiratorial and paranoid narratives about government mind control programs, like those conducted under the aegis of MKULTRA, have proliferated, providing a ready explanation for the experiences with which alleged victims have dealt. The accounts on sites like the Mind Control Forum rarely have happy endings. It is not unusual for there to be updates relating that alleged victim has died, often through suicide.

One example on the Mind Control Forum's area devoted to personal testimonies and experiences is a man named Cary Adcox. Adcox believed that while he had been unsuccessful in his attempts to find employment "because they have stopped every attempt for employment I have had a lead on. These people don't want me to work because it would interfere with the testing they are doing on me." He believed the "testing" was due to his knowledge of electronics and computer technology. Unlike the stories of Project Monarch trauma-based mind control, Adcox claimed to suffer from an implant in the brain stem that allowed the perpetrators to

> access everything my mind is assembling as a thought before I even has a chance to completely think it. They are able to question your mind while you are sleeping and get just about any detail of your past experiences from you while you sleep. This basically opens your entire, what used to be private, life up to them like a book. What ever you see out of your eyes is transmitted to them. Your life has no privacy at all.

Adcox also claimed that these devices did more than simply monitor. They could also produce and manipulate sensations, thoughts and emotions, reporting that "they can send the information to the sensual part of your brain to sexually arouse you." They have the ability to "send information to cause you to cry as they are making you feel guilty at the same time about something you may have done as a child or any number of other things they can say to make you feel guilty about to get you to cry." Adcox ended his discussion of this remote emotional manipulation, saying, "I am 42 years old and have cried more in the last six months then since I was a child." Like most of the testimonials at Mind Control Forum, Cary Adcox was looking for help, telling readers, "If you can shed some light on this as far as what I might be able to do to stop this violation of my life.... I would appreciate any assistance." The help Adcox needed, however, did not materialize. An addendum to the page with his story shared the news report of his 2001 suicide.[57]

In a similar fashion as the Mind Control Forum, the short-lived print magazine *MKZINE* was a venue for discussion of mind control techniques, technology, and cover-up that blended investigations into the historical roots of mind control with personal testimony and conspiratorial speculation. *MKZINE*'s subtitle proclaimed it to be "an examination of coercive mind control, invasive human experimentation, and other abuses" suggesting a broader approach than simply looking at electronic brain implants or claims of Project Monarch abuse. Articles over the five issue run of the magazine included personal testimony of so-called ritual abuse (not necessarily tied to formal mind control programs but, rather, to secret cults to which the wealthy and powerful belonged), reviews of films such as *The Matrix* that the editors perceived to have connections to mind control experimentation, book reviews, and interviews with psychological and counseling professionals who discussed the issues involved with treating alleged mind control victims. Echoing the sad end of Cary Adcox, the editorial in the first issue of *MKZINE* is dedicated to the "memory of Steve Doyle, who last week could no longer resist the voices that told him to kill himself."[58]

While Cathy O'Brien and Brice Taylor were not the first to openly promote mind control conspiracies, their highly personal and emotionally affecting autobiographical exposes—along with the accompanying promotional efforts in the fringe media—were a factor in opening the floodgates of similar testimony in the early twenty-first century.

The dry government records on MKULTRA and similar programs often fail to match the lurid horror of Cathy O'Brien's autobiography. The testimonies online or in small press zines many times lack credible information. One line, however, in that crucial 1963 inspector general's report hovers over these stories: that the victims of MKULTRA were "unwitting subjects in normal life settings." Regardless of the degree to which various aspects of MKULTRA, its predecessors, or its possible successors are known to have been implemented there is solid evidence that intelligence and military entities had such plans in place.

The accounts on the Mind Control Forum are a resource I have used in my U.S. history courses to illustrate the far-reaching consequences of short-sighted federal policy and cover-up. "High risk-low reward" programs such as MKULTRA, along with numerous other examples of state-sponsored experimentation, contributed to the loss of trust between the American people and their government. This loss of trust has fueled conspiracy narratives and these narratives—regardless of their truth or falsehood—may in turn increase the mistrust. There are real victims, as well, such as those on the Mind Control Forum or others whose fragile states are exacerbated by such stories. Often, however, they may be victims of the conspiracy culture itself rather than a conspiracy.

Remote Viewing: Secret Knowledge of the Elite's Psychic Spies

"Remote Viewing" refers to a collection of protocols for using supposed psychic abilities (such as extrasensory perception) to gain knowledge of far distant subjects. On the surface, it is distinctly unlike mind control projects such as those conducted as part of MKULTRA. However, both were the subject of defense and intelligence interest and experimentation. Both became public knowledge after the declassification of reams of documentation. And, like the mind control experiments of MKULTRA, the story surrounding remote viewing has spawned its own genre within the world of conspiratorial narrative. Unlike the lurid and exploitative tales of Cathy O'Brien and other alleged subject of mind control operations, the most prominent figures within the subculture of remote viewing were insiders—people who had a role in the scientific and military establishments that undertook these psychic operations.

In 1995, the CIA revealed that during the 1970s and 1980s it had sponsored and directed experiments in remote viewing. According to Joe McMoneagle, one of the original remote viewing operatives for the American defense establishment remote viewing was distinct from general psychic ability. On a 1997 installment of Art Bell's *Coast to Coast AM* radio program, McMoneagle explained that "what differentiates remote viewing from normal psychic functioning is that remote viewing is usually done within a controlled protocol."[59] Ingo Swann, Hal Puthoff and Russell Targ of the Stanford Research Institute developed this protocol in the mid–1970s.[60] Defense and intelligence organizations would become involved once it became clear that there was at least some indication of positive results. According to Puthoff, the first director of a CIA-sponsored study at Stanford Research Institute, the CIA initiated the study due to "increasing concern in the intelligence community about the level of effort in Soviet parapsychology being funded by the Soviet security services."[61] This is, of course, another similarity between remote viewing and mind control programs—a significant factor in their adoption was the fear that America's enemies could gain an advantage. In effect, they did not want the United States to be on the wrong side of a "psychic gap." Given its alleged effectiveness in a laboratory setting, remote viewing became operational and remained so for quite a few years.

A number of programs run variously by the CIA, the Defense Intelligence Agency, and other entities came with a variety of cryptonyms, including the two most well known and widely used, GRILL FLAME and STAR GATE. The original protocol document developed for the GRILL FLAME project described remote viewing as

> an intellectual process by which a person perceives characteristics of a location remote from that person. RV does not involve any electronic sensing devices at or focused at the target site, nor does it involve classical photo interpretation of photographs obtained from overhead or oblique means. The individual performing RV ... is provided with a unique identifier such as stationary map coordinates, a specific structure, an identifiable vehicle ... or a specific individual.

This technique, the document explained, had a number of crucial benefits for the military and intelligence services. Remote viewing could be used to "target on key enemy military individuals from covert agents to key battle commanders; detect the change in state of military units, to rapidly determine the damage resulting from non-nuclear weapon attack; to determine the access code to computers and other electronic devices; and to determine the general content of documents and other informational items found in military organizations." But because American assets could be targeted by enemy remote viewers, the report's author urged that "Countermeasures must be devised to reduce this vulnerability."[62]

The 1997 interview between Art Bell and several former military remote viewers provided additional insight into the types of work done at Fort Meade. While the targets of remote viewing operations were military or strategic in nature, practice targets could be quite broad. Remote viewer Lyn Buchanan explained that "the best thing we found to ever work with was pictures cut out of National Geographic magazines, sealed in envelopes and you describe what's in the picture, describe what's at the site." When discussing the types of targets with which remote viewers dealt, Bell asked if they could have targeted Saddam Hussein, and "come up with his mood, his intentions." Buchanan replied that they "did in fact do exactly that, to come up with plans and intentions, to come up with background psychological information such as moods, logical ability, his outlook on life, philosophy and so forth. Mainly plans and intentions."[63] Most remote viewing tasks, however, did not require this level of mind reading.

In 2000, the CIA[64] declassified thousands of pages of remote viewing documentation, including many transcripts of actual remote viewing sessions. These documents flesh out the claims made in later by remote viewers regarding the type of work done. In a session, from April 3, 1980, the viewer describes a location and (in accordance with remote viewing protocols) provides a rough sketch of what he is seeing. Analysts assigned to the remote viewing unit would examine these sketches, using them in conjunction with intelligence gathered from more conventional sources. The comments from the remote viewer (known only as "#14") illustrate the level of detail supposedly achieved during their sessions:

> I'm drawing a perimeter wall here which was either brick or concrete block or something like that. [see figure x] It was a solid wall. I'm up in the air now. There appeared to be kind of ... columns or something in there. That's not exactly how they were arranged. They were probably much further apart. But ... and the wall was maybe about a foot thick or so. And I had the feeling like there was almost like a sidewalk around here. And that there was a ... a street that came out here. I didn't feel that there was a sidewalk or anything over on this side.[65]

This assignment required the viewer to report on an area in response to "a request for information on a target of interest."[66] Others were more specific. In the depths of the 1979–1981 Iran hostage crisis, GRILL FLAME was ordered to "provide information relevant to the hostage situation in the U.S. Embassy compound in Teheran, Iran." Unlike most remote viewing sessions, where the viewer is given coordinates and little else (to ensure that they go into the session with no preconceived notions of what they might find), in this case, the remote viewer had "been exposed to open source news media information, classified overhead imagery and photographs of many of the hostages. He knew he would be working against the hostage situation in Iran." Unfortunately the session was not particularly helpful, as it had to be ended early due to "excessive ambient room noise."[67]

In 1995, the results of an independent review determined that the resources used by the government remote viewing programs were not justified by the results of those programs. A report from the American Institutes for Research concluded "even though a statistically significant effect has been observed in the laboratory, it remains unclear whether the existence of a paranormal phenomenon, remote viewing, has been demonstrated. The laboratory studies do not provide evidence regarding the origins or nature of the phenomenon, assuming it exists."

The report further claimed that the programs had never produced any intelligence that was actionable. In other words, the psychics were unable to

C02396730

Approved For Release 2000/08/10 : CIA-RDP96-00791R000200030001-3

~~SECRET~~

DEFENSE INTELLIGENCE AGENCY

WASHINGTON, D.C. 20340-

S-23,025/PAX-TA   10 May 1995

MEMORANDUM FOR THE DIRECTOR OF RESEARCH AND DEVELOPMENT, CIA

SUBJECT: Declassification and Cooperation in Response to Congressionally Directed STAR GATE Program Review (U)

Reference: ORD/CIA Draft Memorandum, 21 February 1995, subject as above.

1. (C/NF) Any decision on declassification actions regarding Project STAR GATE should be made by the CIA. Executive Order 12958 "Classified National Security Information," states that in a transfer of functions, the receiving agency is considered to be the originating agency for any actions affecting program status.

2. (S/NF) DIA has no objection to a declassification of the "fact of" a DIA program to employ paranormal phenomena for intelligence purposes. If CIA decides to declassify this, or any other DIA-specific aspects of the STAR GATE project, please notify this Office two weeks in advance so that we can take appropriate steps to prepare our Public Affairs Office.

FOR THE DIRECTOR:

SG1J

Chief
Office for Counterproliferation,
Nuclear, Biological, and
Chemical Assessments

CLASSIFIED BY MULTIPLE SOURCES
DECLASSIFY ON OADR

~~SECRET~~
NOT RELEASABLE TO FOREIGN NATIONALS
Approved For Release 2000/08/10 : CIA-RDP96-00791R000200030001-3

This 1995 memo discussing declassification of the STAR GATE remote viewing project highlights its convoluted history, involving numerous government agencies.

produce any insights that led to actual intelligence or military operations.[68] Despite the effectiveness of the AIR report in facilitating the shutdown of remote viewing operations in 1995, suspicions persisted that this report was biased. Joe McMoneagle, a military remote viewer, asserted "the people actually doing the review did not have the appropriate clearances for accessing the grand numbers of files, probably 90–95% of the project was never reviewed, they were never allowed access to it. Also, there was [sic] some very specific marching orders given to the scientists initially on what they would review. So, it was a stacked deck. It was a bogus report."[69] With the end of the program and declassification, several former remote viewers came forward with their stories during the late 1990s. Major Edward A. ("Ed") Dames would become the most prominent. Dames had been a member of the military intelligence remote viewing team stationed at Fort Meade, serving as "an analyst, a tasker, managing training and stuff ... he was kind of a jack of all trades."[70] Dames boasts that he "supplied the U.S. President and NSC with proof that the Soviets had clandestinely developed a new generation of biochemical warfare agents. As a result, Congress approved funds for a new DIA Biological Threat Analysis Center."[71] Far from never providing "actionable" intelligence, according to Dames remote viewing provided many crucial pieces of information throughout the program's existence.

At the end of 1995, Dames had the first of many appearances on Art Bell's *Coast to Coast AM* radio show, where he continues to be a popular guest, even after Bell's eventual retirement. On his website, where he sells a variety of instructional aids through which visitors can learn Remote Viewing for themselves, Dames promotes himself as "the world's foremost remote viewing teacher, and creator of Technical Remote Viewing" (a form of remote viewing based on the original "protocols" used by the intelligence and military communities).[72] His reputation, however, is built more on his dire predictions for the future than his educational expertise.

Dames's initial appearances on the show focused on the released government reports and the history of the remote viewing program. Soon, however, he began to offer his own predications of what the future of humanity might hold. By the end of the 1990s, Dames's prognostications had become relentlessly pessimistic, earning him the nickname "Doctor Doom." Initially predicting the emergence of a "plant pathogen" which would destroy food supplies on Earth. Dames introduced this catastrophe in 1997, connecting it to the Hale-Bopp comet. On a January 30, 1997, interview with Art Bell, he claimed that "the meteor showers that will be associated with Hale-Bopp are going to be of a very interesting type because they are bringing in a plant pathogen; an engineered plant pathogen."[73] Dames asserted that the first effects of this massive disaster would strike in early 1998. When 1998 failed to produce the anticipated catastrophe, Dames began to promote a new vision of the future, which centered around a disaster he called the "killshot." This would be, he reported, "a series of solar flares that are so devastating to the Earth, it may cause the death of billions and change life on Earth as we know it."[74]

Hale-Bopp had attracted the attention of another prominent figure associated with remote viewing. Courtney Brown, an associate professor of political science at Emory University, along with colleagues at his Farsight Institute (an institution unaffiliated with Emory) claimed to have remote viewed the comet in 1996. Bolstered by a photograph from an amateur astronomer named Chuck Schramek, as well as verification from an anonymous astrophysicist,[75] Brown and his fellow remote viewers claimed that a "companion" object accompanied Hale-Bopp. Even when the photographs of the companion were denounced, Brown maintained that the remote viewing he and his team had conducted would be borne out by events. In an interview with UFO journalist Michael Lindemann, Brown explained, "this Hale-Bopp thing, it's not us. They were the ones who came, not us.... This Hale-Bopp thing is here for a reason. And they're showing themselves for a reason. It's just a matter of time before something else happens. The remote viewing will be shown as correct."[76] Art Bell hosted Brown and his compatriots several times throughout late 1996 and early 1997, rarely questioning the conclusions they drew from their remote viewing sessions.

When members of a cult called Heaven's Gate committed suicide over several days in mid–March 1997, Brown, the Farsight Institute, and Art Bell came under fire for creating an environment in which the assertion of an extraterrestrial craft accompanying the comet was presented as scientific fact rather than conjecture. This spacecraft dovetailed with Heaven's Gate's existing beliefs. As an article in *Skeptical Inquirer*, the magazine of the Committee for Scientific Investigation of Claims of the Paranormal, explained, "Following the Heaven's Gate suicides, the public learned that news of a 'companion UFO' trailing Comet Hale-Bopp—a rumor spread predominately by late-night talk radio host Art Bell—may well have contributed to cult members taking their lives in an attempt to 'graduate,' as their Web site described it, to a 'higher level' and leave Earth in a spacecraft." Bell denied any responsibility that he or his show may have had for the decisions made by the members of Heaven's Gate, saying, "I'm not going to stop presenting my material because there are unstable people."[77]

The predictions of Ed Dames and the failed prognostications of Courtney Brown highlight the potential dangers of taking psychic predictions too seriously. They also illustrated the role of a conspiratorial mindset in sparking and sustaining the popularity of such things. Remote viewing was a suppressed science, undertaken by intelligence and military authorities (who, in this case, would fit into the role of "elites"). While these elites shut down the remote viewing project in 1995, insiders like Joe McMoneagle claim that remote viewing was, in fact, far more effective than investigators admitted. Remote viewers such as Ed Dames provide (they claim) crucial information about the coming devastation of the Earth and humanity. Dames's discussion of the killshot and related horrors, from a conspiratorial point of view, are shedding light on disasters of which the government does not want the general public to have knowledge. While there is far less of an explicit connection between the claims of remote viewers and the various conspiracy narratives, claims of hidden knowledge carry with them an implicit claim to conspiracy. After all, *someone* must be withholding information about humanity's coming destruction.

5

Mad Science and Forbidden Knowledge

Conspiracies are often disproportionately focused on current political, cultural, and religious trends. Themes of science and history, however, lurk in the background of many of these narratives. The worlds that conspiracy theorists construct contain elements that run contrary to standard, accepted historical narratives. Assertions that the Cold War, for example, was a sham designed to divert public attention away from the reality of extraterrestrials or that various extraterrestrial civilizations have provided technological or other guidance throughout humanity's development challenge the assumptions of those who read them. Similarly, scientific knowledge presented in some conspiracy theories extends beyond what is conventionally acknowledged to be true or known within the scientific community. The persistent claim that intelligent extraterrestrial life visiting the Earth and that powerful forces have suppressed these visits is a well-worn example of this type of "expanded" knowledge.

This chapter deals with conspiracies that are fundamentally rooted in questions of science and other forms of knowledge that conspiracy theorists have deemed to be "hidden" or "forbidden." These include suppressed aspects of human history and scientific knowledge being withheld from the public for sinister purposes. Like the other conspiracies we have examined, these narratives of forbidden knowledge often—but not always—have perpetrators and victims. These conspiratorial perpetrators fall into two broad categories. The first is those who make use of hidden knowledge to increase their power and influence. The second variety of perpetrators is the vast array of scientists, historians, and other scholars who theorists allege are concealing "the truth" about science, medicine, or human history.

Like most of the conspiracy theories and narratives discussed in this book, this broad category contains myriad claims, stories and personalities. Within the realm of science and technology, there are tales of science gone mad. There are also, conversely, allegations of an elite (sometimes shadowy, sometimes quite open) hoarding seemingly miraculous scientific knowledge, denying its benefits to humanity. There is certainly some degree of overlap between some of the topics already discussed and this broad category of "forbidden knowledge." A conspiracy to conceal the existence of extraterrestrial life surely qualifies. Similarly, conspiracies of global domination present idiosyncratic readings of the past that serve to bolster their claims about the present. Claims that elements of the intelligence community are engaged in creating mind controlled slaves fall under this umbrella and assertions that Nazi Germany developed astoundingly powerful weapons that "mainstream" historians refuse to acknowledge touches on both mad science and hidden history. The topics in this chapter are not entirely new ground for us. What, then is the goal for this section of our exploration?

First, there are claims of cover-up and conspiracy that deserve discussion—for their intrinsic significance as well as for their under-representation in the extant conspiracy literature—but not necessarily to the same degree of more sprawling topics such as mind control, UFO cover-ups, or the New World Order. This chapter, however, will not simply be a "mad science miscellany." Rather, the narratives assessed here will serve to illustrate the depth and breadth of a fundamental assumption of conspiracy narrative: commonly accepted knowledge, as presented by credentialed authorities, is at best incomplete and at worst is a deliberate fabrication. While this assumption hovers over every part of this book it is particularly prevalent here.

Second, to an even greater degree, perhaps, than other conspiracies discussed, these allegations of forbidden knowledge, hidden history, and secret science have a marked impact on public perceptions of knowledge and those who work in scientific and academic fields. There is a low likelihood of persuading members of the general public that the U.S. military acquired extraterrestrial technology in 1947 as a result of an alien spaceship crash. Further, those who do accept that claim have few opportunities to apply this view to pressing political, economic, or social issues of the day. Conspiracy theories surrounding science and history are subtler and more ambiguous than tales of Roswell. Internet headlines such as "The Global Warming Hoax—A Convenient Excuse for a New World Order?" use public opinion polls about climate change as evidence that a great deal of "skepticism" exists about widely accepted scientific findings. Few in the public, however, will ever hear about this skepticism, for "The Big Six who control today's mass media in the U.S, and consequently the whole world, are owned by" the "elite" who hope to use the threat environmental catastrophe to implement a global government. Because "the media" will not present this view, we must "be our own researchers and seek the truth."[1]

Here we see accepted scientific claims subjugated to popular opinion and that "research" is something anyone with Internet access can conduct. And while one has few opportunities to express one's views about the Roswell Incident at the voting booth, environmental policy is a prominent component of the political landscape for voters, with topics ranging from fracking to emissions standards often playing a role in electoral campaigns on the local, state, and national levels. The increasing amount of paranoid discourse revolving around scientific, historical, and other scholarly topics batters against the bulwarks of critical thinking and analysis.

This chapter will examine several aspects of forbidden or secret knowledge. First, we will examine conspiracy narratives that address impending environmental catastrophe, claims that such potential catastrophes are hoaxes, and the connection between these phenomena and fears that a global government seeks not only to subjugate humanity but to eliminate large swaths of Earth's population. These stories range from the far-fetched to the deceptively plausible, blending fact and fiction freely. They fill the gaps in our historical and scientific knowledge (particularly environmental and ecological investigations) with speculation that perpetuates similar fears to those we've seen throughout these chapters. We will also explore supposedly hidden or "lost civilizations," allegations of a hollow earth with an inhabitable interior, and the related claims that the same shadowy figures who manipulate our politics, hide the truth about extraterrestrials, and control our minds have been building their own subterranean kingdoms.

Within several prominent conspiratorial narratives, scientific and technological elites along with the elements of the defense and intelligence establishments have consistently concealed knowledge from the general public for their own benefit. Conversely, there is a significant conspiratorial trope involving the forces of science and politics actively attempting to eliminate large swaths of humanity. They will accomplish this destruction will either through concerted action or (in some narratives) concerted inaction. These suspicions often fall upon the same global elites who plot worldwide domination as discussed in Chapter 2. Conspiracy narratives involving the reduction of the earth's population and the subjugation of those who survive have often arisen alongside opposition to increased government regulation and oversight of business and industry related to environmental concerns—specifically climate change. Discussion of overpopulation also underlies several prominent conspiracy theories that connect to a variety of narratives such as underground bases to remote viewing. The narratives presented here bend and warp science to bring it into conformity with conspiracy theories and narratives that had already possessed a well-established history.

5. Mad Science and Forbidden Knowledge   137

The background and development of various scientific models of climate change is vast and complex. While a detailed examination of it is beyond the scope of this study, an important factor to keep in mind is that—in the world of conspiracy narrative—mistakes, errors, adjustments, or reassessments rarely happen. New data that alters models of climate change, the shift in terminology from "global warming" to "climate change" and similar developments in scientific thinking are *not* part of the normal process of investigation. Rather, they are clues that a cover-up exists and that scientists are playing the public for fools. Further, this "hoaxing" is all in aid of sinister goals. Related to the issue of climate change are other environmental and ecological concerns over land use, protection of natural resources, and similar issues. In particular, the political or legal actions taken to address these issues provides fodder for conspiracy theorists. While non-conspiratorial conservative and libertarian-leaning Americans may see these as improper affronts against cherished ideas of private property and personal liberty, more extreme narratives see environmental regulation as a foothold of the New World Order.

As we have with other conspiracy theories and narratives, it is useful to briefly examine the widely-accepted information that serves as a launching point for subsequent paranoid and conspiratorial interpretations. In the case of anti-science conspiracies revolving around population reduction, this launching point is often publicly released scientific papers funded and produced by national governments and, particularly, multinational organizations like the United Nations.

Climate Change, Mortality and the New World Order

The rise of the modern environmental movement in the 1960s led, over time, to increased study by scientists sponsored by a variety of national government as well as international organizations. In late 2014, the United Nations-sponsored Intergovernmental Panel on Climate Change released the "Synthesis Report" which reported,

> Human influence on the climate system is clear and growing, with impacts observed on all continents. If left unchecked, climate change will increase the likelihood of severe, pervasive and irreversible impacts for people and ecosystems. However, options are available to adapt to climate change and implementing stringent mitigations [sic] activities can ensure that the impacts of climate change remain within a manageable range, creating a brighter and more sustainable future.[2]

The report itself provided data on temperature increases and the increased volatility of weather events, with "each of the last three decades has been successively warmer at the Earth's surface than any preceding decade since 1850"[3] and concluded that these temperature increases were due to "Anthropogenic greenhouse gas emissions" which "have increased since the pre-industrial era, driven largely by economic and population growth, and are now higher than ever."[4] This situation is "very likely" to continue to deteriorate with significant impact on the inhabitants of earth, as food production and other factors will be affected. In fact, the report noted, even with a total elimination of greenhouse emissions (which is acknowledged to be unlikely), "it is virtually certain that global mean sea level rise will continue for many centuries beyond 2100."[5] Two ways to respond to these impending catastrophes are adaption and mitigation, finding ways to cope with the coming changes or finding ways to prevent those changes from coming or being as severe as they could be. Such adaption and mitigation would require "effective institutions and governance, innovation and investments in environmentally sound technologies and infrastructure, sustainable livelihoods and behavioural and lifestyle choices" such as "income, asset, and livelihood diversification," "community-based natural resource management," "awareness raising & integrating into education; gender equity in education; extension services; sharing indigenous, traditional & local knowledge," and "household preparation and evacuation planning."[6]

Within this brief summation, drawn from the Synthesis Report's "Summary for Policymakers," we can identify some key terms that might trigger a conspiratorial response. The blame placed on "human influence," when combined with concerns about population growth could be (and, as we will see, often is) extrapolated into a call to reduce the number of humans in order to eliminate these climatological effects. A conspiracist might interpret this report's highlighting of the need for "effective governance" and "income, asset, and livelihood diversification" a call for increased involvement—dictating, even—of how free individuals should live their lives.

Conspiracy narratives centered on the connected issue of population growth, mortality rates, and demographic changes are, likewise, often grounded in official reports from organizations like the United Nations. In 2014, for example, the Department of Economic and Social Affairs of the UN issued its *Concise Report on the World Population Situation* which reported that the planet's population reached 7.2 billion in 2014 and that "the continuation and consequences of these population trends will present both opportunities and challenges for the formulation and implementation of the United Nations post–2015 development agenda and for the achievement of all internationally agreed development goals."[7] Again, from a typical conspiratorial viewpoint, those who are seeking evidence of a global plan to reduce the human population could read this straightforward statement as the expression of a desire to reduce the population to facilitate the implementation of that development agenda. There are other sources, however, that population reduction-oriented conspiracy theorists look. Books such as Paul Ehrlich's 1968 *The Population Bomb* examined the dangers of human population growing to unsupportable numbers (a concern dating back to Thomas Malthus's 1798 *An Essay on the Principle of Population*). Ehrlich's solution to the population problem, presented in the preface, would fuel the concerns of conspiracy theorists for decades to come. While efforts to "stretch" the ability of the earth to feed its population are absolutely necessary, these efforts must be supplemented with "determined and successful efforts at population control. Population control is the conscious regulation of the numbers of human beings to meet the needs not just of individual families, but of society as a whole." Eherlich concluded that "we must have population control at home, hopefully through changes in our value system, but by compulsion if voluntary methods fail.... We can no longer afford merely to treat the symptoms of the cancer of population growth; the cancer itself must be cut out."[8] The output of scientists and the institutions or governments which funded them seemed to be pointing to a need to at best fundamentally change the way that people (especially Americans and western Europeans) had been living their lives since the dawn of the industrial age. At worst, they appeared to call for a reduction in the human population by any means necessary; words like "compulsion" leave a sour taste in the mouth of liberty-loving westerners. In particular, Eherlich's characterization of population growth (but not, note, people themselves) as a cancerous growth requiring removal may be easily twisted into something far more sinister than he intended.

As with many conspiracy theories, those who promote the idea that there is a shadow conspiracy to eliminate or reduce humanity (and enslave those who are left) did not invent their fears out of thin air. They have pushed back against proposed policies to alleviate environmental concerns that actually exist. As with many conspiracy theories, however, those who promulgate them often assert that the environmental and population concerns are a smokescreen, an excuse to eliminate segments of humanity that they find undesirable or to initiate draconian new policies and regulations. This concept of a manufactured event or false catastrophe is a recurring theme, appearing as a response to alien and UFO-oriented conspiracy theories, for example. In the case of environmental and population control conspiracies, these dismissals of widely-accepted problems (climate change, distribution of resources, and so on) have an effect on public opinion and policy formation.

This section is not intended to be a discussion or catalog of "climate change conspiracies" in the sense of climate change denial or general suspicion that the science behind prominent theories of climate change is in some way inadequate. Rather, we will examine examples of conspiracy theories that specifically cite global warming and population growth, disease and plague as weapons that global elites are specifically using to consolidate their control over national and international political, economic, cultural, and social systems. While many of these conspiracy theorists do deny the existence of climate change (or, if they do acknowledge it, they view it as an aspect of a natural warming cycle, unrelated to human activity), they promote detailed and extreme visions of the purpose behind this "hoax." These visions, unsurprisingly, align with broader conspiracy theories concerning globalization. Multinational organizations such as the United Nations figure prominently, with the accompanying fears that the national sovereignty of the United States is at risk.

These conspiracy theories fall into a familiar pattern of attempting to ascertain "what's really going on." No report or announcement can ever be taken at face value for those within the conspiracy genre. Like the narratives themselves, this approach is rooted in paradigms that are sensible and widely accepted. We have seen that, for a time, the U.S. government did downplay the interest it had in UFOs or the fact that intelligence agencies experimented with chemical-based mind control. Conspiracy devotees' extreme skepticism toward official sources of information—academe, the government—is not wrong, but misdirected. This skepticism is, in some ways, critical thinking turned up to 11.

These conspiracy theories also emerge from beyond the political realm. An increasing interest in Bible prophecy and a growing emphasis on eschatology among American Evangelicals has led to overlap between spiritual and secular conspiracy narratives. Ordained Pentecostal minister Irvin Baxter, the founder and president of Endtime Ministries, writes books, publishes a website and a magazine (*Endtime Magazine*), and appears on television and radio programs.[9] The ministry focuses on interpreting current events through the lens of its interpretation of Biblical prophecy. These often have a geopolitical flavor rather than a strictly spiritual one, for example, explaining that the "Mystery Babylon" mentioned in John's Revelation is the Vatican[10] or that the final seven years before the return of Christ to Earth will begin when the Israelis enter into a land-sharing agreement with the Palestinians.[11]

Baxter's coverage of what he sees as the growing power of the United

5. Mad Science and Forbidden Knowledge   141

Nations (the entity he believes to be a key player in enacting the Israeli-Palestinian agreement which will trigger the seven year tribulation) includes discussion of global warming as a tool through which the UN will enhance its control. "The global warming phenomenon," Baxter explains, is "propagated by the United Nations as a real threat to human existence." But, rather, it "is actually a hoax signifying the manifestation of end time events ... designed to enslave the world under the mandate of one world government." Baxter's explanation for the use of a climate change "hoax" in particular echoes things we've seen throughout this study. Baxter asserts that "in order to push the world closer together into a world body, they need to maintain a worldwide threat to humanity that will demand secular action to combat it. Under the guise of worrying about the atmosphere, the United Nations will be able to move the planet toward a biblical prophecy as foretold in Scripture."[12] Though coming from a theological, rather than a political viewpoint, Baxter uses the same basic argument as Bill Cooper did when he claimed that UFO-oriented conspiracy theories were preparing the groundwork for a totalitarian global government or when David Icke interprets major catastrophes (war, assassination, mass shootings, terrorist activities, etc.) as carefully engineered events designed to allow the reptilians and their servants more control over humanity.[13]

A core component within conspiratorial concerns over United Nations environmental and population monitoring efforts is a focus on the UN's Agenda 21, a voluntary action plan introduced at the 1992 Earth Summit. Agenda 21 calls for efforts to implement sustainable development programs, at the international, national, and local levels. Since its introduction, conspiracy theorists have targeted Agenda 21 as being one of the means through which the United Nations will undermine national sovereignty and individual liberty. David Risselada, writing at the website *Freedom Outpost*, labels Agenda 21 as "the human depopulation agenda" and summarizes it as encompassing

> every policy initiative that pushes the world towards total U.N. control. It involves everything from gun control to parental rights. The plan is to strip all individuals of their rights to private property, herd us into dense population centers and control us like cattle. They also intend to drastically reduce the human population from its current number of about seven billion to around 500,000,000, because they fear that human beings consume too much, and the population growth is too much for the planet to handle.

Risselada argues that the widespread availability of abortion and birth control were a vital part of the population reduction plan but when these proved to be inadequate, the more extreme methods of Agenda 21 were necessary.[14] As "resource management" is part of Agenda 21 programs, conspiracy-oriented writers often accuse organizations involved in speculative, sustainability-oriented urban planning of being in league with the United Nations. America 2050, the "infrastructure planning and policy program" of the Regional Plan Association[15] has initiated studies on what it calls "megaregions." The concept of megaregions is a way to think about urban growth and population centers that are connected by "interlocking economic systems, shared natural resources and ecosystems, and common transportation systems." Due to the growth of these megaregions, centered on cities like New York, Chicago, Dallas, or Los Angeles, America 2050 believes that "as continued population growth and low density settlement patterns place increasing pressure on these systems, there is greater impetus to coordinate policy at this expanded scale" recognizing, for example, that "protecting public watersheds that span multiple state and regional boundaries" and other challenges demand "coordination at the megaregional scale." Most of America 2050s policy recommendations focus on infrastructure developments such as special toll lanes on interstate highways for freight hauling trucks[16] and regional high speed rail networks. As innocuous (and, perhaps, dull) as these things may seem on the surface, America 2050 has come under scrutiny by those who fear a global hegemony dominated by the United Nations.

Dave Hodges, host of Internet radio program *The Common Sense Show*, is an example of those who have connected initiatives like America 2050 to Agenda 21 and, in turn, to wider conspiracy theories denouncing supposed depopulation plans. A luridly titled 2014 article, "The Agenda 21 Depopulation of Rural Areas Will Give Obama Stalin-Like Control Over Food," ties America 2050 to the North American Free Trade Agreement, 1970s defense planning and, ultimately, the destruction of America as we know it and the imposition of a "'Hunger Games' nightmare scenario." Hodges declares that America 2050 "is based upon the creation of megacities" and warns that the creation of these urban monstrosities is "well underway." The goal, Hodges claims, is to divide the United States into eleven "large, densely populated urban centers," what he characterizes as "a complete Agenda 21 style of total urbanization." However, for the advent of the megacities "to come to fruition, American suburbs and rural areas must be completely depopulated. This process is underway and the Obama administration is accelerating the process."

This process did not, however, begin with Agenda 21 or America 2050. Hodges draws a thread from Agenda 21 back to the 1994 implementation of the North American Free Trade Agreement between the United States, Canada, and Mexico. NAFTA—part of the globalization of agriculture, bank-

5. Mad Science and Forbidden Knowledge 143

rupted millions of Mexican farmers, who became "the vanguard of ... Mexicans illegally entering the US." He also blames NAFTA for the collapse of small family farms and the rise of "government subsidized corporate farms." This subsidization of agribusiness is equivalent, for Hodges, to outright control of the literal food supply.

He then, in turn, connects "megacities" and NAFTA to a 1974 National Security Council memorandum, "Implications of Worldwide Population Growth for U.S. Security and Overseas Interests." This study examined the degree to which population growth could affect natural resources and, subsequently, geopolitics. The memo raised questions that policy makers would need to face in the event of continued unchecked population control in developing countries. Questions such as "Should the U.S. set even higher agricultural production goals which would enable it to provide additional major food resources to other countries? Should they be nationally or internationally controlled?" and "Would food be considered an instrument of national power?" and "Will we be forced to make choices as to whom we can reasonably assist, and if so, should population efforts be a criterion for such assistance?"[17] as a springboard for speculation that "starvation will be used to enforce the Agenda 21 depopulation of rural areas" and that this is the "'endgame' strategy of the globalists which will depopulate the America's suburbs and rural areas."[18]

Hodge's analysis of the America 2050 initiative is useful as an example not just of the conspiratorial narrative of global control and depopulation but also as a rhetorical model for how, in general, conspiracy theorists present their arguments and evidence. Although he provides a link to the America 2050 page on megaregions, his summation of the concept is at odds with reality. He consistently uses the term "megacity" rather than "megaregion" which—along with his reference to *The Hunger Games*—serves to conjure images of post-apocalyptic tyranny and dystopias typified by material deprivation and brutal subjugation. He also characterizes America 2050's goals as *creating* megaregions/cities, positioning this type of urban growth as a devious plan rather than the result of decades of political, social, economic, and technological development. Hodge's use of Agenda 21 is a reflection of the manner in which the term has evolved into a symbol. "Agenda 21" has become separated from its 1992 origins and—like "Roswell," "REX 84," "FEMA," or "MKULTRA"—serves as conspiracy shorthand. When a reader who has absorbed and been unconsciously conditioned by even a fraction of the conspiratorial literature that has emerged over the past two decades sees the symbol "Agenda 21," the notions of population control and authoritarian resource management enter her mind. Hodges does not define Agenda 21.

Rather, he refers vaguely to the EPA's "Agenda 21 wetlands regulations" or "Agenda 21 urbanization policies." The reader comes to the text with an assumed response to the symbol. That response allows the author to forego crafting a more detailed argument. Similarly, Hodge's outlining of connections between America 2050, NAFTA and the 1974 NSC memorandum on population growth exemplify the conspiratorial practice of "connecting the dots," assembling narrative collages of concepts, statistics, and anecdote which—taken separately—may be grounded in fact and reality. The big picture, painstakingly assembled, is presented as an earth-shattering discovery or revelation. Conspiratorial concerns about Agenda 21 and its relation to national, state, and local policy-making have become widespread enough that the U.S. branch of ICLEI-Local Governments for Sustainability (formerly the International Council for Local Environmental Initiatives) has published a Frequently Asked Questions page "in light of conspiracy theories circulated about ICLEI and Agenda 21." In response to the question "Does ICLEI work behind the scenes in cities and counties to implement or impose a secret agenda?" the organization responds that the "conspiracy theory" is not true and that they have "no authority over its local government members whatsoever, and we do not work in secret or in any way circumvent public input in decision-making processes. We do not mandate, impose, or enforce any national or international policies or initiatives."[19]

Not all environmentally-focused conspiracy narratives deny the existence of climate change. Some theories proclaim that the very real changes in weather patterns in recent decades are, in fact, due to human activity. The activities that cause weather changes are numerous. They include so-called "chem trails"—chemicals sprayed from government aircraft that may look similar to typical aircraft contrail but are, in fact, designed to alter the weather, infect populations with diseases, or other nefarious acts. Some experts fear that conspiracy theories about chem trails, while often disproven, could "poison legitimate debate" about the utility of various geoengineering efforts to combat pollution and climate change.[20] While the very existence of government planted chemicals in the atmosphere is debated, some government programs are very real and well-established. As we have seen, these types of programs are often prime candidates for use as conspiracy fodder.

A government program that came under the recurring scrutiny of conspiracy theorists since the 1990s was the High Frequency Active Auroral Research Program (HAARP). Established in 1990, HAARP was a joint project of the Office of Naval Research, the Air Force Research Laboratory and the University of Alaska. In 1993, the HAARP antenna array in Gakona, Alaska, was completed and its analysis of the ionosphere began. According to the project's official website at the University of Alaska, HAARP's purpose is "to further advance our knowledge of the physical and electrical properties of the Earth's ionosphere which can affect our military and civilian communication and navigation systems."[21] By 2014, when the Defense Advanced Research Projects Agency (DARPA) discontinued the project, its objectives had moved beyond merely studying the atmosphere. According to David Walker, deputy assistant secretary of the Air Force for science, technology and engineering, HAARP had explored the possibility of injecting, "energy into the ionosphere to be able to actually control it." That, Walker announced, had been accomplished.[22] Like the other government projects—both secret and open—that we have examined, HAARP's publicly stated objectives sound science fictional and a bit dangerous—manipulating the atmosphere with a vast antenna installation in far Alaska sounds as much like a villain's plan in a James Bond film as it does a government study.

It is not, then, surprising that conspiracy narratives hold HAARP responsible for changing climate and weather patterns, including so-called "extreme" weather such as extensive droughts and superstorms. HAARP, and other government manipulation of the weather might even be behind the shift in terminology from "global warming" to "climate change." After all, "global warming may be hard to produce; not so 'climate change.'" Also suspicious, supposedly, is Al Gore continuing to speak publicly on climate change: "If indeed the power elite has embarked on a deliberate campaign of climate change (to support various kinds of economic manipulations) then it makes sense to send one of the world's best known drummers back out onto the circuit. Gore's reemergence may coincide with a renewed effort to reignite this dangerous meme." Like Dave Hodges's revelations about America 2050, this brief statement demonstrates a general conspiracy theory pattern. The goals of the conspiracy are vague ("economic manipulation") and the anonymous author employs name-calling and conditional language to give the appearance of solid information. The villains are a shadowy "power elite"; "Gore's reemergence may concede"; "if" the power elite seeks to control the weather. We can describe this kind of phrasing as pseudo-skepticism—the author carefully chooses words designed to deflect accusations when his predictions fail to occur.[23]

Some accusations of HAARP's nefarious activities are more specific:

> One of the first projects for the new HAARP weapon was to cause the accelerated melting of the glaciers in order for the US to get at the vast deposits of oil and mineral deposits in Canada's northern territories. Former vice-president Al Gore is in fact one of the men in the US government responsible for the Global Warming of the planet and his oversight of the development of HAARP has

> made him $millions [sic]. Al Gore and Bill Clinton were the ones who gave government funding for the development of HAARP, which they knew could be used to manipulate the weather, so they are responsible for creating the global warming crisis.... HAARP is a super-powerful ionospheric heater. What does a heater do? It heats things up. What happens when you heat the ionosphere? It causes the gases of the ionosphere to heat up which will cause the Globe to warm—Global warming effect. The United States' experiments with Global weather patterns has [sic] impacted everyone else on the planet.[24]

As with many environmental conspiracy theories, some HAARP narratives invoke the specter of depopulation as a motive for the Alaska-based experiment. Highland1, a pseudonymous poster on *The One Truth* Internet forum, claims that HAARP is threatening "rivers" of vapor in the earth's lower atmosphere. Highland1 claims that "HAARP has been ordered by the current US government (President Obama is the only person who can authorize the use of nuclear weapons, biological weapons and this star wars [sic] weapon of mass destruction) to manipulate the weather and create floods to destroy the World's food supply." President Obama's motivation for this destruction of food stuffs, according to Highland1, is rooted in generally the same sources as Dave Hodges's analysis, explaining that "during the Jimmy Cater [sic] administration ... it was decided that the World population was getting too big and billions of people would have to be killed off" and quotes Henry Kissinger as saying, "Depopulation should be the highest priority of U.S. foreign policy towards the Third World" in what is likely an oblique and exaggerated reference to the 1974 NSC memorandum on population growth. He or she then connects HAARP-based farm destruction to Nazi eugenics programs, erroneously defining eugenics as "the deliberate killing off of large segments of living populations." HAARP, according to Highland1, does more than simply manipulate the weather. Since taking office, President Obama, HAARP has been used "to create earthquakes, tsunamis, floods and heat waves in foreign states and in the US" in order "to covertly kill as many people as possible."[25]

HAARP, chem trails, and government control of farmland target the land, sea, and sky. Depopulation narratives also point to epidemic disease as a tool of the global elite. As AIDS has been the focus of several prominent conspiracy theories since the 1980s and there is a wide array of assertions of the origins of the disease and the supposed purpose of the intentional creation and spread of the disease.[26] Somewhat unusually, conspiracy theories about the origin and spread of HIV and AIDS have come under scrutiny by conspiracy theorists who attempt to sort through the many competing narratives vying for attention. In the early 1990s, G.J. Krupey observed that "confusion still reigns in the public forum on the AIDS question, and bigotry still dominates the discourse" accompanied by "media sensation-mongering and hate-mongering by the religious right." Krupey examines the theory that AIDS had its origin in a biowarfare lab at Fort Detrick, Maryland, and "released, either accidentally or deliberately, on a world unprepared for it." This theory had first surfaced in the 1980s, and used as anti–U.S. propaganda in the Soviet media. Krupey focuses on the connections between the American military and scientific institutions, asking, "Why does the military always seem to be hovering on the periphery of AIDS research, if not in the middle of it? The government's, especially the military's covert experimentation on unwitting American citizens, both individuals and large populations is precedented [sic] and documented.... So it hardly seems responsible to dismiss those who insist upon a military connection to AIDS are mere paranoids."[27]

Conspiracy theories about the origin and spread of HIV and AIDS are not confined to the pages of paranoid magazines and the Internet. In 2005, the *Washington Post* reported the findings of a survey by the Rand Corporation that showed that in polling conducted during 2002 and 2003, 48.2 percent of African Americans agreed "somewhat or strongly" that HIV was artificially created. 26.6 percent believed this creation was done in a government laboratory and 12 percent believed "HIV was created and spread by the CIA." These conspiratorial thoughts extended beyond the creation of the virus to its purpose and supposed management by the powers that be, with 53.4 percent believing that "there is a cure for AIDS but it is being withheld from the poor" and 15.2 percent holding that "AIDS is a form of genocide against blacks."[28] It is this last opinion that correlates most closely with the general trend of science and disease-focused conspiracy narratives. While the generally white mainstream of conspiracy culture addresses the notion of AIDS (or other diseases such as avian flu or Ebola) as a tool of genocide, it does so in a way that does not always highlight ethnicity. Some who specifically identify as white conspiracy researchers, when discussing depopulation schemes also view these plots through a racial lens. The opposite end of the spectrum illustrated by that 15.2 percent is shown in white separatist and white supremacist writings on so-called "white genocide." Where African American conspiracy theorists point to the precedent of the Tuskegee syphilis experiments and "the reality of 300 years of slavery and 100 years of post-slavery exploitation"[29] as supporting their claims of plague-fueled genocide, white genocide theorists rely largely on perceived threats to their existence that are political, economic, and cultural. Christian Miller, in an essay titled "None Dare Call It White Genocide" cites "non-White legal immigration and millions of non-White illegal aliens" as being "inherently destructive" to white Americans. Miller describes non-white immigration and the economic and social chaos he claims accompanies it as "incremental genocide by design," and accuses anyone who opposes immigration restriction as being "pro–White genocide".[30]

These fears of racial genocide are less prevalent than concerns about the more generalized and broad-based reduction of the human population as a whole. These views, while outliers, serve to illustrate the remarkable diversity of opinions and theories about the forces believed to be the perpetrators of global genocide. From HIV to NAFTA, with chem trails and HAARP along the way, these narratives' commonality is similar to others we have examined so far. Elites seek power and control and are, of course, willing to use any means at their disposal to accomplish their goals.

Cases and Connections: The Georgia Guidestones

On March 22, 1980, the Elberton Granite Finishing Company of Elberton, Georgia, unveiled a large monument known as The Georgia Guidestones. Erected on a five acre plot in the northeastern Georgia countryside, this monument consists of four stones that each measure a little over 16 feet high, 6 feet wide, and 19 inches thick and weigh 42,000 pounds. They surround a central stone that is 3 feet narrower. Topping these is a 9 by 6 foot capstone. Nicknamed "The American Stonehenge," it is oriented to align with astronomical features. For example, "the North star is always visible through a special hell drilled from the South to the North side of the center stone." There is also an opening cut in the stones that allows viewing of the sunrise during the vernal and autumnal equinoxes.[31] This monument, placed in a rural county with, at the time, fewer than 20,000 residents,[32] continues to serve as one of the most durable symbols for conspiracy theorists that focus on eugenics, population control, and ecological policy. This is not because of the stones themselves but, rather, because of the messages carved into the granite in English, Russian, Chinese, Arabic, Hebrew, Swahili, Hindi, and Spanish as well as Cuneiform, Sanskrit, Classical Greek, and Egyptian Hieroglyphic.

Calling for the monument to be "guidestones to an age of reason," the stones included ten maxims for humanity:

> Maintain humanity under 500,000,000 in perpetual balance with nature;
> Guide reproduction wisely, improving fitness and diversity;
> Unite humanity with a living new language;
> Rule passion, faith, tradition, and all things with tempered reason;

5. Mad Science and Forbidden Knowledge

Protect people and nations with fair laws and just courts;
Let all nations rule internally, resolving external disputes in a world court;
Avoid petty laws and useless officials;
Prize truth, beauty, love ... seeking harmony with the infinite;
Be not a cancer on earth—leave room for nature—leave room for nature.[33]

The story of the Georgia Guidestones began when a man calling himself R. C. Christian walked into the office of the Elbertson Granite Finishing Company in 1979 claiming to represent "a small group of loyal Americans who believe in God" and who wanted to "leave message for future generations." Christian acknowledged that his name was a pseudonym and that he and his fellow monument sponsors must remain anonymous "in order to avoid debate and contention which might confuse our meaning and which might delay a considered review of our thoughts."[34] They prepared a lengthy statement, published as part of a short illustrated book about the conception and construction of the monument, in which they provided more detailed explanations of and justifications for the ten tenets engraved on the stones. Unsurprisingly, the maxims and the mysterious group's explanations of them are typical of the many that had become prominent in the 1970s. As the authors of the commemorative booklet about the Guidestones wrote, "In 1980, as these stones were being raised, among the many pressing world problem was the need to control human numbers.... Controlling our reproduction is urgently needed.... Population control is a global problem."[35] These statements echo those in Ehrlich's *The Population Bomb* or the 1974 National Security Council memo cited by conspiracy theorists as evidence the United States government had global population reduction as an secret policy goal.

Conspiracy theorists who became aware of the Guidestones during the 1980s and 1990s latched on to the monument's call to "maintain" the human population level at half a billion people carried with it an implication that, somehow, the human population would have to be *reduced* to that level from the 4.3 billion people the planet contained in 1979. Radio host Stanley Monteith, in an essay entitled, "The Population Control Agenda" acknowledged that many people found it "impossible to believe" that there is a global conspiracy to "kill off large segments of the world's population." Monteith admits that he found it difficult to accept as well.

> It was not until I journeyed to Elberton, Georgia, stood within the dark shadows of the great Druid-like monument built there, and read the words engraved on the massive stone pillars of that structure that I finally came to accept the truth. At that point it became obvious that just as our Lord has given mankind Ten Commandments to guide our lives, so, too, those from "the dark side" have been given their instructions from the "one" they worship. The ten programs of the "guides" are inscribed in eight different languages on the four great granite

pillars of the American Stonehenge. That message foretells a terrifying future for humanity.³⁶

Taken in tandem with pronouncements from the United Nations, declassified National Security Council documents, and an increasing focus on the fragile ecological balance of the planet, it is not shocking that those who were predisposed to accept conspiracy theories aw the message of the Guidestones as an agenda rather than a wish list. That the Guidestones had been commissioned and funded by an apparently wealthy, anonymous group under terms of strict secrecy only fueled the belief that the Guidestones were a message from the shadowy elites who controlled the world from behind the scenes.

The Georgia Guidestones would be a persistent presence within conspiracy culture, surfacing as "evidence" of a global depopulation agenda referenced in articles and stories. The non-conspiratorial press have also covered the Guidestones, with outlets like *Wired* producing extensive articles on the monument's existence and influence.³⁷ One enterprising conspiracist has laid claim to thegeorgiaguidestones.com and, as of this writing, uses it to expose the nefarious plans of its creators. One example relates to a time capsule buried beneath the monument and plans—mentioned in the commemorative booklet from Elbertson Granite—to eventually add stones to the monument site "to mark the migrations of the sun and perhaps certain other celestial phenomena."³⁸ Oddly, the inscription noting the presence of the time capsule does not specify when it should be excavated, the inscription reading only that it was "to be opened on" with a blank space where a date should be. The anonymous author of thegeorgiaguidestones.com explains that no date is included on the new stone because

> the Georgia Guide Stones are incomplete. New stones are to be added at the site. That means the sponsors of the stone intend to have a ceremony after the climax event that levels the population of the human race to half a billion. The climax event is going to take place soon. The climax event is going to involve changes in the fixed heavens. The new stones shall mark the earth's orientation to the new heavens. The dates from the new calendar are to be carved in the stone at that time. Hang on! It's going to be a wild ride;)³⁹

Incongruous winking-smiley emoticon aside, this is an example of the level of extrapolation of vast plots from essentially simple statements typical of conspiracy narratives. The Georgia Guidestones serve as a massive target for conspiracy theorists because of its shadowy origins and prominent, tangible, physical presence. Unlike decades old UN recommendations, the Guidestones may be visited and gazed upon. Like Stan Monteith, others have been transformed and convinced by the Guidestones that the plots they may have read about on the Internet are real.

The Hollow Earth

"We are not alone." This statement has guided believers in extraterrestrial visitation (and has been an assumption of those who promote the notion of a cover-up of such visits). That statement has also been directed below the surface of the Earth and, during the late twentieth century, has become just as intertwine with conspiratorial thinking as so many other areas. The concept of an Earth that is hollow and possibly habitable (and inhabited) is not a recent one, nor an exclusively American one. The story of the Hollow Earth in America begins with John Cleves Symmes. Symmes was born in Sussex County, New Jersey, in 1780. He joined the army in 1802 and serve at a variety of posts on the western frontier. He served as an infantry captain in the War of 1812. After the war, Symmes left the army and settled in St. Louis where he had a successful business trading with the Fox tribe. On April 10, 1818, Symmes published a circular and began distributing it. This circular was reprinted in James McBride's 1861 *Pioneer Biography: Sketches of the Lives of Some of the Early Settlers of Butler County, Ohio*. Symmes sets forth his goals right away, saying, "I declare the earth is hollow and habitable within; containing a number of solid concentric spheres, one within the other, and that it is open at the poles twelve or sixteen degrees. I pledge my life in support f this truth, and am ready to explore the hollow, if the world will support and aid me in this undertaking."[40] He also claims the ability to "disclose Dr. Darwin's 'Golden Secret'" and makes a call for "one hundred brave companions, well equipped, to start from Siberia in the fall season, with reindeer and sleights ... [to] find a warm and rich land, stocked with thrifty vegetables and animals, if not men ... we will return in the succeeding spring."[41]

In 1820, Symmes followed up his circular asking for volunteers with a pseudonymous fiction work entitled *Symzonia: A Voyage of Discovery*, writing as Captain Adam Seaborn. The fictional Captain Seaborn, following Symmes's plan, sails through the opening at the North Pole and encounters a comfortable, pleasant interior world. He "had never been in a climate so agreeable to my feelings.... The air was so soft, so elastic and temperate, it was a luxury to sit still and inhale the sweet breath of heaven."[42] Seaborn/Symmes had an inflated view of his discovery of this interior world: "Whose achievements equaled mine? The voyage of Columbus was but an excursion on a fish pond, and his discoveries, compared with mine, were but trifles."[43] Seaborn/Symmes then discusses the government of the interior world and reveals that the humans of the exterior world were the descendants of those who had committed crimes and been exiled from the paradise of this subterranean realm.

Symmes took his ideas on the road, lecturing around the United States about the hollow earth and drawing significant crowds. An 1826 article by "American Traveler" in the Charlestown, Massachusetts, *Zion's Herald* reported that Symmes "has given a public lecture every evening ... and so far as we can learn, all who have heard him have been gratified, and many convinced, of at least, the plausibility of his novel doctrines."[44] That these doctrines, including the existence of a 6000 mile diameter hole at the North Pole and the existed of an inhabited world within were even considered by the audience would indicate that either Symmes was very persuasive or that—more likely—geographical knowledge simply was not wide spread or well known. A desire for geographic knowledge and experience was, however, very prevalent in American society in the early nineteenth century. For most Americans, this desire for exploration and expansion focused on the "west" (especially the Transmississippi west) rather than the interior of the Earth. But was the west a viable place for expansion?

In 1820, the same time in which Symmes wrote Symzonia, Stephen H. Long of the Army Corps of Topographical Engineers made an exploratory trip across the Great Plains to the Rocky Mountains. According to historians Robert Hine and John Mack Faragher, "the account of this expedition concluded that the region was "almost wholly unfit for cultivation, and of course uninhabitable by a people depending upon agriculture for their subsistence," and included a map on which the present states of Oklahoma, Kansas, and Nebraska were labeled the "Great American Desert."[45] This characterization of the Transmississippi west would persist in the American geographical imagination until after the 1860s. Given the widespread acceptance both of this misconception and the notion that America needed to expand to thrive, it is perhaps not surprising that Symmes's notion of an interior world persisted. Particularly unsurprising is the idea that this interior climate and land would be suitable for population and cultivation. Symmes's theories about the hollow earth and his desire to mount an expedition to explore it may look strange from our twenty-first century perspective. To an observer in the 1820s or 30s it might have looked, at most, merely too ambitious and expensive. The stories of explorers such as Lewis and Clark, Zebulon Pike, and Stephen Long were fresh in the American mind. Exploration, expansion, and the discovery of the new and different—be they lands, ideas, literature or technology—were part and parcel of the nineteenth century American experience.

Others took up the Symmes cause, assisting him on the profitable lecture circuit and his theories were compiled and published by his son Americus in 1878, more than a decade after his father's death. By this time, however, many scientific writers had dismissed Symmes's hollow earth ideas. The ideas were not, however, always dismissed. Significantly, American Traveler also noted that "in the course of his lectures [Symmes] sets forth so many facts and incidents which are little known, that we venture to say, there are few persons so well versed in geography."[46] According to McBride's biography, Symmes "received a good, common English education" as a boy and always read enthusiastically about mathematics and science. He did not have any formal education in the sciences or even a college degree. In the twenty-first century world, this would disqualify anyone from speaking as a "scientist." This image of the self-taught scientist, while a staple of nineteenth century America, would fade as the century turned.

The notion of a credentialed society and the attendant divide between educated and non-educated began appearing in earnest in the twentieth century. One of the key events in this process was the formation, meeting, and report of the Committee of Ten on Secondary School Studies of the National Education Association, issued in 1894. This report sought to organize and codify high school science requirements. Beginning in 1894, the NEA would encourage state governments to set specific requirements for formalized science education including chemistry, physics, and astronomy.[47] Before this time, there had been no national standards for science education, resulting it usually being eclectic and incomplete. This reformation of science education coincided with a sharp rise in the professionalization of a variety of scholarly careers. The National Education Association emerged in its present form in 1874. Professional and credentialing organizations such as the American Medical Association (1847) and the American Psychiatric Association (1892) existed, among other reasons, to provide for uniform and enforceable standards among members. These organizations served as gatekeepers—determining the level of education and training necessary to practice particular professions. These measures had not originated in America. European nations, particularly Germany pioneered formal credentialing and professionalization of a variety of fields in the late nineteenth century.

Twentieth and twenty-first century skeptical responses to pseudo-history and pseudo-science illustrate this trend of professionalization and stratification of scholarly professions and contribute to a conspiratorial mindset among those who promote "alternative" historical narratives and scientific theories. The emergence of a credentialed scientific establishment during the twentieth century created an authority that may be characterized as a powerful elite. These scholarly or academic elite—like the political, economic, or religious elites of other conspiracy narratives—serve as targets for suspicion. Why do we not know about the hollow earth? Because such a revelation would upset the academic elite's monopoly on knowledge. This stratification had a specific effect on theories of the Hollow Earth. After John Cleves Symmes and his adherents passed from the scene by the mid-nineteenth century, stories of the hollow earth were limited to the fictional realm, such as Jules Verne's *Journey to the Center of the Earth*. Nonfictional treatment of the notion no longer made appearances in scientific lectures. Rather, nonfictional accounts of the hollow earth appeared in spiritualist texts that discussed the Ascended Masters and lost continents of Mu and Lemuria. Travels to the interior of the earth would persist in novels like John Uri Lloyd's 1898 *Etidorpha* and Willis George Emerson's 1908 novel *The Smoky God*. It would, however, be the 1940s before another devotee of the hollow earth would capture the American imagination as fully as Symmes's speculations.

Richard Sharpe Shaver was born in 1907. Moving to Detroit after graduating high school, he became a student at the Wicker School of Art, working as a nude model to earn money. In the 1930s, Shaver took a job at the Ford auto body plant in Highland Park, Michigan, and held this job for several years.[48] Plagued by disembodied voices in his head, Shaver spent time in Michigan's Ypsilanti State Hospital and a stint from 1938–1943 in the Ionia State Hospital. While there, he began to develop theories about the cause of the voices in his head. He began to believe they emanated from beings below the surface of the Earth, using devices to beam the voices into his mind. Richard Toronto, Shaver's biographer, explains that

> in his spare time, which was plentiful, he learned the nuance of ray technology and eventually classified scores of rays, having experienced them firsthand. Most frequently used were stim ray, ben ray, aug ray, pain ray, crueling ray, police ray, medical ray, and penetray, but there were many others. Shaver came to believe that he alone held the key to a vast secret few others knew.[49]

Shaver began writing in earnest during his time at the Ionia State Hospital, not only about the subterranean mind controllers who were affecting him, but also on more prosaic concerns. In particular, he was on (according to Toronto) "a crusade to expose corruption in the U.S. mental hospital system."[50] In Shaver's view, "fat cats made huge profits from the state, as long as they kept a steady stream of 'crazies' locked up in the nut house. Shaver certainly saw himself as one of those unfortunate patients kept confined without cause."[51]

Shaver's public revelations of hidden history and the mysteries of the Hollow Earth began in 1943 after his release from Ionia. He wrote a letter to editor Ray Palmer at *Amazing Stories* magazine. After some debate within the editorial offices of *Amazing Stories*, Palmer ran Shaver's letter in the January 1944 issue. The letter, signed "S. Shaver," asked that the magazine's editors "have it looked at by some one in the college or a friend who is a student of

5. Mad Science and Forbidden Knowledge

antique time," and provided a key to how the modern alphabet corresponded to ancient meaning. For example, "T—te (the most important symbol used; the real origin of cross symbol—it mean integration force of growth (all matter is growing—the intake is gravity cause—the force is T." Similarly, there was "D—de—detrimental or rather disintegrant energy (the second most important symbol in language)." Shaver asserted that "a great number of our English words have come down intact" from this ancient language and that it was "definite proof of the Atlantean legend." This language, however, was "too deep for modern man." Shaver closed his letter by saying, "It should be saved and placed in wise hands. I can't, will you?" Palmer's editorial response claimed that he had "applied the letter-meanings to the individual letters of many old root words and proper names and got an amazing 'sense' out of them." Palmer asked readers try the language out for themselves and report their results.[52] Palmer, sensing that he might have a commercial sensation on his hands, encouraged Shaver to produce more material in the same vein. Shaver submitted a 10,000-word submission entitled "A Warning to Future Man." Palmer rewrote it (based on *"more than one million words* of further correspondence with Mr. Shaver")[53] and published it in the March 1945 issue of *Amazing Stories* as "I Remember Lemuria!"

In addition to being triple the length of Shaver's original submission to Palmer, "I Remember Lemuria!" blurred the lines between fiction and reality. One line that was blurred was the very origin of the story. Shaver insisted that he directly received his knowledge of the hollow earth from transmissions emanating from the machines below the surface. Palmer did not include this information in "I Remember Lemuria!" Palmer told readers that Shaver's story was an effort to "arrive at *truth* by beginning with what is accepted as fantasy." Shaver's story, Palmer explained, was rooted in "racial memory," which he described as "the feeling that 'this place is familiar, yet I have never been here before!' or 'I know a thing is so, yet I have never learned it!'"[54] Shaver, in his introduction to the story, tells the reader, "What I tell you is not fiction! How can I impress that on you as forcibly as I feel it must be impressed? ... I can only hope that when I have told the story of Mutan Mion as I remember it you will believe."[55]

Shaver presented a history of the Earth that was far different than the accepted narrative and, further, was different from the usual esoteric histories of Lemuria/Mu, Atlantis, and similar regions. Richard Toronto summarizes Shaver's antediluvian worldview thus:

> Shaver's voices explained that prior to the Deluge of Noah, an advanced civilization flourished under the leadership of three races: the Atlans, Titans, and Nortans. These beings came from somewhere in deep space and lived happily

on Earth until the neighborhood went to hell in a handbasket. The sun began to spew radioactive particles that were deadly to their existence. Their bodies—once immortal—began to age. This would never do, and their learned ones sought an immediate solution. At first, they avoided the sun by retreating underground, constructing vast cavern systems within the Earth's crust. This is where they lived and worked for many years, until finally leaving Earth forever, preferring the security of dark space, as far from our deadly sun as possible.[56]

Some, however, stayed behind on the radioactivity-soaked Earth. Some left the subterranean caverns, moving to the surface and (eventually) becoming humans. Others remained below ground. One group, presented by Shaver as positive and benevolent, was the tero. Less helpful were the deros—a term that was an abbreviation of "Detrimental Energy Robots." In a footnote to Mutan Mion's story, Shaver (or, more likely, editor Ray Palmer) explained that the deros' "every thought movement is concluded with the decision to kill. They will instantly kill or torture anyone whom they contact unless they are extremely familiar with them and fear them … to a dero all new things are enemy."[57]

When "I Remember Lemuria" was published in the March 1945 issue of *Amazing Stories*, it sparked a tremendous response from readers. Ray Palmer, knowing a good thing when he saw it, encouraged more material from Shaver and contributed significant parts to the underground saga himself. In the next issue of *Amazing Stories*, Palmer retracted his explanation of "racial memory" and acknowledged that the story "was not a racial memory, but a *thought record!*" that is to say, something directly experienced by Shaver rather than by his distance ancestor. Palmer also revealed that "I Remember Lemuria!" was a blend of fiction and reality and that he had "detracted not one single whit from the 'facts' that Mr. Shaver's original manuscript might have contained." This reality was borne out by the letters received from readers which Palmer claimed revealed that, among other facts, "that mankind does know about the 'dero' people living now in the caves and is tormented by them."[58] Shaver contributed a new story ("Thought Records of Lemuria") in which he recounted hearing voices in his head while working on the automotive line and his subsequent contacts with those dwelling below the surface.[59]

For several years, Shaver's tales appeared in the pages of *Amazing Stories*, angering science fiction fans that believed the entire Shaver saga to be a hoax that was bringing science fiction into disrepute. Leadership at Ziff-Davis, the publisher of *Amazing Stories*, ordered Palmer to make clear to the readers that the Shaver Mystery (as it was now known) was fictional in nature. Palmer did so, little by little, until in 1948 the topic all but faded from the pages of

Amazing Stories. Ray Palmer had begun to shift his workload to the establishment of a new publication, *FATE*, which allowed him the freedom to indulge in occult topics like hidden civilizations and his new topic of special interest, flying saucers.[60] Palmer, politically on the outs with Ziff-Davis due to the controversy over the Shaver mystery and frustrated that he was not allowed to publish a flying saucer-oriented issue of *Amazing Stories* (in his view, due to pressure from the government),[61] was soon to leave the science fiction magazine.

Unlike the stories of Symmes and other tales of the hollow earth, Shaver's vision of the subterranean was a land that had fallen into chaos and disorder rather than a preserved paradise. Further, under the guidance of Ray Palmer, Shaver's tales of the deros and teros became "a record of an era of hidden truth." The degree to which Palmer accepted Shaver's ideas has always been unclear. What is more certain is that Palmer believed that "science fiction and provocative ideas inspire people to think for themselves," enabling them to emerge from the "mental enchainment" of formal, state-sanctioned education.[62] Palmer and Shaver both conveyed this sense that the scientific and educational establishment was not the be all and end all of knowledge. In correspondence with some skeptical science fiction fans who doubted his claims, Shaver related that before he knew of the deros and teros, he could not comprehend the "wonder-science" to which he had been exposed, believing it to be "modern secret science—things that science had developed and kept to itself as a monopoly, for the power and wealth the advantages of using these apparatuses would give them."[63] The assertion that a hidden elite (scientific, political, or financial) controlling secret technology to solidify and maintain their dominance is a common conspiratorial trope. Shaver's assertion that human science was inferior to that of the residents of the hollow earth adds a layer to the typical science or technology conspiracy. When considered in conjunction with Richard Toronto's discussion of Shaver's suspicion of corruption within the mental health system (corruption of which Shaver believed he was a victim), a frightening and paranoid vision emerges. The dero tormented Shaver with their technology and the only response for those in power on the surface world was to imprison him in a mental hospital.

Interest in the Shaver Mystery as well as the broader topic of a hollow, inhabited earth, has continued over the decades. Fanzines like Richard Toronto's *Shavertron* and Mary Jane Martin's *Hollow Hassle* created a space for conversation and speculation about the possibility of a habitable space inside the planet. In these publications we continue to see elements of the skeptical attitude toward accepted science that Shaver and Palmer had demonstrated in the 1940s. In an interview for an edited collection of *Hollow*

Hassle articles, Mary Jane Martin claimed, "science is wrong a lot.... And then still don't really know much about what is going on below our feet."[64] As with Palmer and Shaver's tales of the inner earth, this skepticism approached the level of "conspiracy theory" but was targeted at scientific and academic elites rather than political, economic or government figures. Whatever cover-ups existed were rooted in the denial of the hollow earth. As discussed in Chapter 3, by the 1960s, non-extraterrestrial explanations for unidentified flying saucers—including the notion that they were connected to inhabitants of the inner earth—had faded. By the 1980s, however, the conspiratorial mindset intertwined with darker and more paranoid issues began to permeate some corners of hollow earth research and, once again, supposed alien craft would become connected with things below the planet's surface.

Fred Nadis, in his 2013 biography of Ray Palmer, attributes two specific strands of 1980s and 1990s conspiracy thought to the pulp author and editor. The first of these is "the flying saucer community's certainty of a governmental cover-up" and the second is "the hollow earth tradition" promulgated by Shaver and Palmer's writing.[65] He specifically highlights the tales of the supposed underground base near Dulce, New Mexico, as a prominent inheritor of the Shaver/Palmer tradition, characterizing Paul Bennewitz's stories of alien experimentation as "a dero scene right out of a Shaver story."[66] One strand Nadis briefly touches upon, however, shares in the spirit of Shaver's writings more fully. This is the connection made by some in Christian fundamentalist circles between alien abductions, the "fallen angels" of the Old Testament, and the history of the antediluvian world.

Underground Bases

The narratives that discuss the supposed dark deeds of government, military, and corporate conspirators in seeking to control the destiny of humanity highlight a variety of technologies and techniques that persist throughout the 1990s and into the twenty-first century. There is a particular constellation of technological manifestations that particularly epitomize this era—mysterious underground bases, and the nearly ubiquitous black helicopters that, supposedly, terrorized those who threatened to expose the plans of the New World Order. These two conspiratorial memes have been connected to others such mysterious livestock "mutilations" and UFOs.

UFOs, in particular, have long been associated with underground bases and the connected narrative of an inhabitable hollow Earth. In his extensive survey of conspiracy culture, Michael Barkun states,

> The inner-earth materials place the alien presence underground—in tunnels, installations, and caverns. in some cases, the aliens come from outer space and merely choose a subsurface realm because they feel more secure there. In other instances, they are said to be native to this netherworld.... The underground denizens are always described as malevolent ... perhaps a reflection of the long-standing identification of underground realms with the domain of the dead. Hell is always below, heaven above.[67]

Barkun's examination of subterranean conspiracy theories—particularly to sinister underground bases—is tightly bound up with UFO and extraterrestrial conspiracy narratives. As we will see, there is certainly a strong alien connection to this topic. Reports of an alleged base near Dulce, New Mexico, emerged in the 1980s from the research and writing of Bill Moore, John Lear, John Grace, and others (see Chapter 3). Stories of occurrences at the Dulce base would be come a strange sub-genre of alien conspiracy narrative during the 1990s.

As with many areas of conspiracy narrative in the 1990s, questions of alien visitors and their quisling collaborators in the American government cast a long shadow. There are, however, aspects of underground bases to which Barkun (and others) have paid far less attention. This is the connection between these supposed underground bases and other firmly terrestrial and political conspiracy narratives. During the 1990s, tales of mysterious underground military bases became blended with reports of unmarked black helicopters as well as the persistent fears of martial law or the subjugation of the United States by the United Nations as promoted by Bill Cooper, Linda Thompson, and others. This relatively prosaic approach to the investigation of underground bases also highlights the ambiguous and shifting nature of the question of extraterrestrial visitation and the ways in which predominantly political conspiracists contorted the issue in order to bolster their own claims.

Like many conspiracy theories and narratives that have emerged since World War II, the suspicion that the United States government—particularly its military—is engaged in constructing hidden subterranean installations for unknown and possibly malign purposes is rooted in the geopolitical realities and assumptions of the Cold War. With the possibility of a large scale nuclear exchange between the United States and the Soviet Union, the American military—as well as other agencies such as the Department of Energy—investigated the possibility of moving key elements of industrial production and military operations into underground, "hardened" sites. A 1961 report recounted that in the early 1950s, the head of the U.S. Army's Corps of Engineers commissioned a study to "'determine the feasibility and cost of constructing and operating strategic defense plants under ground.'" Based on "our experience in World War II as well as the experience of our enemies and allies" the Corps of Engineers determined that "installing our critical industries underground affords increased opportunity to protect our defense production against sabotage, practically eliminates the costs of replacing bombed-out activities, and offers better assurance of continued production in the event of persistent enemy bombing." This need was even more pressing in an age of potential nuclear warfare. The advantages for corporations of preparing to move their facilities underground were, to the Army, obvious. Advanced planning was preferable to the potential for "frantic and expensive efforts to combat the effects upon both civilian and military morale (let alone materiel production) after the first atom bomb has fallen in our midst." The time to build your bomb shelter is not when the bombs are falling. After all, "New York, San Francisco or Washington may very likely be the Pearl Harbor of World War III. Insurance that our national life will continue, despite the ravages of atomic warfare, is a vital stimulus for planning (and constructing) underground defense plants." This report was focused on the construction of industrial production facilities so it is was, of course, aimed at corporate America and the defense work they would doubtless provide in World War III as they had in World Wars I and II. It is telling, however, that the authors equate the survival of corporate assets to the survival of "our national life."[68]

Other belowground elements implemented during the Cold War are less obscure than underground industrial facilities. Nuclear-tipped ICBMs were sunk below the surface of the Earth in launch silos throughout the United States, placed on farms and ranches as well as more remote areas.[69] Like many other conspiracy tropes and narratives, there is a degree of truth underlying stories of mysterious underground facilities built around our country without our knowledge. At the very least, the technological means existed from the opening decades of the Cold War to construct such installations.

In addition to nuclear missile silos and bomb-resistant manufacturing facilities, a key purpose for underground facilities—and one which would be the most prone to conspiratorial elaboration—is the preservation of vital government functions in the event of catastrophic disaster such as a nuclear war. Defense officials undertook planning for numerous "continuity of government" programs in the late 1940s after the Soviet Union detonated their first atomic device. Since 1959, the Mount Weather Emergency Operations Center, located within the Blue Ridge Mountains 48 miles from Washington, D.C., has served as one of the key installations that would house key officials and figures that would keep the United States functioning in the event of disaster. Declassified documents from the early 1960s paint a picture of a facility that

5. Mad Science and Forbidden Knowledge   161

was clearly designed to be a long-term home for the military and political figures that might inhabit it. One 1961 memo outlined existing recreational facilities including an indoor driving range, four ping pong tables, and "the capability of producing special entertainment 'shows' and releasing them over [the facility's] own closed circuit channel."[70] Also emerging in the 1950s—and far less well known—is the Raven Rock Mountain Complex, which was established as an "alternate Pentagon" by President Harry Truman.[71] While these facilities had purposes that were sensible given the geopolitical realities of the time, there were some necessary aspects of such continuity of government planning that would, in later decades, contribute to the conspiratorial narratives, particularly those of martial law descending upon the United States.

In 1958 President Dwight D. Eisenhower established a system that designated emergency administrators who would be placed in charge of the American economy and infrastructure in the event of a massive disaster. The Emergency Censorship Agency, the Emergency Food Agency, and the Emergency Manpower Agency, were three of the ten agencies that would take control of vast portions of American life.[72] This plan was the procedural ancestor of the series of Executive Orders that would emerge in the 1960s and 1970s that had substantively the same goals as Eisenhower's plan. Those Executive Orders would be used in the 1980s and 1990s as "evidence" that the subjugation of the American people was a pen stroke away. the Federal Emergency Management Agency was often targeted as the villain in such a scenario, since "it has the power to suspend laws, move entire populations, arrest and detain citizens without a warrant and hold them without trial, it can seize property, food supplies, transportation systems, and can suspend the Constitution."[73] While these contingency plans and the facilities to support them were arguably sensible given the nature of the Cold War, as that conflict wound down in the first half of the 1990s, the contingency plans stayed in place, fueling the suspicions of conspiracy theorists.

But during the mid–1990s, the increase in the frequency of political conspiracy narratives. Given the prevalence of extraterrestrial conspiracy theories during that time, it was inevitable that political topics would bleed into areas that—while consistently conspiratorial—had shied away from overt political narratives. Bill Cooper's writings highlighted these connections and, along with Bob Lazar's tales of secret testing facilities in Nevada related to extraterrestrial technology, a link between hidden government installations and the extraterrestrial question emerged. As discussed in Chapter 4, the alleged underground facility near Dulce, New Mexico, became a staple of UFO lore in the 1980s. Rumors that the base was jointly occupied by alien forces as well as American military personnel were a crucial component of one of paranoid ufology's key narratives: that the U.S. government was in league with evil aliens. These aliens, however, were untrustworthy and a breakdown in this interplanetary relationship led to a firefight at the Dulce base in which several Americans lost their lives. Due in large part to the prominence of the Dulce base story, the entire concept of "underground bases" became sundered from its factual Cold War/Continuity-of-Government basis and became firmly lodged within the realm of the extraterrestrial and conspiratorial.

Because of the explosion of writers and researchers who focused on the political aspects of various conspiracies we see these writers having to address the question of an alien conspiracy even in their most resolutely terrestrial and political work, despite the fact that many of them saw tales of alien infiltration as a distraction from more pressing concerns.

This is certainly true in the case of underground bases and secret government facilities. Richard Sauder's 1995 book *Underground Bases and Tunnels: What Is the Government Trying to Hide?* is, despite its lurid title—a remarkably sensible book. It focuses, largely, on the factual existence of below-ground government and military installations using declassified documents to demonstrate that such bases are possible to build. The back cover copy of the book attempts to sensationalize this, inviting the reader to "go behind the scenes into little-known corners of the public record and discover how corporate America has worked hand-in-glove with the Pentagon for decades—dreaming about, planning, and actually constructing secret underground bases." The prevalence of the underground base mythos within UFO circles in the mid–1990s, however, demanded at lead some nod to the topic within Sauder's tome.[74]

Sauder opens his book with "A Cautionary Note to UFO Buffs" in which he acknowledges that there are "persistent rumors" that secret underground bases are constructed and staffed by "both covert human agencies *and* aliens working together in secret" (emphasis author's). To let UFO-minded readers down gently, Sauder goes on to report that his "research has not revealed whether or not Little Greys even *exist*, much less whether or not they are living and working in underground installations. Perhaps the Little Greys really do exist; perhaps they do not."[75] Sauder quickly moves on from the UFO topic and into the nuts and bolts of subterranean construction. The need for such a caveat for UFO fans was necessary, as the book was presented as quite extraterrestrial in focus. A flash on the front cover boasts "additional chapters on UFO-like technology" and back cover blurbs for Underground Base and Tunnels emphasize the supposedly alien-orientation of the book with quotations from Don Ecker—the Research Director for *UFO Magazine*—and prominent "abductee" Whitley Strieber.[76]

The chapters on "UFO-like technology" mentioned on the front cover address several questions that were, at the time, becoming prominent in conspiracy circles. One of these was speculation on whether or not it is feasible that so-called "alien abductions" could, in fact, be abductions by terrestrial forces who needed access to unwitting human test subjects for experimentation. Sauder discusses implantable microchips and radio transponders (a common topic among conspiracists discussing mind control technology) and notes the similarities between aspects of abductee accounts and extant (if not well-known) technology. These transponders could be used to "electronically monitor, in real time, the whereabouts and movements" of those who had been implanted for the purposes of possible "social or political control." Implantable devices that enable nefarious forces to engage in surveillance or outright remote control of large numbers of people were becoming a common fear in conspiracy literature, providing a technological parallel to concerns about hypnosis and brainwashing that were prominent in the 1950s and 1960s. Sauder concludes that

> we find ourselves stuck in a bizarre hall of mirrors full of constantly shifting, bizarre images, each one more improbable than the next. Are the images alien? Human? Are the perpetrators hiding behind disinformation or propaganda masks? Hypnotic masks? Electronically or chemically induced masks?[77]

Sauder also delves into the issue of cattle and livestock "mutilations," which had occurred in the American west and southwest and had become associated with UFO sightings during the 1980s and 1990s. The 1988 papers, for example, asserted that "millions of cattle have been killed in the process of acquiring biological materials" and that "both aliens and the U.S. government are responsible for mutilations, but for different reasons."[78] Sauder contends that there is "no hard proof" of alien involvement in these attacks on livestock and notes "the presence of mysterious, unidentified helicopters in the vicinity of many cattle mutilations."[79] He asserts that the supposed "alien" technology that produced such precise, laser-like incisions in the victims is, in fact, earthly. As is typical throughout the book, Sauder does not offer any solid conclusions, acknowledging that questions about the purposes of these experiments are "tremendously difficult" to answer.[80] Despite Sauder's relative restraint in drawing poorly-founded conclusions, he does relate this conjecture to a broader, global conspiracy:

> if the possibility of being implanted and electronically tracked and monitored (perhaps without your knowledge or consent) makes you feel a trifle uneasy, just try repeating the following words softly to yourself until you feel more relaxed: "'New World Order ... New World Order ... New World Order....'"[81]

Sauder's tone possesses a grudging character as he discusses the links between subterranean military and government facilities and wilder, more paranormal topics. Even this reference to the New World Order seems a bit tongue-in-cheek. Other authors, however, took extreme and paranoid assertions much more seriously.

One of the most prominent of these authors was Jim Keith. During the 1990s, Keith wrote over a dozen books on subjects ranging from mind control to the JFK assassination and was one of the most well-known proponents of the notion that the so-called UFO phenomenon (and the constellation of theories that had developed around it) was a useful smokescreen for sinister, Earth-based conspiracies. Keith addressed several themes raised by Sauder—particularly mysterious unmarked helicopters and cattle mutilations in *Black Helicopters over America: Strikeforce for the New World Order* (1994) and *Black Helicopters II: The Endgame Strategy* (1997). Keith traces the phenomenon of black helicopters to 1971, in which a farmer in Colorado sighted a "mystery chopper" flying over a flock of sheep, among whom were 40 that were "found dead and 'blistered' in some unknown manner."[82] Much of the book is a catalog of these mysterious sightings from the 1970s to the mid-1990s when the craft began to emerge into the conspiratorial consciousness. In 1994, Michael Benn, who created a petition to impeach President Bill Clinton, reported that a number of black helicopters buzzed his house and fired missiles which (presumably mistakenly) set fire to the home of Benn's neighbor. According to the report quoted by Keith, Benn had "just collected his 12,000,000th signature for the petition to impeach Clinton, and believes it is quite possible that someone wanted him out of the way."[83] Benn, one the first prominent "victims" of what would come to be colloquially known as "Black Helicopters" soon faded from the conspiracy scene, fueling speculation. On a militia-focused Usenet discussion group, one poster reported that

According to neighbors, a team of apparent government people dressed in firesuits immediately arrived, claiming it was an accident, and warned people not to talk about the incident. According to some reports, the neighbor was paid off for the house and warned not to talk about it. The neighbor moved away and has not been heard from again. The destroyed house was rebuilt within days by a team of what did not appear to be ordinary commercial contractors, and all evidence of the missile attack removed. The house was reportedly later sold, apparently to a government employee.

Perhaps, the poster said, "we can add yet another name to the 80 some enemies of Clinton who have died or disappeared mysteriously."[84]

Keith, like Sauder, connects black helicopter sightings to the "mutilation" of cattle and other livestock, saying that this connection "has confused the

5. Mad Science and Forbidden Knowledge 165

issue—perhaps purposely" and that "at least a substantial number of the sightings are of aircraft involved in covert government operations on domestic soil." As the book goes on, Keith draws connections between black helicopters and the presence of non-U.S. troops taking part in maneuvers and training in the United States under the aegis of the United Nations. While the black helicopters "are government craft, dispatched from one agency or another" their anonymous nature is the result of the fact that "within the last year or two virtually all military aircraft have had their service insignia removed." Why? "It has been suggested that these craft are being prepared for incorporation into the United Nations military command." Keith goes on to invoke the same fears that Bill Cooper, Linda Thompson, and others promulgated in the early 1990s, alleging that "in addition to numerous reports of troop and materiel movements ... there are also reports of 'detention centers' being set up in the country."[85] Keith admits that the potential detention sites he lists need on-the-ground investigation to be confirmed. He does not think, however, that the purported centers are designed to hold vast amounts of people. they are designed, he argues for "select" groups of prisoners including "prison overflow, unbending patriots, random dissidents, anti–New World Order loudmouths and ... groups and individuals who are not willing to go along with the next 'baby step' of totalitarian control in the United States." That "baby step," according to Keith, is the confiscation of firearms from the population. the vast majority of Americans, he argues, do not need to be put into camps because they are "in one of the most devilishly effective concentration camps ever devised: a 'free' society ... in which all of the institutions are controlled by small cliques of moneyed [sic] elite."[86] Terrestrial, not alien, advanced technology, such as signal-transmitting implants, or massive tunneling equipment serve as tools of those domestic and international forces which would subjugate the people of the United States. In keeping with a common theme within the conspiracy genre, the basic shape of these narratives share features both specific and broad.

In his 1997 sequel, *Black Helicopters II: The Endgame Strategy*, Keith expands on a suggestion in his first book that the sinister black helicopters and the livestock mutilations that had been occurring for several decades as part of a wider U.S. government program that was developing and testing a variety of chemical and biological weapons. Using solidly documented, publicly available evidence, he outlines the lamentable history of defense officials authorizing tests of chemical compounds on (often unwitting) civilian populations, such as the spraying of parts of St. Louis, Missouri, with zinc cadmium sulfide during the 1950s and 1960s.[87] Keith uses these established cases to bolster the claims of those who witnessed "black chopper spraying toxic substances on populated areas, particularly in areas where political activists live."[88] Keith assumes a continuity and continuum between the experimentation done in the 1950s and 1960s (experimentation that, like attempts at mind control and manipulation was reported to have ceased) and the actions reported in the 1990s. Like many conspiracy-oriented authors, there is an expectation that if the government (or military, or church, or other organization) had at one time engaged in a behavior, that this behavior will continue to occur. For Jim Keith, one of the strongest pieces of evidence that the government continued to exploit civilians against their will was the fact that they had done it before.

These experiments, according to Keith, focus on biological warfare agents that could be targeted specifically to individual ethnic groups. Citing a Salt Lake City reporter, he asserts that "an anti–Oriental biological weapon ... had been tested at Dugway [proving ground]." Could these experiments, Keith asks, "provide confirmation for the persistent allegations that the AIDs [capitalization as in original] virus was released as a race-specific depopulation device?"[89] As *Black Helicopters II* continues, Keith expands his view beyond the mysterious craft themselves and weaves together numerous threads that should be deeply familiar to us. He discusses the executive orders that would give FEMA control over every aspect of American life and discusses the REX 84 plans.[90] He discusses the possibility of the military being given law enforcement responsibilities.[91] he connects alien abductions to MKULTRA and related mind control programs.[92] He denounces the NAFTA and GATT trade agreements as "elitist violations of American sovereignty"[93] and warns of an impending United Nations takeover of the United States, citing "super-secret organizations like the Illuminati, the Rhodes Round Table, and the Skull and Bones society, and merely secretive ones such as the Bilderbergers, the Trilateral Commission, and the Council on Foreign Relations." Their goal (since "the early 1700s") has been to "destroy national sovereignties worldwide and to globalize government in an unelected dictatorship of the rich."[94]

The black helicopters themselves make little more than a token appearance in *Black Helicopters II*. The real focus is on the impending subjugation of the United States by the hideous forces of globalism, embodied in the United Nations and—ultimately—in groups such as the Illuminati. So what makes this tale different than that of William Cooper or the films of Linda Thompson? How is Keith's approach or that of Richard Sauder distinct from other fears of a tyrannical American government or no American government at all?

One crucial factor, in the case of Sauder, is his almost relentless focus on technology and government activities that are astoundingly well-documented, particularly within the context of conspiracy writing. Further, Sauder rarely draws conclusions about the underground facilities being constructed by various branches of the government and military establishment. The furthest he goes in Underground Bases and Tunnels is to acknowledge that suspicions exist within various conspiratorial circles. For Sauder, the heart of the conspiracy lies in the fact that such a vast array of projects has been undertaken in secret over the course of decades. The sinister nature of these underground bases is not rooted in whether or not they house an invasion force from beyond the stars but, rather, that such a base exists at all. Anticipating readers' objections "to the publication of information about military facilities," Sauder responds that "the aims and ideals of representative democracy are poorly served by secrecy in government, especially in the policies of the armed services." Citing examples such as the Iran-Contra affair and "super-secret nuclear bomb testing in Nevada," Sauder asserts that "secret policies and agendas" result in "an ever present danger of [the] military taking control of the government.... Dictatorships are born when power is usurped by the military."[95] Sauder sees secrecy and power as threats in and of themselves, harbingers of democracy's end.

Jim Keith's work, while addressing many of the same concepts and concerns as Sauder's, takes a different approach, one that is far more aligned with the all-encompassing, all-connecting compulsions of conspiracy narratives. Keith, in his two books on black helicopters, draws together a broad assortment of conspiratorial memes beyond these craft including mind control, UFOs, alien abduction, underground bases, detention camps for Constitution loving Americans, and a UN-led multinational invasion force. Significantly, Keith strips these narratives of most of their esoteric and supernatural trappings. He is saying little that is substantively different than Bill Cooper or David Icke but Keith's assessment lacks Cooper's ultimate villain of the ancient mystery religions. Unlike Cooper, Keith does not ask the reader to rely upon his own unsupported witnessing of sinister government documents. Keith spins a tale of global domination by a super-rich elite, and he does so without casting anyone in the role of head lizard person. Jim Keith may considered a materialist—rather than an idealist—conspiracy theorist. For Jim Keith, the most crucial aspect of this mad science is that it is truly scientific in the sense that human reason and knowledge are at the root of these conspiracies.

Richard Shaver and Ray Palmer's use of the inhabited hollow earth as a tool to recast human history finds parallels in some examinations of the Old Testament creation account and efforts to determine the physical location of the Garden of Eden. Rodney Cluff, for example, drawing on nineteenth century Mormon writings, explains that by passing through the earth's cavern systems from the earth's "womb" inside to come to the surface, Adam and Eve were "born" into this world by "mother" earth. Their second home on the earth's surface was near the cavern that brought them here. The Garden of Eden IS in Jackson County, Missouri, but NOT on the surface. It is located 800 miles down—on the inner surface of the earth on the highest mountain plateau of the Inner Continent.[96]

Contributors to *The Hollow Hassle* fanzine, continuing the tradition begun by Shaver and Palmer, used stories of the hollow earth as a medium for questioning accepted religious and scientific accounts of humanity's origins and the physical nature of the earth. In 1980, Tal LeVesque—a driving force behind *The Hollow Hassle*—connected the suppression of humanity's knowledge of the subterranean world to the twin villains of the Catholic Church and the scientific establishment:

> In ancient Pagan times the superior race who inhabits the earth's interior frequently contacted surface dwellers, and temples were built for their occupancy during their visits. But with the establishment of the Church of Rome, these temples were destroyed and the existence of the "gods of the Underworld" was denied.... And just as religionists taught that it was an inferno of everlasting fire, so scientists preserved the error in their theory that the earth has a fiery core, basing this on the flimsy evidence that the further down one goes, the hotter it becomes. however, this evidence has now been proved false and scientist are looking more closely at the Hollow Earth theory as they find that most things in nature are Hollow.[97]

LeVesque sees a campaign to rewrite ancient history to obfuscate the existence of a habitable realm within the earth. Arguing that "over 100 Bible verses teach that the world is Hollow," he asserted that "the whole interior of the Earth is called 'Eden,' the garden of God ... out of which our race came from ... we are on our way back to Paradise inside the earth. We shall fulfill the covenant; when we go back into the garden; into the abode of LIGHT, wherein there is NO DARKNESS."[98]

We can draw a line from the theories of John Cleves Symmes through the esoteric discussions of Aghast and Shambala to Shaver (and Palmer's) Dero and Tero. Devotees of the Shaver Mystery took up the mantle, developing those stories and theories. One branch of inner earth thought, however, connects to a remarkable number of other conspiratorial pathways: the intersection of Christian doctrine and theology (particularly the fringes of evangelical Protestantism), UFOs, alien abductions, demon possession, end times prophecy, and other obscure blends of religion and the paranormal. While there are a number of writers and speakers who, especially over the past two decades, have attempted to integrate UFO and extraterrestrial conspiracy theory with Christian doctrine, a writer and researcher named Jim Wilhelmsen has blended a remarkable array of paranormal, conspiratorial, and theological tropes in his work. His approach provides a useful example of the degree to which conspiracy theorists have appropriated notions of the hollow earth.

Jim Wilhelmsen operates a website called *Echoes of Enoch* which provides readers with "answers to questions and explanations of Bible stories misunderstood for centuries or completely unknown until now." These explanations encompass "every aspect of the paranormal and supernatural." He offers "deliverance" from alien abduction and similar troubles such as "Orbs, ghosts, shadow people, black eyed kids, sleep paralysis, constant humming noises or clicks in the night distracting you from healthy sleep or anything unwanted and not believed by others?" While Wilhelmsen has no formal medical training, "working in the city of Detroit with the gangs and drug community," he has "experienced many supernatural workings using the gifts of God's Holy Spirit to see many delivered and restored to productive members of society."[99]

Wilhelmsen's teachings about the hollow earth utilize the familiar conspiratorial technique of calling acknowledged scientific and theological authorities into question. He asserts that "Modern Science will tell you that it is impossible for the earth to be 'Hollow.' This same Modern Science will tell you man came from a monkey and there are no such things as UFO's [sic]." Scientific authorities, Wilhelmsen suggests, are wrong about a hollow earth because he believes they are wrong about evolution and extraterrestrial life (although his characterization of these views is so simplified as to be nearly useless). In an echo of Tal LeVesque's hollow earth writings, Wilhelmsen claims that "the 'official' position of the Church (Holy Roman [sic] version) was that the earth was flat" linking the religious establishment to the scientific establishment of a later time in an ahistorical conspiracy. He then provides a brief overview of various hollow earth theories and stories (omitting the Shaver Mystery, oddly) as well as a survey of Bible verses (or, sometimes, only parts of verses) with explanations of how they prove the earth is hollow. For example, Wilhelmsen cites Job 38:30 ("The waters are hid as with a stone, and the face of the deep is frozen.") and provides the following interpretation:

> This is very interesting in deed [sic]. The waters "hid" are the internal waters of the deep or abyss. Like a stone on top the excess floodwaters frozen now covers the face or opening of the abyss. This ice covering is what we call the Arctic and Antarctic circles. Frozen like a rock to cover the openings of the inner earth and the waters "hid" within. This was only a resulted [sic] effect after the flood.

He also explains Amos 9:2 ("Though they dig into hell, thence shall mine hand take them; though they climb up to heaven, thence will I bring them down") as a Biblical prophecy that foretells the existence of the supposed Nazi Antarctic base at Neu Schwabenland since, "in the mindset of the Nazi's Theosophical ideas, they believed themselves to be the diluted genetic strain of a subterranean super race.... Their goal was to form an alliance with their underground 'brothers' ... to form new super weapons and lead the World into a New Age for the Aryan."

As for who inhabits these hollow spaces in the earth, Wilhelmsen explains that the lands under the surface of the earth are what the Bible refers to as the land of Nod, to which Cain was exiled after killing his brother Abel. Wilhelmsen argues that "Cain was removed from the surface of the earth into a subterranean realm" and that the "mark" placed upon him was his physical size, connecting Cain to the giants or Nephilim of the sixth chapter of Genesis (a popular portion of the Bible for those who seek to connect aliens with fallen angels or demons). The descendants of Cain, Wilhelmsen suggests, are connected to the beings commonly referred to as aliens, carrying out their abductions on an unsuspecting populace. This is only possible because of Cain's true nature and that of his descendants. Wilhelmsen asserts that the commonly accepted narrative of the Garden of Eden (Adam and Eve eat from the tree of the knowledge of good and evil and, as a result, sin enters the world and the couple is expelled from Eden) and the subsequent births of Cain and Abel are the result of mistranslations and misinterpretations. Rather, Cain's birth was the result of

> the inability of the serpent or the Gray's [sic] to have sexual intercourse with animals or mankind. Does this not suggest that something sexual must have been part of the fall or the act of partaking of the fruit of the tree of the knowledge of good and evil? The forbidden fruit then, is actually a figurative expression of the result of an act or decision to choose a different dimension. Part of this decision changed the very biology and may also have introduced the seed of the serpent into mankind's lineage as a part of the plan of Satan to overthrow all of creation.[100]

Wilhelmsen interprets "the fall" as a point of bifurcation between two dimensions, conveniently making possible the interaction (including genetic interaction) between the "aliens" and humans. Despite not acknowledging the Shaver Mystery in his summary of hollow earth ideas and theories, his characterization of the subterranean dwelling demon/alien creatures carries echoes of the dero.

Theories and narratives that rely on the revelation of previously concealed scientific knowledge represent an important aspect of the wider conspiracy culture. Overtly political conspiracies provoke questions about the overt and covert power structures in "free" societies. Economic and financial conspiracy theories explore modern industrial (and post-industrial) capitalist systems, seeking to impose order on often-chaotic processes. Narratives of hidden knowledge are, like political and economic conspiracy theories, a product of and a reaction to the modern age. The privileged assumptions of the Enlightenment came under scrutiny in the twentieth century in a variety of ways. Scientific conspiracy theories propose and promote a subversion and, often, inversion of the rigidly hierarchical and categorized systems of knowledge that characterize academic and scholarly learning.

Conspiracy theories that call into question not only the findings of scientists, historians, and other scholars but also cast doubt on their positions of authority. Systems of argumentation and evidence are diluted with standard tools of the conspiratorial trade. Whispered rumors are freighted with disproportionate amounts of meaning; the testimony of experts and the findings of researchers are sifted through and diverse, decontextualized morsels of confirmation are woven into a tapestry of fear. Knowledge conspiracies are also interdisciplinary, with ancient poetry used as "proof" of an inhabited hollow earth or New Testament prophecy manipulated into an explanation of genetic experimentation.

These theories also connect to other sub-genres of conspiracy culture, with depopulation schemes being tied particularly closely to fears of a World Government or New World Order. Suspicions of a hollow earth have, since the 1940s, been linked to UFOs and, in recent times, have been tied to alien invasion and abduction fears, as with the work of Jim Wilhelmsen. At times, it is very difficult—if not impossible—to draw clear lines between political, economic, racial, and scientific conspiracy theories. what distinguishes them, however, is that they are more clearly concerned with larger questions of epistemology, focused not only on who has political power but also who has the power to determine the manner in which human societies produce knowledge and how that knowledge is integrated into technology and policy.

6

The Hidden World of the Nazis

Conspiracy theories surrounding the Nazi regime—encompassing their rise and fall (or survival) as well as their technology—are a suitable topic for the end of this study. Nearly all the conspiracy narratives we have touched on up to these points intersect with Nazi Germany in some way. From mind control to flying saucers to underground bases, a dark fascination with and suspicion of National Socialism is a recurring feature of many conspiracy theories. While some of these are blatantly Nazi-oriented, involving literal continuations of the Third Reich, often times the shadowy presence of the Nazi regime is subtler. The Nazis serve as an *influence*, inspiring whatever cabal a particular theorist is attempting to expose. In some ways, conspiratorial use of Nazism resembles a thread that often runs through the "counterfactual" genre of science fiction. Taking "what if" as a starting point, historians and novelists alike have reimagined a North America that never left British control, a triumphant Confederacy in the American Civil War, or a sixteenth century England under the thumb of Spain's Phillip II. Often, a counterfactual approach can serve to illustrate *real* causes and effects more clearly. By understanding what *did not* happen, a reader or researcher can more fully understand how events unfolded. Historically oriented conspiracy narratives take the question of "what if" and expand it. Thus, an intriguing jumping-off point for historical study or fictional speculation becomes an accusation of a cover-up. In the hands of the conspiratorial historian the question "What if history had taken a different path?" becomes "Why are we being lied to about the path history has taken?" Perhaps no historical counterfactual has received as much attention from conspiracy-oriented writers of history than the origins, conduct, and aftermath of the Second World War. The popular counterfactual query "What if the Nazis had won World War Two?" becomes "Why does everyone not realize that the Nazis won World War Two and are at the heart of the secret power structure that controls the world?" Because of these deep and intricate connections, it is not useful, in this chapter, to discuss these connections independently of the core Nazi-based conspiracy theories. Rather, we will address them as they arise. Much of the conspiracy literature involving Nazi Germany and the post-war persistence of Nazi influence ranges from the relatively sedate to incredibly lurid. Often these theories and narratives will use the notion of a global Nazi underground as a common denominator connecting together such disparate conspiracy tropes as alien abductions, the suppression of free energy, and the coming end of the world. One of the more widely circulated illustrations of this is *The Omega File: Greys, Nazis, Underground Bases, and the New World Order* by Bruce Alan Walton using the pseudonym Branton. This is a work that began its life in the mid–1990s as a series of text files circulating on Internet message boards and conspiracy-focused websites and, eventually, making its way into print. *The Omega File* presents a history of the twentieth century in which the Nazi regime was merely one aspect of a much farther reaching conspiracy involving familiar conspiracy actors such as the Bavarian Illuminati, the Central Intelligence Agency, the gray aliens, "central banking" systems and a vaguely defined "military-industrial complex."

The following passage, while lengthy, provides a superb overview of Branton's approach in *The Omega File* and his other works. While many of the concepts he addresses have surfaced multiple times in this book, the high degree of "conspiratorial overlap" displayed here is not unusual when the Nazis are involved. Branton, discussing the Nazi presence in the Antarctic, writes:

> VIPs and scientists started to show up with a compliment of ULTRA, a highly specialized Nazi SS team like our MJ-12. ULTRA has always been in control of Antarctica. ULTRA is the name of a secret alien interface agency in the NSA. Remember that the NSA has connections to both the Nazi S.S. and the Dulce base. According to Contactee Alex Collier, the upper level members of the NSA-ULTRA group are cloned replicates or have been so heavily implanted, virtual cyborgs, that they could be considered as being barely human—automatons who are remotely controlled by the Greys' group ego or group mind. It is also noteworthy that ULTRA is also the name of the Above Top Secret CIA-NSA-Alien base under the Archuleta plateau and peak northeast of Dulce, New Mexico.... Could Antarctica be the real power behind the New World Order? If the Nazi bases still exist in Antarctica then they would no doubt still have secret contact with the Bavarian cults, which sponsored and were an integral part of the Nazi party, like the Bavarian Thule society for instance.... The Illuminati have its base in Germany, and Germany has been the most active country in the international drive for Internet censorship and control.[1]

In one paragraph, Branton combines and conflates a number of memes that have occupied the conspiracy world over the past several decades. In addition to the survival of the Nazi regime beyond the end of World War II, Branton invokes MJ-12, the use of the codeword "ULTRA" evoking the CIA's MKULTRA brainwashing experiments, cloned duplicates of senior government officials, reminiscent of Peter Beter's organic robotoids, the underground base at Dulce and, of course, a New World Order. Branton's overblown assertions of everything in the conspiracy world being interconnected, however, are not fully representative of contemporary conspiracy theorists' approaches to Nazi Germany, and Branton's work fits less well in the Nazi Conspiracy framework than it does within the framework of attempts by conspiracists to craft vast master narratives linking diverse strands and stories. The Nazi regime becomes a common denominator in these narratives, connecting diverse events, people, and concepts.

Works by conspiracy writers such as Peter Levenda and Joseph Farrell are much more sedate. They extensively cite and reproduce declassified government documents from the United States, Germany, and other nations. While their claims (such as Hitler living beyond his supposed 1945 suicide, Nazi infiltration of the American government, or connections between secret Nazi technology and the supposed UFO crash in New Mexico) are certainly outrageous, conspiracists like Levenda and Farrell are careful to distance themselves from the wilder claims of Branton and similar theorists, often taking on a debunking tone. The more extreme claims serve as a sort of straw man, demolishing the *very* outrageous arguments establishes a credibility of which conspiracists can take advantage when presented their own *slightly* outrageous arguments.

Like many conspiracy narratives, however, theories about elements of the Nazi regime surviving beyond 1945 take full advantage of the secretive manner in which both Allied and Soviet intelligence and defense establishments exfiltrated useful German scientific and technical personal at the end of the war. As we will see, paranoia and conspiracy thinking in this case, as in many others, are not rooted merely in simple errors of fact. Rather, many conspiracy narratives bolster their claims with accurate facts extrapolated far beyond the supportable evidence.

Nazi Germany's efforts to push the envelope of technological development during the Second World War led to innovations such as rocketry and jet engines. Speculation ranging from the solidly supported to the wildly conjectural, however, has muddied the waters of the Nazi regime's scientific and technological efforts. Antarctic voyages to secure the future of the German whaling industry are combined with typically vague and blustery quotations from Nazi party officials. These conflations lead to the recurring conspiracy trope of a Nazi base in the Antarctic. Conspiracy writers have associated this base, which served as a bolt hole for the escaping Nazi leadership following the war, within larger narratives such as the threat of a resurgent Fourth Reich to tales of alien invasion. This is only one example. From disc shaped flying craft to nearly magical death rays, conspiratorial and "alternate" historians have associated Nazi engineering, technological, and scientific skill with a variety of fringe narratives. These have intersected with both the esoteric spiritual belief of the party leadership as well as connecting it to the post-war wave of UFO and flying saucer belief. All of these concepts and events, have been based, to some degree, on factual information. From the American government acquiring the services of former Nazi personnel to the party leadership's interest in occult spiritualism, conspiracy researchers and writers have blurred the boundaries between supportable fact and unsupportable speculation.

Adolf Hitler's Postwar Career

Adolf Hitler's April 30, 1945, death in his Führerbunker has long been shrouded in, if not mystery, then certainly uncertainty. This uncertainty is due less to a sinister conspiracy to hide Hitler's survival after the war than to the geopolitical realities of the war's closing days in Europe. Although Berlin, the German capital, had been under assault by the Soviet army only since mid–April, Hitler had been in the Führerbunker since January of 1945. As the Soviets moved to take the city, Hitler (along with wife Eva Braun and, later, other members of the Führerbunker staff) committed suicide on the 30th of April. While historians accept this basic timeline, uncertainty enters the picture for a number of reasons. There are differing accounts of the means of Hitler's suicide. Did he die by poison? Gunshot? Poison and gunshot? Witnesses and historians have suggested all three at various times. Forensic examination, which could answer that question, is difficult—if not impossible—to undertake due to the known circumstances of the Fuhrer's death. Hitler's body was burned after his suicide and, while the Soviet government claimed to have recovered Hitler's remains, this claim has long been under scrutiny.

Given the increasing tensions between the United States (and its allies) and the Soviet Union, it is not surprising that the Soviet Union was less than forthcoming with details of what they found in the garden outside of Hitler's bunker. Numerous stories circulated, many judged to be Soviet propaganda (such as the claim that the western allies were hiding Hitler and plotting against the USSR), all of which served to muddy the waters surrounding Hitler's demise. Stalin, suspicious that Hitler might have survived the war, authorized additional post-war missions to recover as much of Hitler's remains as possible. The KGB cremated most of the remains in 1970, retaining only a portion of Hitler's jawbone and a fragment of skull. Following the end of the Cold War, intelligence archives became more open and in 2000, a public exhibition displayed the extant fragment of Hitler's skull. A Russian archivist, confident in the skull's authenticity, claimed "it is not just some bone we found in the street, but a fragment of a skull that was found in a hole where Hitler's body had been buried." In 2005, however, doubt was cast on that skull fragment. American researchers conducted studies on the skull fragment and concluded that it belonged to a female less than 40 years of age. Manifestly not Adolf Hitler.[2]

The uncertainty over Hitler's ultimate fate led, naturally, to speculation over what that fate might have been. This is reflected in FBI records from throughout mid- to late 1945, as various tips and suppositions about the very-much-alive Adolf Hitler's whereabouts. The suggestions—always politely responded to by FBI officials—were often nothing more than guesses, such as this handwritten note received by the Bureau on October 15, 1945:

> I'll bet a dollar to a doughnut that Hitler is located right in New York City!
> There's no other city in the world where he could so easily be absorbed. No doubt you have considered the possibility, but I mention it for what it is worth anyway [emphasis in original].[3]

While New York City might have seemed obvious to that writer, Argentina was a much more popular subject of suspicion. This was due to the considerable German influence over the country despite its official neutrality throughout most of the war and its eventual entry into the ranks of the Allies. In the ensuing decades, of course, Argentina was found to have harbored a considerable number of fleeing Nazis, including Eichmann, Mengele, and Barbie, who took refuge thanks to the right-wing government of Juan Perón.[4]

A September 9, 1945, report from the Los Angeles FBI office entitled "[Redacted] Report on Hitler Hideout" provides the following synopsis:

> [Redacted] reports contact with [redacted], claims to have aided six top Argentine officials in hiding ADOLPH HITLER upon his landing by submarine in Argentina. HITLER reported to be hiding out in foothills of southern Andes. Information obtained from [redacted] unable to be verified because of [redacted] disappearance. Attempts to locate [redacted] negative. No record of him in police or INS files.

The redacted subject of the report, according to agents, had gone to a reporter from the *Los Angeles Examiner* with his story. The reporter then contacted the FBI. Ultimately, the reporting agents concluded that there was a "lack of sufficient information to support the story" and that it was "impossible to

6. The Hidden World of the Nazis

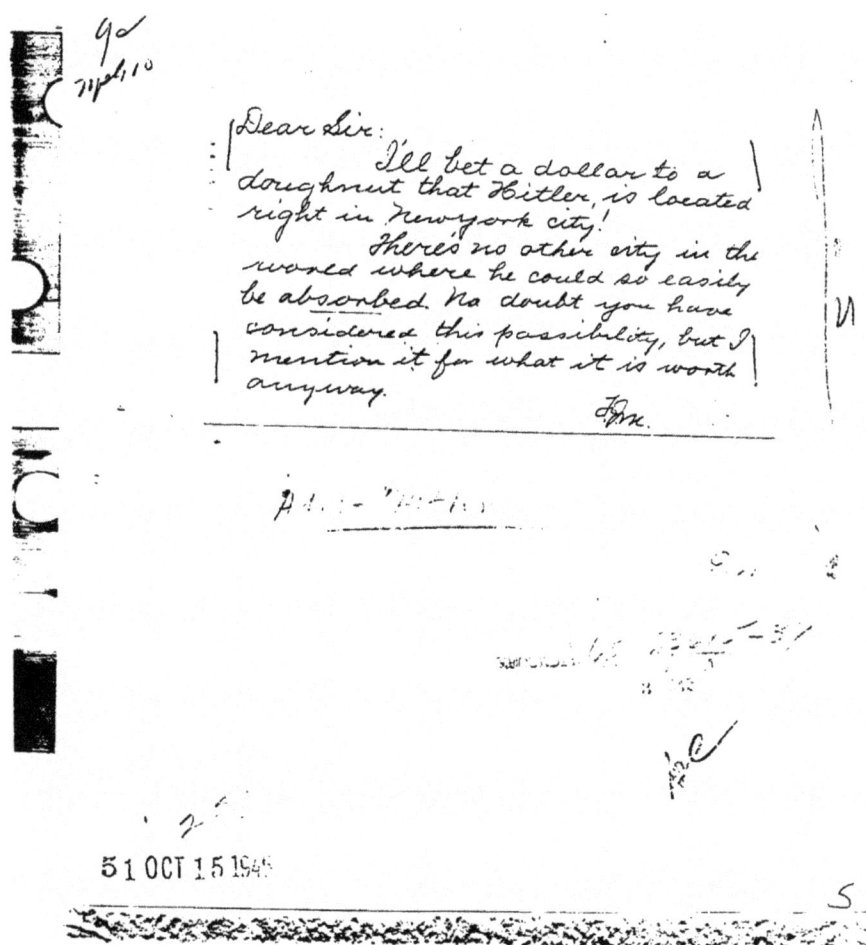

Above and following page: These brief notes to FBI director J. Edgar Hoover illustrate the range of theories about the supposedly living Hitler's location after World War II, from New York City to Argentina to "a monastery in Tibet."

continue efforts to locate HITLER with the sparse information available"[5] (capitalization as in original) Many of the leads that surfaced in the FBI's records on Hitler's supposed survival contained either pure speculation (as in the October 15 note) or convoluted stories with non-credible informants.

A November 3, 1945, letter addressed to "Edgar J, Hoover [sic]" from a redacted correspondent illustrates a very early connection between the persistent Hitler-survival myth with a setting that would not have been out of place in a James Bond villain's lair:

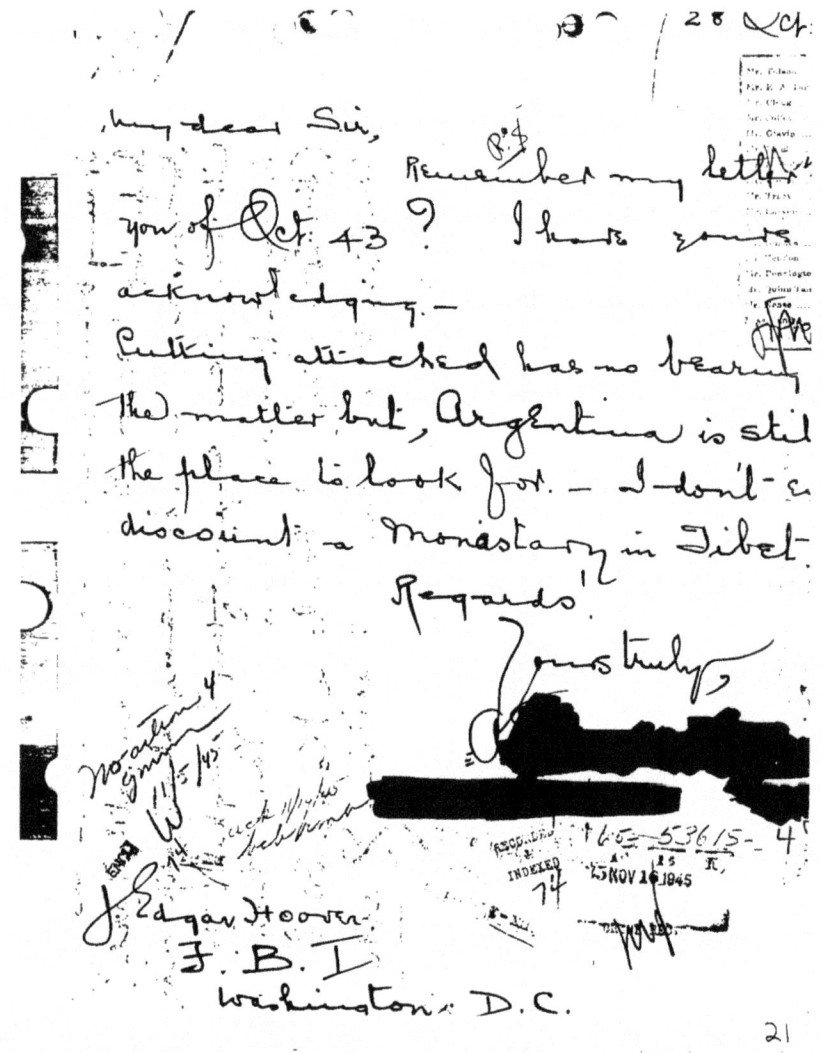

I have some news in my passion [sic] whitch [sic] I believe to be true and would interest you very much. I canot [sic] devulg [sic] the mans [sic] name at present who gave me the news but I will geve [sic] you the news I have and if you think it worth while then you can have one of your men contact me, for further information.

Hitler is in Argentina. He is liveing [sic] in a great underground establishment beneath a vast hacienda—675 miles vest [sic] fromm [sic] Florianopolis; 450 miles northwest of Buenos Aires; and that 'two doubles' are there with Hitler. The western enterence [sic] to elevators leading to Hitlers [sic] new underground is a wall operated by photo-electric cells, and that by code signals of

6. The Hidden World of the Nazis

even dim flash lights, wall slides to left, lets autos speed in, and instantly slides back into place.

Do not believe the British lie that Hitler is dead I am a full blooded American and think this should be investigated at once.[6]

Mr Edgar J. Hoover   Nov 3rd 1945

Dear Friend,

I have some news in my possion whitch I believe to be true and would interest you very much. I canot devulg the mans name at present who gave me the news but I will geve you the news I have and if you think it worth while then you can have one of your men contact me, for futher information. Hitler is in Argentina, He is liveing in a great underground establishment beneath a vast hacienda- 675 miles vestfrpm Florianopolis; 450 miles northwest of Buenos Aires; and that 'two doubles' are there with Hitler. The western enterence to elevators leading to Hitlers new underground is a vall operated by photo-electric cells, and that by code signals of even dim flash lights, wall slides to left, lets autos speed in, and instantly slides back onto place.

Do not believe the British lie that Hitler is dead I am a full blooded American and think this should be investigated at once.   Your Friend,

---

This letter to Hoover, written scarcely six months after the war's end, places Hitler in an underground Argentinian "establishment."

This letter introduces a number of tropes that would remain a constant in the most outlandish conspiracy theories over the decades, including those theories that are unrelated to Hitler. Underground bases are a staple of paranoid narratives and, while they are often identified with the secret bases of malevolent extraterrestrials (such as the mythical base in Dulce, New Mexico), underground bases often figure into more Earth-bound conspiracies. While Hitler often does not figure into these other underground bases, they are often the domain of a manipulative ruling cabal. The letter writer's reference to Hitler having two doubles is evocative of the work of 1970s conspiracist Peter David Beter, with his assertions that Jimmy Carter, Walter Mondale, and other high ranking government officials had been replaced by "organic robotoids." One of the first accounts of Hitler's death to emerge after the war was British historian Hugh Trevor-Roper's 1947 book *The Last Days of Hitler*. Serving in the intelligence services during the War, Trevor-Roper was assigned to investigate Hitler's death in 1945. While he did conduct some personal interviews, most of his research relied on the hundreds of interviews, interrogations, and debriefings conducted by U.S. and British officials. *The Last Days of Hitler* established the narrative of Hitler's suicide as thoroughly as possible given the lack of forensic evidence. Over the decades following the Second World War, however, suspicions that Hitler had escaped from Germany persisted. Otto Skorzeny, a German commando who aided Mussolini's escape from captivity was the subject of a book by Glenn Infield in 1981. In this book, Skorzeny claimed that "It was entirely possible for the Führer to leave he bunker by a subterranean passage under the Reich Chancellery" and detailed a potential escape route out of Berlin. Some conspiracy theorists have, over the years, worked from the assumption that because Hitler *could* have escaped, that Hitler *did* escape.[7]

Project Paperclip: Welcoming the Nazis?

As noted, Nazi officials, including Josef Mengele and Adolph Eichmann escaped the war crimes tribunals after World War II and were able to flee to Argentina. Others eluded Allied prosecution through collusion with covert elements of those Allied forces, particularly the United States and the Soviet Union. The revelation of the extent of this collusion has fueled extensive speculation and has been a particularly rich source of conspiracy thinking from the 1980s to the present. Chief among these efforts to bring Nazi scientists to the United States was Project Paperclip, many details of which came to light between the late 1970s and mid–1980s thanks to declassification and journalists' use of the Freedom of Information Act in their investigations. Through Paperclip, War Department officials made the determination that it was in the national security interests of the United States to bring some Nazi scientists, weapons experts, and aeronautical engineers to the United States rather than subject them to the war crimes tribunals and punishments of their less technically talented Nazi colleagues.

In a 1985 edition of the *Bulletin of the Atomic Scientists* soon after information about Paperclip became publicly known, Linda Hunt wrote that "the War Department was intent on using Nazi specialists and was not about to let other government agencies or even a policy signed by President Truman get in its way."[8] Political scientist John Gimbel, however, argues that this was far from a rogue operation. Paperclip had its roots in an earlier wartime project (Overcast) that aimed to extract hundreds of German rocketry and munitions experts with a view toward shortening the brutal war against Japan (as well as aid post-war weapons and technology development). Gimbel also credits Tom Bowers's 1987 book *The Paperclip Conspiracy: The Hunt for the Nazi Scientists* and Christopher Simpson's 1988 *Blowback: America's Recruitment of Nazis and Its Effects on the Cold War* with bringing much of the background on these operations to public attention. Gimbel asserts, however, that these books are often "less than models of balanced historical analysis." Their accusatory, conspiratorial tone is limited in its approach. A book such as Bowers's may "bash the Pentagon, but give little or no attention to the broader base of the policy" resulting in a "distorted view of the policy" and a "false interpretation of the role of President Truman and several other agencies of the government." Far from being a dark conspiracy on the part of a few crypto-fascists, Gimbel argues that

> German scientists and technicians were brought to the United States under a national policy that was developed and implemented by duly authorized, responsible agents of the US government, including cabinet officers who consulted with and received the approval of the president. Under that national policy, the scientists were brought from Germany—when it was deemed to be in the US national interest—either in disregard of or in violation of denazification procedures that the United States insisted upon for other Germans.[9]

This is not to say that the process of denazification was smooth or without exception. Gimbal notes that it was not unusual for American interests to override the general policies and practices of denazification in the case of Germans who had particularly necessary skills.

Many historians and other scholars have spent the decades since World War II debating the morality of welcoming (or even allowing) scientists affiliated with the Nazi regime into the American fold following the war, regardless of the pragmatic and strategic value of their knowledge and the perceived necessity of keeping their knowledge and skills from being utilized by the Soviet Union. Werner von Braun, a key figure in the American space exploration efforts of the 1950s and 1960s, has elicited a variety of opinions from historians. "In the eyes of his associates and hero-worshippers, he is still seen as an apolitical space enthusiast who was not a 'real' Nazi and had nothing to do with the crimes of the Third Reich." However, "many critics and many survivors of the Mittelbau-Dora concentration camp, on the other hand, see him as an unprincipled opportunist or even a convinced Nazi who was directly responsible for the deaths of 20,000 prisoners."[10]

A less ambiguous figure, Klaus Barbie, was an SS officer known for torturing prisoners, particularly in occupied France. In 1983, Barbie was found in Bolivia and extradited to France to stand trial for war crimes. During this process, rumors of his connections with the U.S. military establishment arose. Investigations by the Justice Department revealed that at the close of the war, Barbie was protected from prosecution by the U.S. government. Documents uncovered in 1991 revealed that the U.S. High Commission for Germany repeatedly evaded French requests to help find and prosecute Barbie. Barbie, unbeknownst to the French, was an active asset of the U.S. Army Counterintelligence Corps. In light of his aid, the High Commission concluded that

> to have exposed BARBIE to interrogation and public trial would not have been in consonance with accepted clandestine intelligence operational doctrine.... [II]e was knowledgeable of high level operations and operational procedures, which would have been compromised. Through procedures in effect at that time, BARBIE was therefor [sic] assisted in 1951 in leaving Europe for resettlement.[11]

The U.S. military's protection and exploitation of Barbie at the expense both of our ally and the broader cause of justice highlighted the moral quagmire wrought by the fight against Nazism and the looming fight against Soviet Communism.

The historical record—both in its primary sources and the analyses undertaken by scholars over the past seven decades—has not hidden or sanitized the morally ambiguous actions of the U.S. government in protecting and using some of the most heinous figures of the Nazi regime. Despite the title of Bowers's book, Paperclip was not, in the commonly accepted sense, a "conspiracy." It was hidden from the public, like most wartime operations. Like most acts undertaken in times of conflict, it privileged strategic and tactical dominance (as well as) pragmatism over more seemingly-abstract concepts such as law and justice. If, as Christopher Simpson argues in *Blowback*, these policies promoted a culture of lawlessness and disregard for democratic institutions within elements of the American intelligence and military systems, this was likely an unintended consequences. The conspiratorial viewpoint, such as that offered by writer and broadcaster Mae Brussell. In a 1984 article examining Nazi connections to the assassination of John F. Kennedy, she scrutinizes J. Edgar Hoover. "As America stood on the threshold of World War II," she wrote, "Hoover continued a friendly relationship with the nazis who dominated Interpol, the Berlin-based international secret police." This relationship continued after the war and bore fruit with Hoover's complicity in the Kennedy assassination, for "with ... J. Edgar Hoover in control of the Kennedy assassination investigation ... nazi connections were buried."[12] Often, however, the Nazi regime becomes a symbol in conspiracy writing, a shorthand for the sort of tyranny that the New World Order seeks to impose upon humanity. For example Bill Cooper claimed that, because his organization published a "scathing exposé" of the Oklahoma City bombing, "U.S. Attorney Janet Reno, the butcher of Waco, ordered the Nazi Gestapo to go after us which immediately launched investigations by the FBI, IRS, Financial Crimes Network, and many others." He did not, of course, mean that the *literal* Gestapo had been unleashed. Rather, Cooper uses Nazi references as a rhetorical device to inflame his readers and to reinforce their opinions that the federal government and its agencies exist in opposition to freedom and liberty.[13]

Nazi Secret Weapons

The existence of Nazi Germany's research into both nuclear powered weapons and other advanced technologies during the Second World War has proven to be a fertile subject for writers of conspiratorial "alternative" history. Historians have documented the development of German nuclear physics research in the years prior and during the war, providing a fairly comprehensive picture of why the United States developed (and used) atomic weapons while the Germans (and the Japanese, who were also engaged in nuclear research) did not. A key factor in the non-development of nuclear weapons in Nazi Germany was the allocation of resources and a lack of political will rather than any deficiencies in technological knowledge.

Writing in 2005, Walter E. Grunden, Mark Walker, and Masakatsu Yamasaki explored the extent to German and Japanese nuclear research during World War II. The authors note that Nazi officials such as Albert Speer saw value in nuclear research (certainly in its military applications but also in terms of power generation) and that the Nazi regime provided resources, including exemption from military service, for those involved in nuclear research. As the war ground on, however, resources for this research were increasingly shifted to areas of higher priority:

> Resources were limited and became increasingly difficult to obtain as the war deteriorated; at the same time, massive amounts of such resources were swallowed up by projects such as rocket research. Germany probably had the requisite industrial capacity to develop nuclear weapons but was using it for other, more immediate concerns. Moreover, it appears unlikely that, even with a tremendous effort, Germany would have had atomic bombs before being defeated by the Allies. Similarly, Germany had many qualified scientists and engineers (despite the fact that so many had been forced out of Germany at the start of the Third Reich), but they were working on other projects, such as ballistic missiles and jet planes. The scientists involved in the uranium project did not believe they could make nuclear weapons in time to win the war.

It is also unclear whether or not the Nazi regime would have been willing to deploy nuclear weapons, for "even Adolf Hitler, one of the most ruthless men of recent history, refrained from deploying biological and chemical weapons because Germany had insufficient defenses if the Allies replied in kind."[14]

Other attempts at Nazi secret weapons, which they referred to as Wunderwaffe or "wonder weapons," such as enhancements to existing jet engines or rocket technology, were a logical extension of existed technology. Others were far more exotic. The so-called "sun gun," for example which consisted of "a big mirror in space which would focus the sun's rays to a scorching point at the earth's surface" which could have been used to "burn an enemy city to ashes or to boil part of an ocean"[15] Despite plans for an orbital weapon and Werner von Braun's work with rocketry, there is no solid evidence of even a nascent space exploration program. According to the Smithsonian's Michael Neufeld, "people equate a rocket program with a space program, and the German rocket program was about building weapons only. That was the only reason Nazi Germany supported rocketry. Their objective was to build the V-2 and, if possible in the future, larger and longer-range weapons."[16] This assumption of Nazi space travel capabilities often includes the possibility of Nazi moonrises. As Usenet poster Robert K. Rouse wrote in 1993, "The Germans landed on the Moon as early as probably 1942, utilizing their larger exoatmospheric rocket saucers.... Welcome to Alice in Saucerland." Echoing conspiratorial assumptions of U.S./Soviet/Nazi cooperation, Rouse explains

> when Russians and Americans secretly landed jointly on the Moon in the early fifties with their own saucers, they spent their first night there as guests of the ... Nazi underground base. In the sixties a massive Russian–American base had been built on the Moon, that now has a population of 40,000 people, as the

rumor goes. After the end of the war in May 1945, the Germans continued their space effort from their south polar colony of Neu Schwabenland.[17]

Joseph P. Farrell is a conspiracy-oriented writer and "alternative" historian whose work generally focuses on allegedly hidden or lost technology. His earliest books, such *The Giza Death Star: The Paleophysics of the Great Pyramid and the Military Compound at Giza* and its sequels (*The Giza Death Star Deployed* and *The Giza Death Star Destroyed*) dealt with topics familiar to those who watch television documentary series such as *Ancient Aliens*. Farrell's broad approach to history and technology is that ancient texts—such as passages in the Mahabharata—that discuss flying machines and powerful weapons should be approached more literally than figuratively. Farrell's work spans the breadth of the often related scenes of fringe science and fringe history, ranging from ancient mysteries to supposedly occult aspects of global financial systems. Farrell is, perhaps, most well-known in conspiracy circles for his exploration of the supposedly suppressed exotic technologies of the Nazi regime. In his 2004 book *Reich of the Black Sun: Nazi Secret Weapons and the Cold War Allied Legend*, Farrell alleges that Nazi Germany had, in fact, produced an atomic bomb by 1944 as well as "a whole host of second and third and even fourth generation weapons technologies even more horrific in their destructive power." These investigations and inventions were "intimately linked to the Nazi racial and genocidal ideology."[18] Farrell, however, carefully positions *Reich of the Black Sun* as a work neither of history nor "merely of fiction." He describes it as "an attempt to make sense, by means of a radical hypothesis placed within a very broad context, of events during and after the war that make no sense."[19]

Farrell's account of the Nazi atomic effort is highly technical and detailed, with explanations of the differences in refining uranium as opposed to plutonium. He asserts that the synthetic rubber plant operated by I.G. Farben at the Auschwitz concentration camp was a cover for a Manhattan Project style nuclear research facility. While there is a great deal of detail in this section of *Reich of the Black Sun*, the conclusions Farrell draws from them are largely speculative, filled with the hedging language typical of conspiracy writers who are, to some degree, attempting to allow for the possibility that they might be wrong. Farrell's explanation of the use of Nazi secret weapons and their possible use on the Eastern Front is a fairly thorough example of his "speculative" approach:

> If the Germans had the bomb, why didn't they use it? ... If they had it, they were far more likely to use it on Russia than on the Western allies, since the war in the East was conceived and intended by Hitler to be a genocidal war from the outset.... The use of such weapons on the Eastern Front by the Germans

would also tentatively explain why more is not *known* about it, for it is highly unlikely that Stalin's Russia would have publicly acknowledged the fact.[20]

"*If* the Germans had the bomb"; "would *tentatively* explain"; such phrases pepper Farrell's work. The manner in which Farrell uses and cites sources is also typical of conspiracy research. Crucial quotations are obtained from other secondary sources rather than primary sources, often omitting potentially crucial context. Background, foundational ideas, theoretical frameworks and evidence are often taken from other fringe history publications rather than making use of more traditional scholarship. This is not, of course, surprising given that Farrell's (and other alternative historians') view is that academia has ignored or hidden such evidence. They *must* rely on such fringe sources because those sources (and their authors) are fellow travelers on the road of truth. However, one of the purposes of citation in scholarly historical explorations is to allow readers to investigate the sources for themselves, in full. In doing so, they are able to more fully evaluate the claims an author makes. In his use of sources and evidence, then, Farrell's research is much more akin to other conspiracy tomes than to scholarly historical work. One footnote, for example, reads:

> Researcher Frank Joseph[21] has found another source for a reactor and I consider his information to be so crucial to this story and so sensational that I cannot in good conscience mention it in this work. I believe that it is a story that he best tells himself, since it is his discovery.[22]

Essentially, this is a footnote that says, "I've seen Frank Joseph's evidence for this, but I'm not going to tell you about it. Yet, you should accept that it corroborates my work." We must, however, recall that Farrell does not claim that this is a straight history of Nazi technology during the Second World War. This is a useful dodge that allows him to make historical arguments while avoiding the scrutiny usually applied to such historical arguments.

This speculative, hypothetical approach and the conclusions Farrell draws from the evidence he presents shift from the details of plutonium enrichment to exploring the connections between Nazi science and Nazi esoteric and occult beliefs. Farrell's "thesis and methods is that there is an 'occulted physics' hidden—sometimes deliberately—within various mythological and ancient texts, including tests [sic] of the esoteric or occult traditions both of the Orient and the Occident." These texts must be interpreted in a "proto-scientific" manner rather than a "metaphysical" manner. The myths into which are encoded this occulted information includes "all legends, texts, scriptures … of various cultures. The cultures chiefly in view are the classical Sumerian, Egyptian, Hindu, Maya, Olmec, Scandinavian-Teutonic,

Chinese, and of course the later standard Graeco-Roman European culture."[23] The cultural bias of this listing is clear, with Farrell considering "Graeco-Roman European culture" to be the human default, a "standard."

Reich of the Black Sun and several of Farrell's later books including *SS Brotherhood of the Bell*—which details additional Nazi secret weapons which utilized this occulted physics—would continue to explore the connections between Nazi technology and Nazi ideology. This notion of ancient civilizations holding the key to modern power does—in a general sense—mesh with the Nazi party's ideological roots in organizations such as the Thule Society, with their focus on the deep historical roots of the so-called Aryan race. These mythological approaches, however well worn they might be, rarely intersect with the historical and archaeological record. For the fringe historian this serves as proof of a larger conspiracy to conceal the truth. In *Roswell and The Reich*, Farrell posited that the Roswell Incident was "terrestrial but anomalous," arguing that surviving and thriving Nazi forces had continued to refine their wartime weapons technology, developing the craft that would become identified as "flying saucers."[24]

Nazis in Antarctica

One other aspect of Nazi science and technology that has gained a great deal of traction in conspiratorial history is the notion of a vast Nazi stronghold in Antarctica. During the 1930s and 1940s there was a great deal of exploration of the Polar Regions. The circumstances surrounding the existence of a supposed Nazi base in Antarctica have a solid basis in historical fact. Colin Summerhayes and Peter Beeching, in a 2007 article entitled "Hitler's Antarctic Base: the Myth and the Reality" sought to establish the facts of German expeditions to the region during the late 1930s as well as Allied operations to counter the establishment of a German presence.

In early 1939, a secret German naval expedition sought to establish a base at Queen Maud Land in Antarctica. The need for the expedition and this base of operations, according to Summerhayes and Beeching "arose out of concerns within the German government about the future of the German whaling industry. At that time, whaling was an important activity supplying oil, lubricants, glycerin (for nitroglycerine used in explosives), margarine and other essential products." Such products were increasingly vital to German industrial and military needs. There was a geopolitical aspect to the German expedition as well. "Great Britain asserted the right to charge heavy fees for whaling concessions, and imposed restrictions on whaling activity.

A secret expedition was therefore planned to claim a piece of Antarctica for Germany, and to find there a place suitable for a base for the German whaling fleet."[25] A supposed German Antarctic base also figured in stories—beginning in the late 1940s—asserting that Hitler and other Nazi officials had been secretly taken from Europe to Antarctica via Argentina onboard the submarine *U-530*. Such speculation stemmed mainly from *Hitler is Alive*, a 1947 book by Ladislas Szabo, a Hungarian refugee who had escaped to Argentina. While the United States Navy sent expeditions to Antarctica after World War II, Summerhayes and Beeching assert that there is no evidence that this mission was dedicated to destroying the mythical Nazi base.[26] The work of Summerhays and Beeching is a direct response to the claims of Nazi establishment of a major base in Antarctica. In each of the case studies on Nazi-era conspiracy theories that follow, the Antarctic plays a role in embellishing the Nazi myth.

There are some generalizations about Nazi-oriented conspiracy theories that underlie the specific examples we will examine here. Conspiracy theories about the survival and persistence of the Nazi regime beyond the end of the Second World War—and conspiracy narratives about the Nazi regime more broadly—often possess one or more of these five characteristics:

1. The Nazi regime itself, and the officials comprising it, are rarely the heroes of the story. Conspiracy writers present these people as a threat to liberty, freedom, and—often—to life itself. They are an evil force that the public thought was defeated in 1945.

2. The Nazi regime, especially its leadership, was powerful, almost supernaturally so. They sought support and strength from ancient rituals that were infused with magical properties, mostly based on the *Volkish* spiritualities popular in the early Twentieth century but also connected to the Theosophical tradition. Technologically, the Nazi *Wunderwaffe* were even more magical, ranging beyond advanced rocketry to encompass nuclear energy, space travel, and flying saucers.

3. The Nazi party and the nation it controlled were, in turn, under the control of powers even more vast and powerful. These powers are incredibly ancient and have manifested themselves in the form of various secret societies and organizations throughout history. Bill Cooper, for example, asserted that

> most modern secret societies ... are really one society with one purpose. You may call them whatever you wish—the Order of the Quest, the JASON Society, the Roshaniya, the Qabbalah, the Knights Templar, the Knights of Malta, the Knights of Columbus, the Jesuits, the Masons, the Ancient and Mystical Order of Rosae Crucis, the Illuminati, the Nazi Party, the Communist Party, the Executive Members of the Council on Foreign Relations, The Group, the Brother-

hood of the Dragon, the Rosicrucian's, the Royal Institute of International Affairs, the Trilateral Commission, the Bilderberg Group, the Open Friendly Secret Society (the Vatican), the Russell Trust, the Skull & Bones, the Scroll & Key, the Order—they are all the same and all work toward the same ultimate goal, a New World Order.[27]

4. The Nazi movement survived the end of the war and their desire for domination persists. Key figures within the regime fled to South America of course, but also to secret bases in Antarctica. The United States and other nations have known about these bases since the end of the war.

5. There are many conspiracies at work. There is the Nazi's own conspiracy to survive their supposed defeat. There is the collusion of the American and other government to hide the continued existence of the Nazi movement. Finally, there is the willful ignorance of the historical community who persist in presenting the "false" story of Allied victory in 1945.

While not *all* Nazi-focused conspiracy narratives rely on all of these tropes, most make use of at least one of them.

Conspiracy theorists also, as a general rule and not just in the case of speculation about the Third Reich, make use of the same primary sources as historians who hold to the accepted narrative of historical events, including those concerning the Nazi regime's rise and fall. Often, however, the conspiracists' use of these documents attempts to fill in gaps in the record that might or might not exist. To illustrate this, recall the FBI documents cited earlier in this chapter. In those reports, FBI agents conveyed information about rumors of Hitler's escape from Germany to South America at the close of the war. These documents could, on the other hand, be interpreted as an FBI endorsement of these claims rather than the mere reporting of these claims. When the FBI declassified these documents, stories—particularly on Internet conspiracy sites emerged which cast them in a different light than the Bureau's archivists probably intended.

One article, with the headline "FBI Quietly Opens Secret Files That Attest HITLER WENT TO ARGENTINA Rather Than Commit Suicide" (capitalization in original), implies that the very presence of FBI records with claims of Hitler's survival are substantial evidence of that survival. The FBI report from Los Angeles is described as revealing "that the agency was well aware of a mysterious submarine making its way up the Argentinian coast dropping off high level Nazi officials. What is even more astonishing is the fact that the FBI knew he was in fact living in the foothills of the Andes." While the report did not actually establish anything of the sort that, and other FBI documentation opened a door for the writer to claim that

> with all of the new found evidence coming to light, it is possible and even likely that not only did Hitler escape from Germany; he had the help of the international intelligence community. Released FBI documents prove that they were not only aware of Hitler's presence in Argentina; they were also helping to cover it up.... Did Hitler escape to Argentina? The answer is yes.[28]

This manner of pulling more from government (and other) sources than may actually exist is a hallmark of conspiracy theories. The merest suggestion of evidence is taken to extremes and, often, stretched beyond their ability to bear.

Peter Levenda and Joseph Farrell are but two authors who have addressed conspiracy theories surrounding Nazi Germany. While they are far from the only conspiracists to have written on the subject, their works provide substantial coverage of the major Nazi-oriented conspiracies. Their works cover the supposed cover-ups of exotic Nazi technology, survival of the regime past the end of the Second World War, and the infiltration of the United States by a Nazi-dominated conspiracy. They also, to varying degrees, connected the Nazi regime to other mainstay topics of conspiracy theory such as UFO cover-ups and fears of a New World Order. These particular authors—and Nazi-oriented conspiracy theories in general—provide a useful segue into an examination of the connections between the various strands of conspiracy belief. Concerns about the survival and secret power of Nazi Germany are a consistent concern for conspiracy writers of all stripes.

Peter Levenda and the Occult Roots of Nazism

Peter Levenda's work, while largely concerned with a variety of dark forces manipulating American and, indeed, global history and politics, has also delved deeply into conspiratorial narratives on the rise, development, and survival of the Nazi regime,. He has focused on their esoteric beliefs and practices as well as more prosaic political and economic matters. Levenda's first work on Nazi Germany was *Unholy Alliance*, a 1994 book exploring the roots and significance of the Nazi leadership's belief in and use of folkloric traditions and supposedly "occult" practices. In particular, *Unholy Alliance* places a great deal of emphasis on the role these beliefs and practices played in the formation of the Nazi movement and its rise to political power in Germany during the 1920s and 1930s.

The question of the occult and esoteric roots of National Socialism, particularly with regard to pan-German nationalism as well as the anti–Semitic and otherwise racialist beliefs and policy goals of the part of the time. It is well established that, to a certain degree, the origins of the Nazi party are connected to organizations such as the Thule Society (also known as the Study Group for German Antiquity), which promoted the investigation and promulgation of stories of a mythical deep history of the Germanic peoples, linking them with the ancient peoples such as the Aryans. Theories about the mythical homelands for these Aryan peoples persisted as well. The extent to which organizations such s the Thule Society was directly responsible for the emergence of the Nazi party as a political force is a subject of debate. There were, of course, commonalities between the Thule Society and similar groups—chiefly anti–Semitism and a pan-German nationalism, both of which had their roots in the nineteenth century. The National Socialist movement began to coalesce around a number of organizations following World War I. On April 30, 1919, during a conflict between Communist and anti–Communist factions in Munich seven members of the Thule Society were killed by Communists. This event helped to form a bond between the Thule Society and the nascent National Socialist movement. In books published during the early days of the Nazi regime in the 1930s, the connection between the Thule Society and Nazi leadership was heavily emphasized, with one writer claiming "Thule members were the people to whom Hitler first turned, and who first allied themselves with Hitler."[29]

Conspiracy theorists have used claims such as these to bolster their assertions that the Nazi party and the political regime that emerged from it was, thus, primarily an esoteric occult organization that was plugged into mysterious powers from ancient times. And, naturally, that academic historians have sought to suppress or cover-up this information. On the contrary, historians have—for decades—examined the role that organizations such as the Thule Society as well as the Nazi's broader use of folklore and mythology as a tool to unify the German people. Christa Kamenetsky, for example, has argued that Nazi use of folklore and mythology was deeply significant not because of the inherent power of the dark forces they supposedly attempted to control but rather because the regime's use of folklore as a political tool as well as their manipulation of the study of the subject at the university level played a role in discrediting folklore as a field of study in the post-war era.[30] The use of mythology and folklore to bolster claims of racial superiority, however, was only one factor in the rise of Nazisim. Reginald Phelps's examination of the Thule Society and other organizations' connections to the rise of the Nazi regime led him to conclude that these organizations

> made conspicuously little headway in Munich and Bavaria until war, revolution, the Munich Soviets, and the killing of the hostages provided the festering soil for them to grow in. Only then did violent racist antisemitism become "popular"

in Bavaria, only then could Munich become the logical center for national socialism. But, to repeat: It was less the theories of racist cranks than concrete national and local conditions, plus the remorseless propaganda of Hitler, that enabled national socialism to make its start at the place and time it did.[31]

Thus while pseudo-historical, pseudo-scientific assumptions about German ethnic and cultural origins certainly played a role in the development of National Socialism in general and the Nazi party in general, it was only one of many factors leading to the rise and dominance of Hitler and the Nazi regime.

Peter Levenda's *Unholy Alliance: A History of Nazi Involvement with the Occult* is, on the whole more restrained than many examinations of Nazi occultism, his thesis being "the refusal of historians to view the Nazi Party as a religious—or at least a mystical organization, a *cult* ... has contributed to so much confusion" (italics in original) with regard to neo-Nazism and other revivals of Nazi racial belief. Lavenda concentrates on exploring the degree to which Nazi folkloric and occult beliefs informed Nazi racial policies, asserting that "the Nazi Party was never merely a political party; it was always much more."[32] He traces the origins of these beliefs to such movements as Helena Blavatsky's theosophical movement and, of course, the Thule Society. Levenda argues that the powerful mystique of the Nazi regime following the war may be attributed the racialist occult beliefs the Party promulgated:

> Whereas Communism set itself up in opposition to *all* religions, Nazism supported a pagan revival to *replace* the existing religions. It is perhaps this strategy *more than any other* that has allowed Nazism in various forms to survive its calamitous defeat in World War II[33] [italics in original].

It is this "survival" of Nazism that illustrates the conspiratorial inclinations of *Unholy Alliance*.

In keeping with conspiratorial patterns of "connecting the dots" and imbuing seemingly disconnected, random events with almost supernatural levels of meaning, Levenda draws parallels between the April 30, 1919, murder of the Munich Thule Society members with the April 30, 1945, suicide of Hitler and the April 30, 1975, fall of Saigon to the North Vietnamese. April 30, Levenda argues, is a day of occult significance to the Nazi regime, and events such as the fall of Saigon represent a synchronicity rather than a coincidence. A thorough understanding of the occult, he argues, is necessary to understand the survival of Nazi ideals "from the Skinheads of Germany and America to Colonia Dignidad in Chile and from the underground SS organization in South America, Asia, and Africa, to the domestic racial violence of the United States." Such things cannot be fully understood in political, economic, or sociological terms. The mystical and religious aspects of Nazism are key to its survival.

Thus Nazism, Levenda claims, was spirited out of Europe via a number of escape routes, many of which were operated by the Roman Catholic Church. These escape routes, known as "ratlines," were the means by which Nazi war criminals such as Adolf Eichmann, Joseph Mengele, and Klaus Barbie escaped to South America. While these escape routes are well-established in the historical record, Levenda—both in *Unholy Alliance* and later books such as *Ratline: Soviet Spies, Nazi Priests, and the Disappearance of Adolf Hitler* and *Sinister Forces: A Grimoire of American Political Witchcraft*—argues that the Nazi escape routes were much more organized and extensive than usually thought. One example is the Colonia Dignidad settlement in Chile. Levenda, in *Unholy Alliance*, recounts a story of how he visited this village, inhabited by a population largely of German descent. The connections between Colonia Dignidad and the dictatorial regime of Augusto Pinochet are well documented, with the village serving as a center of torture for enemies of the regime. In 2005, Paul Schaefer, a prominent leader in Colonia Dignidad and a former Nazi medic, came under scrutiny for accusations of sexual and physical abuse of young boys from the surrounding area. Political prisoners of the Pinochet regime testified to "a warren of stone-walled tunnels under the colony, where they were taken to be tortured with electric shocks to the strains of Wagner and Mozart," a claim substantiated by outside investigators, including Amnesty International.[34] Levenda, relying on testimony from Chileans who lived near Colonia Dignidad, argues that its former Nazi residents were more than convenient allies for the Pinochet regime but were, rather, a fully functioning exponent of the international Nazi movement.[35]

He also asserts that these Nazi tendrils extended further into the United States than historians acknowledge. For example, Levenda argues that the goals of Project Paperclip went far beyond the acquisition of top rocket scientists and, in fact, was used to bring other Nazi scientists to the United States, particularly to work on various government mind control programs. In doing so, Levenda begins the process of blending several conspiratorial notions. First, that the Nazi movement survived the War in a more organized manner than the "official" histories admit. Second, that American dealings with Nazi officials after 1945 was far more expansive than an attempt to corner the market on German aerospace expertise. Levenda highlights connections between Nazi scientists and CIA mind control programs such as MKULTRA that was, to a degree, a continuation of Nazi mind control experiments begun in the 1930s. There is little direct evidence of these experiments, however, due to the fact that "documentation on Nazi psychological warfare and mind control research was also either destroyed—by the Nazis themselves—or concealed under very high security classifications by the US military and intelligence establishment."[36]

Peter Levenda's explorations of the influence of Nazi ideals and beliefs beyond the confines of the Second World War is, in some ways, notable for the relatively low-key approach to Nazi-oriented conspiracy theory. Levenda's work on the Nazis stretches the boundaries of the more widely accepted historical narrative. The basic shape of that narrative, however, remains. While there is no question that the Nazi regime embraced esoteric and occult beliefs that both influenced and reinforced their racial policies. This was, however, only one of many factors in their rise. While the ideologies of Nazi Germany are held to be good and right by some on the fringes of the political spectrum, that is not due to an organized and global Nazi movement. Rather, as Nicholas Goodrick-Clarke observes in his study of modern Aryanism and Neo-Nazi belief, "more than half a century after the defeat and disgrace of Nazism and fascism, the far right is again challenging the liberal order of the Western democracies for political space. Radical ideologies are feeding on the threats of economic globalization, affirmative action and Third World immigration."[37] Just as in the early twentieth century, social, economic, and political factors are key.

Assumptions about the extent to which elements of the Nazi regime persisted beyond the end of the Second World War or the nature of their secret and suppressed technology exist far beyond the work and theories of those conspiracists for whom this is a main focus. In a June 2015 appearance on *The Prophecy Club* radio program, Jim Wilhelmsen, the alien abduction researcher who believes Cain was exiled to the hollow earth, tied together aliens, Bible prophecy, a secret Nazi base in Antarctica, Nazi time travel technology, and a global plot by the United Nations and the Illuminati.[38] Nazi lore penetrates nearly every corner of the conspiracy world. Mark Phillips, self-proclaimed mind control expert wrote in 1993 (two years before he and Cathy O'Brien published *TRANCE Formation of America*), that Nazis pioneered Project Monarch's "trauma-based" mind control:

> The original documentation which spawned this project was derived from collected intensive research previously performed by top SS German Nazi scientists (1927–1941) as the result of their interest in the multigenerational affects of occult psychology as applied in the nuclear family of known pedophiles. The identified leader of this research was an SS officer by the name of Himmler.[39]

In the 1995 book, Phillips expands on this theory and ties mind control and the Nazi regime more deeply into popular conspiracy theories:

> I had remembered the Nazi mind-control research performed under Himmler's command on the families of northern European multi-generational Satanists. Christianity, particularly Catholicism, was Himmler's pick of the religions' litter

for targeting "Chosen Ones" for his hideous mind-control experiments. These Chosen Ones were to be the robotic leaders of Hitler's New World Order.[40]

Phillips and O'Brien were not the only alleged mind control victims that made an explicit connection between their plight and the actions of the Nazis. Arizona Wilder, whose mind control slave testimony has been promoted by David Icke, recalled in an interview with the conspiracy theorist that during her childhood mind control conditioning, she encountered a very important individual:

> There was a programmer that was programming me, a very infamous person in history who actually has been in this country, and he was known as Dr. Green. He actually was Dr. Joseph Mengele from the concentration camps in Germany. And he stayed a lot at China Lake Naval Weapons Station out here in Southern California, in the desert area. And I would be around this man a lot.[41]

The Nazis server as a kind of nexus point for a wide variety of conspiracy claims. These claims often place the Nazis (or their predecessors or their successors) at nearly every significant event of the past century. However the Nazi regime arose within a specific political, cultural, social, and economic context. To attribute that rise to fringe forces such as a vast, far-reaching plot hatched centuries before by the Illuminati or other trans-national bodies or to supernatural power or advanced technology is to undermine the historical role and agency not only of the Nazi party apparatus but of the German people—supporters of the Nazi movement or otherwise. Similarly, explanations of the geopolitical landscape of the post-war, Cold War world that cast it as an illusory construct designed to mask the ongoing rule of the Nazi regime or their American proxies carry a risk as well. The years following the Second World War were indeed a time of deceit and double-dealing. The United States engaged in overt and covert operations of questionable legality and ethics—such as the toppling of democratically elected regimes in Iran and Guatemala and the arming of various insurgent groups around the world—in their epic struggle against the Soviet Union.

As Lance deHaven-Smith's work illustrates, there are more than enough conspiracy theories (or, to use deHaven-Smith's term, State Crimes against Democracy) at home and abroad for historians may bring to the public's attention. Narratives about a Fourth Reich, occult Nazi technology being mistaken for alien craft or other stories often serve only to mask real wrong-doing, wrong-doing that may still be corrected, prosecuted, or otherwise assuaged. There are extant cover-ups more fully supported by the historical records yet little-known or poorly understood by the general public. Fanciful tales of Antarctic bases full of Nazi troops, or Hitler's underground Argentinian lair, while entertaining, are not the secrets with which we should be concerned.

Conclusion

Conspiracy theories and the narratives to which they have contributed during the twentieth and twenty-first centuries share a number of tropes and trends. This is despite what, on the surface, may appear to be incompatible differences. These theories involve beings from the inner earth, reptilians from the lower fourth dimension, extraterrestrials friendly and un-friendly, tyrannical national governments operating complex systems of control, utilizing everything from underground bases to mind controlled sex slaves. Some of the theories explicitly contradict each other. Are "aliens" truly alien or are they from the inner earth? Are they from neither place but, rather, a complex hoax designed to condition the population to accept a global government? Is the Catholic church the evil force behind these conspiracies, or are all these conspiracies part of a plot to destroy a virtuous church? When they are not contradictory, they are often excessively confirmatory, with the same evidence and documentation used to support a variety of different stories. One of these involves something called "Alternative 3."

"Alternative 3"[1] is a fitting topic on which to close this book. "Alternative 3" was broadcast as an installment of *Science Report*, a documentary science series produced by Anglia Television in the United Kingdom. Its paranoid tale seems tailor made for the conspiracy narratives which would emerge in the 1980s and 1990s and persist until today. A variety of researchers have used it as support for their various theories or used it as a springboard for further speculation. While it was broadcast on June 20, 1977, the planned airdate was April 1. If it *had* gone out on this date, this televisual April Fools' joke might have had a significantly different legacy. This "documentary" detailed an investigation into a supposed "brain drain" in the UK that saw top scientists dropping off the grid. The investigation led to paranoia about disappearing scientists, global ecological catastrophe, and the secret plans of the elite saving them at the expense of the great mass of humanity. According to "Alternative 3," scientists had determined that the surface of the earth would—within a few decades—be incapable of supporting human life, as industrial pollution drastically affects the earth's climate. The brain drain is revealed to be part of a U.S./Soviet plan to remove the most "valuable" humans from a rapidly dying earth, using them as the foundation of a new human civilization away from our doomed planet. This was the "third alternative" elites planned to save a remnant of humanity, hence the title. Fictional astronaut "Bob Grodin" reported seeing artificial constructs on the Moon—evidence that the technology to move selected humans off Earth indeed existed.

"Alternative 3" in typical documentary style—made on film rather than video, featuring a talking head host in studio and an investigator/camera operator duo doggedly pursuing the truth on normal, 1970s documentary film stock. Visually, it looks a 1970s *Doctor Who* story combined with an episode of *In Search of....* Peter Wright, in his review of the "Alternative 3" DVD release for the journal *Science Fiction Film and Television*, holds up "Alternative 3" as "an exemplary illustration of how the documentary mode—albeit subverted—can challenge complacency."[2] "Alternative 3" was a hoax in the mode of the Orson Welles *War of the Worlds* broadcast, prompting dozens of calls to television stations either complaining about the obvious fake story on what was supposed to be a science program or demanding more information about the frightening cover-up.

It was intended to be broadcast on April 1 and, indeed, the closing credits make references to April Fools' Day. The "scientists" and "astronauts" interviewed were played by known actors, and credited as such on screen. A novelization, *Alternative 003* explicitly states that it was based on a television script. Despite this, "Alternative 3" took on a life after broadcast and publication as a recurring piece of supporting evidence in a variety of conspiracy theories, largely in the United States where "Alternative 3" (and its textual counterpart, *Alternative 003*) had not been broadcast, and for years was largely unavailable to interested viewers or readers. Instead it existed in a zone of shadowy rumor, another supposed example of the elites letting information (or disinformation) slip into the public consciousness to arrogantly broadcast their nefarious plans. It would be reworked over and over, the basic concepts deformed and stretched to provide support for a number of different theories and narratives. For example, this poster to an online bulletin board wrote:

> According to well-informed U.S. intelligence sources, Alternative 3 is a plan to colonize the planet Mars with a cross-section of persons from all major areas of human knowledge and culture. This project has been ongoing and under development for many years.... Is the foregoing all true? I don't know, I wasn't there. But the people who DO know are now speaking up—because what you

are reading is most likely just the "tip of the iceberg" of what is really going on with our Manned Missions and our presence in space.³

Summaries such as this were the most exposure to "Alternative 3" that most people could find. One sees the same quotations from the novelization surface in a number of online documents which précis the story.

Never one to shy away from coopting bits and pieces of poorly sourced internet lore into his own theories, Bill Cooper wrote the following concerning "Alternative 3" in his 1991 book *Behold a Pale Horse*:

> ALL THREE ALTERNATIVES included BIRTH CONTROL, STERILIZATION, AND THE INTRODUCTION OF DEADLY MICROBES TO CONTROL OR SLOW THE GROWTH OF EARTH'S POPULATION. AIDS is only ONE result of these plans. It was decided BY THE ELITE that since the population must be reduced and controlled, it would be in the best interest of the human race to rid ourselves of undesirable elements of our society. Specific targeted populations included BLACKS, HISPANICS, and HOMOSEXUALS.⁴

Cooper, returning once again to the secret briefing documents he claimed to have seen while in the Navy, informs his readers that he "can say that the book *Alternative 003* is at least 70% true from my own knowledge and the knowledge of my sources." The presumably untrue remaining 30% "was an attempt to compromise the British TV expos) [sic] with information that could be proven false."⁵ The television and print versions of the "Alternative 3" mythos, for example, did not extensively discuss the use of biowarfare or engineered diseases to reduce unwanted sectors of the population. In the relative absence of anything against which readers could check these claims, theories could use "Alternative 3" to support a large number of claims that did not, necessarily, appear in the original sources. Tellingly, Cooper never once acknowledges that "Alternative 3" was presented as fiction, instead consistently referring to it as a documentary or exposé.

Cooper was not, of course, the only conspiracy researcher who made use of the "Alternative 3" phenomenon. Mae Brussell, a prominent conspiracy theorist in the 1970s and 1980s, may have been the first in the United States to bring public attention to the television show and, especially, the novelization (which expanded on the television production in terms of the level of detail about the plot). In a 1979 broadcast of her program *World Watchers International,* she claimed that *Alternative 003*

> made me nauseous and I wanted to vomit, and I wanted to faint. I wanted to cry, I wanted to bang the walls down, I literally had the shakes for about a week. It was so scary because it just could be the bottom line of these conspiracies. I belief it probably is the most important book I've read in many, many years…. I don't have any doubt in my mind that this is a very dangerous document to

have, probably the most dangerous thing which I possess in my library at this point."⁶

Conspiracy researcher and writer Jim Keith discussed Brussell's feelings in his 1994 book *Alternative 3: UFOs, Secret Societies, and World Control* and took a nuanced view of the story. Much like his approaches to UFOs, mind control, and black helicopters, he argues that even if "Alternative 3"—the episode and book it spawned—were fiction (which Keith believed they probably were) many of the concepts it presented—environmental collapse, government cover-ups, and a plot to save the elite at the expense of the masses—were documented facts.⁷ As we have seen, however, "documented facts" are a somewhat artful term when dealing with conspiracy culture. On message boards and websites, mentions of "Alternative 3" often spark a firestorm of debate over its truth or falsehood. This controversy has continued despite a 1970s-era letter from Leslie Watkins (one of the authors/screenwriters) circulating on the Internet very patiently explaining it was fiction. Except—as is often the case with conspiracy theories—the waters became muddied enough even in something as seemingly straightforward as the case of *Alternative 003*.

Muddying the waters, in the late 1980s, a letter from "Alternative 3"/*Alternative 003* writer Leslie Watkins surfaced on various Bulletin Board Systems. Allegedly, Penguin Books had *Alternative 003* listed in its non-fiction catalog while Watkins's agent insisted on the original claim that the story was entirely fictional. Watkins's attempt to clarify this issue actually led to increased speculation among conspiracy researchers. Watkins claimed that *Alternative 003* was "based on fact, but uses that fact as a launchpad for a HIGH DIVE INTO FICTION," darkly asserting that

> Documentary evidence provided by many ... correspondents decided me to write a serious and COMPLETELY NON-FICTION sequel. Unfortunately, a chest containing the bulk of the letters was among the items which were mysteriously LOST IN TRANSIT some four years when I moved from London, England, to Sydney, Australia, before I moved on to settle in New Zealand. For some time after Alternative 3 was originally published, I have reason to suppose that my home telephone was being tapped and my contacts who were experienced in such matters were convinced that certain intelligence agencies considered that I probably knew too much.⁸

The mysterious disappearance of the confirming documentation certainly added to the conspiratorial mood surrounding the book. Even later (and one suspects he was beginning to enjoy this) Watkins wrote that he might, in fact, have been used to convey disinformation after all.

If the conspiracy theories and facts surrounding MKULTRA serve as a crucial example of how documented history may be used to bolster wildly undocumented claims, the saga of "Alternative 3" illustrates that conspiracy theorists can appropriate nearly *anything* that conforms to their assumptions. One of those assumptions, of course, is that nothing is truly as it seems. Documentaries presented as fact are disinformation, designed to maintain the status quo of "reality" as the elites wish us to understand it. Mockumentaries presented as fiction are fact (except for the parts that are not), designed to hide the truth in plain sight, the elites mocking the lowly sheeple.

As I write this, in the spring of 2015, the spirit of those 1990s era conspiracy theories involving REX 84, or Operation Market Garden is experiencing a resurgence and fears of tyrannical over-reach by the federal government are making headlines once again. The focus of this fear is "Jade Helm 15," a training exercise described by the Department of Defense as "routine training to maintain a high level of readiness.... Soldiers will use this opportunity to further develop tactics, techniques and procedures for emerging concepts in Special Operations warfare."[9] This operation, taking place across several states in the American southwest, triggered fears that the Obama administration was undertaking the first steps in initiating Martial Law—Operation Market Garden and its cousins in action. A writer for *Infowars*, a website affiliated with conspiracy-oriented talk show host Alex Jones claimed that Jones

> never said this was going to be martial law. But given the history of 9/11, 7/7 (the London subway bombing) and other drills where first responders were involved in a training exercise and a real attack happens at exactly the same time, place and manner as the training scenario, we should keep a watchful eye on any training exercise outside of military bases.[10]

If such speculation had been confined to the usual corners of the conspiracy community, this would not be particularly noteworthy. However, Governor Greg Abbot of Texas ordered the Texas National Guard to observe the exercises, ostensibly to ensure that "Texans know their safety, constitutional rights, private property rights and civil liberties will not be infringed."[11] Jumping into the fray was Republican presidential candidate Ted Cruz, a Texas senator, who, while not validating the fears, certainly fueled the paranoia of subterfuge by the Obama administration, saying, "We are assured it is a military training exercise. I have no reason to doubt those assurances, but I understand the reason for concern and uncertainty, because when the federal government has not demonstrated itself to be trustworthy in this administration, the natural consequence is that many citizens don't trust what it is saying."[12]

Some within the conspiratorial world have well-developed narratives into which Jade Helm fits very neatly. Stan Johnson, host of the *Prophecy Club* radio program, promotes a number of guest speakers who have connected many of the conspiracy theories we've discussed in this book to their interpretations of Biblical prophecy. On occasion, these radio guests have connected standard conspiracy narratives to their own prophecies, which they alleged to have received from God. One of the prophets is the late Dumitru Duduman who claims that in the 1980s, he had a vision of the end of the United States, shown to him by the angel Gabriel:

> He said, "Remember this, Dumitru. The Russian spies have discovered where the nuclear warehouses are in America. When the Americans will think that it is peace and safety—from the middle of the country, some of the people will start fighting against the government. The government will be busy with internal problems. Then from the ocean, from Cuba, Nicaragua, Mexico...." (He told me two other countries, but I didn't remember what they were.) "they will bomb the nuclear warehouses. When they explode, America will burn!"[13]

Johnson connects this prophecy to a number of current events, including Jade Helm. Jade Helm, he explains, is an acronym. While "Jade" is an acronym for "Joint Assistance for Development and Execution"—a typically bureaucratic phrase—"Helm" stands for "Homeland Eradication of Local Militias." While variations of this acronym exist on many websites (and Johnson claims that he learned of this acronym through a Google search), Johnson connects it with the prophecies of Duduman and others, weaving it into a tapestry that is often more revelatory of views that are as much political as religious. Johnson predicts that Jade Helm is part of a wider plan which will begin with a "global currency reset," which will erase the U.S. government's national debt, but forbid it from ever going into debt again. According to Johnson, this will lead to a cessation of government entitlements, resulting in rioting (he cites the unrest in Ferguson, Missouri, and Baltimore as an example). Because of the rioting, President Obama will declare martial law, "suspending the Constitution for five years," preventing the 2016 presidential elections from taking place. Militias will rise up to resist this tyranny, which is where Jade Helm comes into play: to eliminate that resistance before it begins. The emergence of the Jade Helm conspiracy theories did not change Johnson's vision for the future, but it did serve as evidence, bolstering his claims.[14]

Whether the foe is the federal government, an international army, or a cabal of freemasons and Jesuits, the fear of subjugation persists into the present day and will, likely, continue into the future. These fears of will be a significant component of other well-known conspiracy narratives, including suspicions that a secret government is covering up proof of alien life, or continuing to conduct horrifying mind control experimentation and manipulation. Perhaps, some stories go, this secret government is just the Nazi party in a new guise. The fear of a tyrannical government, beholden not to the people but to shadowy, foreign forces, is one of the fundamental building blocks of conspiracy theory in the United States. As we have seen, however, it is not new—it extends back to the birth of the republic, finding targets in the unpopular groups and individuals of the day, from King George III to Barack Obama.

Chapter Notes

Introduction

1. Richard Hofstadter, "The Paranoid Style in American Politics," *Harper's Magazine*, November 1964, 84.
2. *Ibid.*, 77.
3. *Ibid.*, 86.
4. "Trust in Government," *Gallup*, n.d., http://www.gallup.com/poll/5392/trust-government.aspx.
5. Mark Fenster, *Conspiracy Theories: Secrecy and Power in American Culture* (Minneapolis: University of Minnesota Press, 1999), 3.
6. *Ibid.*, 11, 21.
7. *Ibid.*, 108.
8. *Ibid.*, xv.
9. *Ibid.*, xiii.
10. Michael Barkun, *A Culture of Conspiracy: Apocalyptic Visions in Contemporary America* (Berkeley: University of California Press, 2003), ix.
11. *Ibid.*, 4–6.
12. *Ibid.*, 8–9.
13. *Ibid.*, 13.
14. Fran Mason, "A Poor Person's Cognitive Mapping," in *Conspiracy Nation: The Politics of Paranoia in Postwar America* (New York: New York University Press, 2002), 43–44.
15. Lance DeHaven-Smith, *Conspiracy Theory in America* (Austin: University of Texas Press, 2014), 1.
16. *Ibid.*, 2.
17. *Ibid.*, 3.
18. *Ibid.*, 197, 199.
19. *Ibid.*, 129–131.
20. *Ibid.*, 9.
21. *Ibid.*, 195.
22. *Ibid.*, 183.

Chapter 1

1. David Icke, *The Biggest Secret: The Book That Will Change the World* (Scottsdale: Bridge of Love, 1999), 259.
2. Jonathan Israel, *Democratic Enlightenment: Philosophy, Revolution, and Human Rights, 1750–1790*, 1st ed. (New York: Oxford University Press, 2011), 826.
3. Daniel Pipes, *Conspiracy: How the Paranoid Style Flourishes and Where It Comes From* (New York: Touchstone, 1999), 66.
4. "Matthew Cooke Manuscript," n.d., http://en.wikisource.org/wiki/Matthew_Cooke_Manuscript.
5. Ric Berman, *Schism: The Battle That Forged Freemasonry*, electronic ed. (Brighton: Sussex Academic Press, 2013).
6. Israel, 827–828, 833.
7. John Robison, *Proofs of a Conspiracy* (New York: George Forman, 1798), 84.
8. Lance DeHaven-Smith, *Conspiracy Theory in America* (Austin: University of Texas Press, 2014), 56–57.
9. William Morgan, *Illustrations of Masonry by One of the Fraternity* (Batavia, NY: David C. Miller, 1827), viii.
10. *Ibid.*, ix.
11. A Citizen of Massachusetts, *Free Masonry: A Poem in Three Cantos* (Leicester, MA: Samuel A. Whittemore, 1830), 58 [emphases in original].
12. Lyman Beecher, *A Plea for the West* (Cincinnati: Truman and Smith, 1835), 11–12.
13. *Ibid.*, 51.
14. *Ibid.*, 55–57.
15. *Ibid.*, 61.
16. *Ibid.*, 60.
17. "A Relic of the War: How the Pope Recognized the Southern Confederacy—His

Letter to Jeff. Davis," *New York Times*, August 18, 1876.

18. Charles Paschal Telesphore Chiniquy, *Fifty Years in the Church of Rome* (New York: Fleming H. Revell Company, 1886), 705, 710.

19. *Ibid.*, 720.

20. Jack T. Chick, *The Awful Truth* (Ontario, CA: Chick Publications, 2011), 19.

21. Edith Starr Miller, *Occult Theocrasy* (Abbeville, France: F. Paillart, 1933), 8.

22. *Ibid.*, 623.

23. *Ibid.*, 619–620.

24. Jim Keith, "Jim Keith on the Biggest Secret," n.d., http://www.konformist.com/1999/icke-keith.htm.

25. "About David," David Icke, n.d., http://www.davidicke.com/about-david/.

26. David Icke, *Truth Vibrations: David Icke's Journey from TV Celebrity to World Visionary: An Exploration of the Mysteries of Life and Prophetic Revelations for the Future of Humanity*, rev. electronic ed. (Dublin: Gill and Macmillan, 2014), Introduction.

27. *Ibid.*, Chapter 1.

28. *Ibid.*, Chapter 8.

29. David Icke, *The Robots' Rebellion: The Story of the Spiritual Renaissance* (Bath: Gateway Books, 1994), xvii.

30. *Ibid.*, 12.

31. *Ibid.*, 89.

32. *Ibid.*, 38.

33. *Ibid.*, 90.

34. *Ibid.*, 138.

35. For a detailed history of the debunking of the *Protocols*, see "A Hoax of Hate: The Protocols of the Elders of Zion," *The Antidefamation League*, n.d., http://archive.adl.org/special_reports/protocols/protocols_intro.html#.VYhYwRNVhBc.

36. *Ibid.*, 138–139.

37. *Ibid.* 157.

38. *Ibid.*, 161–164.

39. *Ibid.*, 194.

40. *Ibid.*, 293.

41. *Ibid.*, 299–301.

42. *Ibid.*, 337.

43. *Ibid.*, 340.

44. David Icke, *The Biggest Secret: The Book That Will Change the World* (Scottsdale: Bridge of Love, 1999), 21–22.

45. Steve Lohr, "Bush, They Say, Is Indeed a Connecticut Yankee from King Henry's Court," *New York Times*, July 5, 1988, sec. U.S., http://www.nytimes.com/1988/07/05/us/bush-they-say-is-indeed-a-connecticut-yankee-from-king-henry-s-court.html.

46. Kate Kell, "Kerry's Royal Roots Will Give Him Victory, Says Burke's," *The Guardian*, August 17, 2004, http://www.theguardian.com/world/2004/aug/17/uselections2004.usa1.

47. Icke, *The Biggest Secret*, 1.

48. *Ibid.*, 42.

49. *Ibid.*, 31.

50. *Ibid.*, 33.

51. *Ibid.* 443.

52. *Ibid.*, 450.

53. David Icke, *Children of the Matrix: How an Interdimensional Race Has Controlled the World for Thousands of Years-And Still Does* (Ryde, Isle of Wight: David Icke Books, 2001), xxiii.

54. *Ibid.*, xv.

55. *Ibid.*, 428.

56. *Ibid.*, 431–432.

57. *Ibid.*, 431.

58. Jon Ronson, "Jon Ronson on David Icke," *The Guardian*, March 17, 2001, http://www.theguardian.com/books/2001/mar/17/features.weekend.

59. Icke, *Children of the Matrix*, 412.

60. Richard Warman, "The Official Website of Richard Warman," http://www.richardwarman.ca/.

61. David Icke, *Human Race Get Off Your Knees: The Lion Sleeps No More* (Ryde, Isle of Wight: David Icke Books, 2010), 386.

62. M0JFK, "Re: David Icke Update on Settlement……The Warman Case Is Over—Here Is the Background," accessed April 21, 2015, http://projectavalon.net/forum4/showthread.php?80600-David-Icke-update-on-settlement……The-Warman-case-is-over-here-is-the-background&p=941556&viewfull=1#post941556.

63. "Conspiracy Theory Poll Results," *Public Policy Polling*, April 2, 2013, http://www.publicpolicypolling.com/main/2013/04/conspiracy-theory-poll-results-.html.

Chapter 2

1. John Stormer, *None Dare Call It Treason* (Florissant, MO: Liberty Bell Press, 1964), 7.

2. *Ibid.*, 226.

3. Gary Allen, *None Dare Call It Conspiracy*, electronic ed. (Seal Beach, CA: Concord Press, 1972).

Notes—Chapter 2

4. *Ibid.*

5. Peter David Beter. "Audio Letter No. 46," May 28, 1979, http://www.peterdavidbeter.com/docs/all/dbal46.html.

6. Peter David Beter, "Audio Letter No. 45," April 27, 1979, http://www.peterdavidbeter.com/docs/all/dbal45.html.

7. Alfonso Chardy, "Reagan Advisers Ran 'Secret' Government," *Miami Herald*, July 5, 1987, Final edition, sec. Front, 1A.

8. Gyeorgos C. Hatonn, *Space—Gate: The Veil Removed*, 3d ed. (Las Vegas: Phoenix Source, 1993), 1.

9. Hatonn, "Martial Law Plans for USA," *The Phoenix Liberator*, July 7, 1992, 33–35.

10. Linda Thompson, *America Under Siege* (American Justice Federation, 1994).

11. Department of the Army, "DA Civil Disturbance Plan 'GARDEN PLOT,'" August 3, 1978, i, 1.

12. *Ibid.*, C-7–9.

13. *Ibid.*, 2.

14. *Ibid.*, February 15, 1991, C-1–8.

15. Clyde Haberman, "Idaho Family, and Federal Tactics, Under Siege," *New York Times*, October 27, 2014, NA(L). *New York Times*. Web. 29 April 2015.

16. Joe Rosenbloom III, "Waco: More than Simple Blunders?" *Wall Street Journal*, October 17, 1995.

17. Haberman.

18. Jon Ronson, *Them: Adventures with Extremists*, reprint ed. (New York: Simon & Schuster, 2003), 79.

19. David Thibodeau and Leon Whiteson, *A Place Called Waco: A Survivor's Story* (New York: HarperCollins, 1999), 205.

20. Haberman.

21. "Primetime: McVeigh's Own Words," March 29, 2001, http://abcnews.go.com/Primetime/story?id=132158&page=1&singlePage=true.

22. Dee Finney, "MCVEIGH—THE PATSY," December 17, 2006, http://www.greatdreams.com/mcveigh-patsy.htm.

23. Dave Hodges, "We Won't Get Fooled Again!" July 22, 2012, https://www.freedomsphoenix.com/Article/115348-2012-07-22-we-wont-get-fooled-again.htm.

24. Ronson, 96.

25. "Operation Vampire Killer 2000," in the finest traditions of both conspiracy culture and the Internet, has been transcribed and reproduced in numerous places. My quotations are from "Operation Vampire Killer 2000," n.d., http://www.lawfulpath.com/ref/vk2k.shtml.

26. Mark Potok, Larry Keller, and David Holthouse, *The Second Wave: Return of the Militias* (Montgomery, AL: Southern Poverty Law Center, August 2009), 7.

27. "About," n.d, http://oathkeepers.org/oktester/about/.

28. Jim Keith, *Black Helicopters II: The Endgame Strategy* (Lilburn, GA: Illuminet Press, 1997), 165, 170.

29. "Declaration of Orders We Will Not Obey," n.d., http://oathkeepers.org/declaration-of-orders-we-will-not-obey/.

30. Milton William Cooper, "THE SECRET GOVERNMENT: The Origin, Identity, and Purpose of MJ-12," Textfiles.com, May 23, 1989, http://textfiles.com/ufo/mj.12.

31. *Ibid.*

32. William Cooper, "The Release of the Cooper Material," July 5, 1990, http://textfiles.com/ufo/addit.txt.

33. In the documentary about Cooper's life and work (James Jankiewicz, *The Hour of Our Time: The Legacy of William Cooper* [Ether Films, 2005]), Cooper acknowledges that he had only "Ever Been Wrong Once." It is reasonable to assume that he was referring to his one-time belief in an extraterrestrial angle to the global conspiracy.

34. Milton William Cooper, "MAJESTY-TWELVE," *Hour of the Time*, 1997, http://www.hourofthetime.com/majestyt.htm.

35. *Ibid.*

36. *Ibid.*

37. Manly P. Hall, *The Secret Teachings of All Ages: An Encyclopedic Outline of Masonic, Hermetic, Qabbalistic and Rosicrucian Symbolical Philosophy* (Courier Corporation, 2010), xxxvi.

38. Cooper, "MAJESTYTWELVE."

39. The notion of "Legal Fictions" or "Straw Man Theory" is a prominent one within the right wing extremist community, particularly tax protesters. The Internal Revenue service (in a bulletin warning of various tax avoidance schemes) has described this theory as being "Premised on the Erroneous Theory That Most Government Documents Do Not Actually Refer to Individuals. Users of the 'Straw Man' Theory Falsely Claim That Only Documents Using an Individual's Name with 'Standard' Capitalization, I.E., Lower-

Case with Only the Beginning Letters of Each Name Capitalized, Are Legitimate. These Individuals Erroneously Argue That the Use of the Individual's Name in All Upper-Case Letters, Which Is Common in Some Government Documents, Refers to a Separate Legal Entity." Internal Revenue Service, "Internal Revenue Bulletin—April 4, 2005—Rev. Rul. 2005–21," April 4, 2005, http://www.irs.gov/irb/2005–14_IRB/ar13.html.

40. Milton William Cooper, "Cooper Family Targeted by Feds," July 6, 1998, http://www.hourofthetime.com/targeted.htm.

41. Milton William Cooper, *Cooper Family Targeted by Feds*, Hour of the Time, 1998.

42. Cooper, "Cooper Family Targeted by Feds."

43. "Arizona Militia Figure Is Shot to Death," *Los Angeles Times*, November 7, 2001, http://articles.latimes.com/2001/nov/07/news/mn-1182.

44. "William Cooper Predicted 9/11 Less than 11 Weeks Before Attacks Happened—June 28, 2001," June 11, 2014, http://www.sott.net/article/280317-William-Cooper-predicted-9-11-less-than-11-weeks-before-attacks-happened-June-28-2001.

45. Broctune, "William Cooper," *Above Top Secret*, March 6, 2013, http://www.abovetopsecret.com/forum/thread931526/pg1#pid 16039938.

46. kyviecaldegs, "William Cooper," *Above Top Secret*, March 6, 2013, http://www.abovetopsecret.com/forum/thread931526/pg1#pid 16040172.

Chapter 3

1. The term "ufology" (with various capitalization and spellings) first appeared in print in 1956 on page 9 of Morris K. Jessup's *UFO and the Bible* (New York: Citadel Press) and is arguably the most common term in use up to the present time. I am using it as a convenient shorthand for the wide variety of viewpoints, beliefs, and approaches in that area of interest.

2. For a thorough study of the Contactees and their influence see Gulyas, *Extraterrestrials and the American Zeitgeist: Alien Contact Tales Since the 1950s* (Jefferson, N.C.: McFarland, 2013).

3. Jerome Clark, *The UFO Book: Encyclopedia of the Extraterrestrial* (Detroit: Visible Ink Press, 1997), 412

4. "Condon Report, Section I: Conclusions & Recommendations," http://files.ncas.org/condon/text/sec-i.htm.

5. James W. Moseley and Karl T. Pflock, *Shockingly Close to the Truth: Confessions of a Grave-Robbing Ufologist* (Amherst, N.Y: Prometheus, 2002), 218.

6. Ibid., 140.

7. Donald Keyhoe, *The Flying Saucer Conspiracy* (New York: Henry Holt, 1955), 7.

8. Ibid., 24.

9. Ibid., 189–194.

10. Frank Edwards, *Flying Saucers: Serious Business* (New York: Bantam, 1966), 135.

11. Department of the Air Force, "Air Force Regulation No. 200–2: Unidentified Flying Objects (UFO)," February 5, 1958.

12. Donald Keyhoe, *Flying Saucers: Top Secret* (New York: Putnam, 1960), 160.

13. Curtis Peebles, *Watch the Skies! A Chronicle of the Flying Saucer Myth* (Washington, D.C.: Smithsonian Institution Press, 1994), 128–130.

14. Keyhoe, *Flying Saucers: Top Secret*, 154.

15. Elaine Tyler May discusses the idea of domestic containment in *Homeward Bound: American Families in the Cold War Era* (New York: Basic, 1988). Alan Nadel takes a wider look at American culture in an age of containment in *Containment Culture: American Narratives, Postmodernism, and the Atomic Age* (Durham: Duke University Press, 1995).

16. Robert S. Ellwood, "Spiritualism and UFO Religion in New Zealand: The International Transmission of Modern Spiritual Movements," in *The Gods Have Landed: New Religions from Other Worlds*, ed. James R. Lewis, SUNY Series in Religious Studies (Albany: State University of New York Press, 1995), 141.

17. Albert K. Bender, *Flying Saucers and the Three Men* (London: Neville Spearman, 1963).

18. Ibid., 134–135.

19. Gray Barker, *They Knew Too Much About Flying Saucers*. (Liliburn, GA: Illuminet Press, 1997), 114.

20. John G. Fuller, *The Interrupted Journey* (New York: Dell, 1967).

21. J. Allen Hynek, *The UFO Experience: A Scientific Inquiry* (New York: Da Capo Press, 1998), 156.

22. Whitley Strieber, *Communion: A True*

Story, rev. ed. (New York: Avon, 1988), 301–302.

23. David M. Jacobs, *The Threat: Revealing the Secret Alien Agenda* (New York: Simon & Schuster, 1999), 252–253, 258.

24. Richard Dolan, "Introduction," in *The Best of Roswell: From the Files of FATE Magazine*, ed. The Editors of FATE (Lakeville, MN: Galde Press, 2007), ix—xii, x.

25. *Ibid.*, xi.

26. "Majestic 12," *FBI*, n.d., http://vault.fbi.gov/Majestic%2012.

27. Like most UFO related conspiracy theories, the saga of the MJ-12 papers is incredibly convoluted. A seeming unrelated document known as the "Cutler-Twining memo" mentions "the MJ-12 SSP briefing." UFO researchers supposed found this document in the National Archives but it, also, has been denounced as a hoax.

28. Greg Bishop, *Project Beta: The Story of Paul Bennewitz, National Security, and the Creation of a Modern UFO Myth* (New York: Pocket Paraview, 2005), 127.

29. Bishop, 157–163.

30. William L. Moore, "UFOs and the U.S. Government: Part I," *MUFON UFO Journal*, November 1989, 8–14.

31. Greg Bishop, "'They Told Me to Say This!' An Interview with Ufologist Bill Moore," in *Wake Up Down There! The Excluded Middle Anthology*, ed. Gregory Bishop (Kempton, IL: Adventures Unlimited Press, 2000), 37–46, 38.

32. John Lear, "Statement Released by John Lear," December 29, 1987, http://textfiles.com/ufo/alear1.txt.

33. Bishop, "'They Told Me to Say This!'"

34. Bill Cooper, "Bill Coopers [sic] Reasons for Going Public," n.d., http://textfiles.com/ufo/UFOBBS/1000/1855.ufo.

35. Bill Cooper, "The Krill Reports Introduction," *UFO Casebook Files*, n.d., http://ufocasebook.com/krillintro.html.

36. Don Allen, "O.H. Krill intro/README," *Alt.Alien.Visitors*, August 8, 1991, http://wiretap.area.com/Gopher/Library/Fringe/Ufo/krill.txt.

37. I.M. Feddup [pseudonym], "Behold a Stale Horse," n.d., https://web.archive.org/web/20000510202212/http://homeworldonline.nl/~karel/ufo/people/cooper-lear/stale-horse.html.

38. "John Lear Tells All—02," *Bibliotecapleyades*, April 2008, http://www.bibliotecapleyades.net/sociopolitica/sociopol_lear03b.htm.

39. Don Ecker, "This Was Written by Don Ecker in the Summer of 1990 for UFO Magazine, in Which It Appeared," http://www.skeptictank.org/files//ufo2/cooperex.htm.

40. Milton William Cooper, UFO #2, *Hour of the Time*, 1994.

41. Jason Bishop III, "The Dulce Base," *Sacred Texts*, accessed June 16, 2015, http://www.sacred-texts.com/ufo/dulce.htm.

42. Keith's work as part of the "Commander X" group was revealed after his 1999 death. Robert Sterling, "Konformist: Jim Keith (AKA Commander X) 1949–1999," *Konformist Newswire*, September 24, 1999, https://groups.yahoo.com/neo/groups/konformist/conversations/messages/703.

43. Commander X [pseudonym], *Underground Alien Bases* (Wilmington, DE: Abelard Productions, 1990), 33.

44. Milton William Cooper, "MAJESTYTWELVE," 1997, http://www.hourofthetime.com/majestyt.htm.

45. Milton William Cooper, *Behold a Pale Horse* (Flagstaff: Light Technology, 1991), 235.

46. Cooper consistently used the spelling (and pronunciation) "ufoology" rather than "ufology." Readers should assume that unless noted, this is the spelling Cooper employed.

47. *The Imperial Japanese Mission 1917: A Record of the Reception Throughout the United States of the Special Mission Headed by Viscount Ishii* (Washington, D.C.: Carnegie Endowment for International Peace, 1918), 105.

48. William Cooper, "The War Of The Worlds," December 17, 1999, http://www.hourofthetime.com/warofthe.htm.

49. "MAJESTYTWELVE."

50. Jacques Vallee, "The Bill Cooper Briefing," *Bibliotecapleyades*, n.d., http://www.bibliotecapleyades.net/sociopolitica/esp_sociopol_cooper14.htm.

51. Milton William Cooper, Reply to Bill English, *Hour of the Time*, January 11, 1999.

52. Cooper, *Behold a Pale Horse*, 235.

53. Jim Keith, *Saucers of the Illuminati* (Kempton, IL: Adventures Unlimited Press, 2004), 45.

54. Kenn Thomas, "Foreword," *Saucers of the Illuminati* (Kempton, IL: Adventures Unlimited Press, 2004), 5–6.

55. *Ibid.*, 117.
56. Keith, *Saucers of the Illuminati*, 14–15.

Chapter 4

1. Jaye Beldo, "I Was a Sex Slave for the CIA!!!" *The Konformist*, n.d., http://www.konformist.com/mkkafe/ciaslave.htm.
2. Alison Winter, "Manchurian Candidates: Forensic Hypnosis in the Cold War," *Grey Room* 45 (Fall 2011): 106–27, 107.
3. Timothy Melley, "Brainwashed! Conspiracy Theory and Ideology in the Postwar United States," *New German Critique* 103 (January 1, 2008): 145–64, 145.
4. *Ibid.*, 146.
5. *Ibid.*, 147.
6. Edward Hunter, *Brainwashing: The Story of Men Who Defied It* (New York: Farrar, Strauss and Cudahy, 1956). 309.
7. *Ibid.*, 310.
8. Dick Anthony, "Pseudoscience and Minority Religions: An Evaluation of the Brainwashing Theories of Jean-Marie Abgrall," *Social Justice Research* 12, no. 4 (December 1999): 421–56, 424–425.
9. The earliest documentation uses this capitalization/spacing (MKULTRA) and this is how I will refer to the project. Quotations that use variations (Mk Ultra, MK Ultra, MK ULTRA, etc.) are presented as in the original.
10. U.S. Senate Select Committee to Study Governmental Operations with respect to Intelligence Activities, *Final Report of the Select Committee to Study Governmental Operations with Respect to Intelligence Activities: Book 1, Foreign and Military Intelligence* (Washington, D.C.: Government Printing Office, 1976), 403–404.
11. *Project MKULTRA, the CIA's Program of Research in Behavioral Modification* (Washington, D.C., 1977), 1.
12. *Ibid.*, 5.
13. J.S. Earman, "Report on Inspection of MKULTRA," July 26, 1963, 1–2.
14. *Ibid.*
15. *Ibid.*, 6.
16. *Ibid.*, 27.
17. *CIA V. Sims*, 471 U.S. 159 (1985).
18. Earman, 10.
19. Cathy O'Brien and Mark Phillips, *TRANCE Formation of America*, rev. Kindle electronic ed. (Las Vegas: Reality Marketing, 2005), location 89.
20. *Ibid.*, location 337.
21. *Ibid.*
22. Michael Barkun, *A Culture of Conspiracy: Apocalyptic Visions in Contemporary America*, 1st ed., Comparative Studies in Religion and Society (Berkeley: University of California Press, 2003), 77.
23. O'Brien and Phillips,, location 7186.
24. *TRANCE Formation of America*, location 1395.
25. *Ibid.*, location 2695.
26. *Ibid.*, location 922.
27. *Ibid.*, location 895.
28. The topic of Satanic Ritual Abuse and the resulting panic is covered well in Mary De Young, *The Day Care Ritual Abuse Moral Panic* (Jefferson, N.C: McFarland, 2004).
29. O'Brien and Phillips, location 46.
30. *Ibid.*, location 2319.
31. *Ibid.*, location 2331.
32. Kenn Thomas and Jim Keith's *The Octopus: Secret Government and the Death of Danny Casolaro*, rev. ed. (Berkeley: Feral House, 2003), is the most thoroughly researched account of Casolaro's involvement in the Inslaw affair and the numerous other alleged cover-ups to which he connected it.
33. "Interview with Gurudas," *Sightings on the Radio*, April 20, 1997.
34. Beldo, "I Was a Sex Slave for the CIA!!!"
35. Jim Keith, *Mind Control, World Control*, 2d ed. (Kempton, IL: Adventures Unlimited Press, 1998). 299.
36. "Cathy O'Brien | the Richie Allen Show," http://richieallenshow.com/cathyobrien/.
37. Brice Taylor, *Thanks for the Memories ... the Truth Has Set Me Free! The Memoirs of Bob Hope's and Henry Kissinger's Mind-Controlled Slave* (Landrum, SC: Brice Taylor Trust, 1999).
38. *Ibid.*, 35.
39. *Ibid.*, 36.
40. *Ibid.*, 42.
41. "Who We Are," *The Tavistock Institute*, http://www.tavinstitute.org/who-we-are/.
42. "Key Texts," *The Tavistock Institute*, http://www.tavinstitute.org/who-we-are/key-texts/.
43. Taylor, 15.
44. John Coleman, *The Tavistock Institute of Human Relations: Shaping the Moral, Spiritual, Cultural, Political, and Economic*

Notes—Chapter 4

Decline of the United States of America (Palmdale, CA: Omni Publications, 1999), v.

45. Taylor, 293.

46. Ray Bilger, "The True Story About Mark Phillips," July 12, 2000, http://educate-yourself.org/mc/markphillipstruestory12jul00.shtml.

47. O'Brien and Phillips, location 4872.

48. *Ibid.*, location 4976.

49. David Icke, *I Am Me I Am Free: The Robots' Guide to Freedom* (Poway, CA: Bridge of Love, 1996), 69.

50. Alex Constantine, *Psychic Dictatorship in the U.S.A.* (Portland, OR: Feral House, 1995), ix-xi, 189–194.

51. *Ibid.*, 21.

52. Alex Ansary, "Mass Mind Control Through Network Television," December 29, 2005, http://rense.com/general69/mass.htm.

53. Barkun, 76–77.

54. The original mind control forum is housed at http://www.randomcollection.info/mcf/, but has not been updated since 2012. There are other sites called "The Mind Control Forum" but many of these are repositories of pornographic stories that feature mind control as a key element and are not, strictly speaking, relevant to mind control-oriented aspects of conspiracy culture.

55. Edmund Light, "Beginnings of the Mind Control Forum," 1998, http://www.randomcollection.info/mcf/light2.htm.

56. Edmund Light, "Ed Light: Mind Control Forums' Founder," 1995, http://www.randomcollection.info/mcf/v/light.htm.

57. Cary Adcox, "Cary Adcox," n.d., http://www.randomcollection.info/mcf/v/adcox.htm.

58. Columbia Jones, "Editorial," *MKZINE*, Spring/Summer 2003.

59. "Interview with Lyn Buchanan, Joe Mcmoneagle, and Paul H. Smith," Coast to Coast AM, March 25, 1997.

60. Richard S. Broughton, *Parapsychology: The Controversial Science* (New York: Ballantine, 1991), 117.

61. H. E. Puthoff, "CIA-Initiated Remote Viewing at Stanford Research Institute," n.d., http://www.biomindsuperpowers.com/Pages/CIA-InitiatedRV.html.

62. John W. Kramar, "GRILL FLAME Protocol" (United States Army, Materiel Systems Analysis Activity, July 7, 1978).

63. "Interview with Lyn Buchanan, Joe Mcmoneagle, and Paul H. Smith," Coast to Coast AM, March 25, 1997.

64. The history of the various remote viewing programs is fairly convoluted. In 1978, the US Army absorbed the SRI remote viewing program and designated it GRILL FLAME. In 1985, control was transferred to the Defense Intelligence Agency's Scientific and Technical Intelligence Directorate and re-designated SUN STREAK. In 1991, the program was moved to the Science Applications International Corporation, a private corporation but with continued oversight by the DIA. At this point it was assigned the STAR GATE cryptonym. Responsibility for STAR GATE shifted to the Central Intelligence Agency in 1995 The Federation of American Scientists has published a concise history of the various projects. "STAR GATE [Controlled Remote Viewing]," Federation of American Scientists, December 29, 2005, http://fas.org/irp/program/collect/stargate.htm.

65. "GRILL FLAME Program Session Report" (US Army, INSCOM, n.d.), Release approval CIA-RDP96–00788R000200360001–1, 6.

66. *Ibid.*, 2.

67. "GRILL FLAME Program Session Report" (US Army, INSCOM, n.d.). Release approval CIA-RDP96–00788R00080071 0001–6, 2–3.

68. Michael D. Mumford, Andrew M. Rose, and David A. Goslin, "Executive Summary," *An Evaluation of Remote Viewing: Research and Applications* (The American Institutes for Research, September 29, 1995), 3–4.

69. "Interview with Lyn Buchanan, Joe Mcmoneagle, and Paul H. Smith,"

70. *Ibid.*

71. "Who Is Ed Dames?," accessed October 20, 2014, http://www.learnrv.com/eddames.cfm.

72. *Ibid.*

73. "Interview with Ed Dames," Coast to Coast AM, January 30, 1997.

74. "The Killshot: Approaching the Moment," accessed October 20, 2014, http://www.thekillshot.com/.

75. Olivier Hainaut, "Hale-Bopp Companions?!?," January 22, 1997, http://www.ifa.hawaii.edu/images/hale-bopp/tholen-sep1/.

76. Michael Lindemann, "Courtney Brown

Speaks on Hale-Bopp Photo Hoax," January 16, 1997, http://www.theanomalieschannel.com/archive/cni-news/CNI.0619.html.

77. Thomas G. Genoni, Jr., "Art Bell, Heaven's Gate, and Journalistic Integrity," http://www.csicop.org/si/show/art_bell_heavenrsquos_gate_and_journalistic_integrity/.

Chapter 5

1. Omar Cherif, "The Global Warming Hoax—A Convenient Excuse for a New World Order?" June 4, 2013. http://consciouslifenews.com/global-warming-hoax-convenient-excuse-new-world-order-2/1158164/.

2. Florencia Soto Nino, "Climate Change Threatens Irreversible and Dangerous Impacts, but Options Exist to Limit Its Effects," *UN and Climate Change*, November 2, 2014, http://www.un.org/climatechange/blog/2014/11/climate-change-threatens-irreversible-dangerous-impacts-options-exist-limit-effects/.

3. Intergovernmental Panel on Climate Change, *Climate Change 2014: Synthesis Report. Contribution of Working Groups I, II and III to the Fifth Assessment Report of the Intergovernmental Panel on Climate Change* (Core Writing Team, R.K. Pachauri and L.A. Meyer, eds. Geneva: IPCC, 2014), 2.

4. *Ibid.*, 4.

5. *Ibid.*, 16.

6. *Ibid.*, 26–27.

7. Department of Economic and Social Affairs Population Division, *Concise Report on the World Population Situation in 2014* (New York: United Nations, 2014), iii.

8. Paul R. Ehrlich, *The Population Bomb* (New York: Ballantine, 1968), xi-xii.

9. Irvin Baxter, "About Irvin Baxter," *Endtime Ministries*, n.d., http://www.endtime.com/irvin-baxter/.

10. *Ibid.*

11. *Ibid.*

12. Irvin Baxter, "Global Warming: UN Hoax Driving Us to One World Order," *Endtime Ministries*, April 22, 2014, http://www.endtime.com/blog/global-warming-phenomenon-real-hoax/.

13. David Icke, "Problem-Reaction-Solution Explained," Davidicke.com, September 8, 2014, http://www.davidicke.com/headlines/david-icke-problem-reaction-solution-explained-2/.

14. David Risselada, "Human Depopulation Is the Real Agenda," Freedom Outpost, August 9, 2014, http://freedomoutpost.com/2014/08/human-depopulation-real-agenda/.

15. "About Us," *America 2050*, n.d., http://www.america2050.org/about.html.

16. "Megaregions," *America 2050*, n.d., http://www.america2050.org/content/megaregions.html#more.

17. National Security Council, "Implications of Worldwide Population Growth for U.S. Security and Overseas Interests," December 10, 1974, 83.

18. Dave Hodges, "The Agenda 21 Depopulation of Rural Areas Will Give Obama Stalin-Like Control Over Food," *The Common Sense Show*, August 26, 2014, http://www.thecommonsenseshow.com/2014/08/26/the-agenda-21-depopulation-of-rural-areas-will-give-obama-stalin-like-control-over-food/.

19. "FAQ: ICLEI, the United Nations, and Agenda 21," *ICLEI Local Governments for Sustainability USA*, n.d., http://www.icleiusa.org/about-iclei/faqs/faq-iclei-the-united-nations-and-agenda-21.

20. Puneet Kollipara, "How a Group of Conspiracy Theorists Could Derail the Debate Over Climate Policy," *Washington Post*, January 22, 2015, http://www.washingtonpost.com/news/energy-environment/wp/2015/01/22/how-a-group-of-conspiracy-theorists-could-derail-the-debate-over-climate-policy/.

21. "Frequently Asked Questions About HAARP," *The High Frequency Active Auroral Research Program*, n.d., https://web.archive.org/web/20130205012118/http://www.haarp.alaska.edu/haarp/faq.html.

22. Dermot Cole, "Air Force Prepares to Dismantle HAARP Ahead of Summer Shutdown," *Alaska Dispatch News*, accessed June 3, 2015, http://www.adn.com/article/20140514/air-force-prepares-dismantle-haarp-ahead-summer-shutdown.

23. "Climate Change and HAARP—a Working Relationship?" *The Daily Bell*, February 24, 2014, http://www.thedailybell.com/news-analysis/35055/Climate-Change-and-HAARP—A-Working-Relationship/.

24. "U.S. Global Climate Change Weapon Called HAARP," *PRESS Core*, December 31, 2010, http://presscore.ca/haarp-responsible-for-the-accelerated-melting-of-the-glaciers-aka-global-warming.

25. Highland1, "HAARP Being Used to Create Floods to Destroy World's Food Supply," *The One Truth*, February 11, 2014, http://jandeane81.com/threads/2041-HAARP-being-used-to-create-floods-to-destroy-World%EF%BF%BDs-food-supply?s=9c3aaa69f06bd11b72f7f3dc9f08b819&p=13138&viewfull=1#post13138.

26. Jack Braitch provides an extensive chart of nine of the most prominent AIDS conspiracy theories in Jack Bratich, "Injections and Truth Serums: AIDS Conspiracy Theories and the Politics of Articulation," in *Conspiracy Nation: The Politics of Paranoia in Postwar America*, ed. Peter Knight (New York: New York University Press, 2002), 133–56.

27. G.J. Krupey, "AIDS: Act of God or the Pentagon?" in *Secret and Suppressed: Banned Ideas and Hidden History*, ed. Jim Keith (Portland, OR: Feral House, 1993), 241, 253.

28. Darryl Fears, "Study: Many Blacks Cite AIDS Conspiracy," *Washington Post*, January 25, 2005, http://www.washingtonpost.com/wp-dyn/articles/A33695-2005Jan24.html.

29. Ibid.

30. Christian Miller, "None Dare Call It White Genocide," *Majority Rights*, August 25, 2010, http://majorityrights.com/weblog/comments/none_dare_call_it_white_genocide/.

31. Elbertson Granite Finishing Co., Inc., *The Georgia Guidestones* (Hartwell, GA: The Sun, 1981), 37.

32. Richard L. Forstall, "Georgia: Population of Counties by Decennial Census," *Census.Gov*, March 27, 1995, http://www.census.gov/population/cencounts/ga190090.txt.

33. Elbertson Granite Finishing Co., Inc., 13.

34. Ibid., 17.

35. Ibid., 19–20.

36. Stanley K. Monteith, "The Georgia Guidestones," n.d., http://www.radioliberty.com/stones.htm.

37. Randall Sullivan, "American Stonehenge: Monumental Instructions for the Post-Apocalypse," *Wired*, April 20, 2009, http://archive.wired.com/science/discoveries/magazine/17-05/ff_guidestones?currentPage=all.

38. Elbertson Granite Finishing Co., Inc., 18–19.

39. "Opening the Times [Sic] Capsule," *The Georgia Guidestones*, n.d., http://www.thegeorgiaguidestones.com/When.htm.

40. James McBride, *Pioneer Biography: Sketches of the Lives of Some of the Early Settlers of Butler County, Ohio* (Cincinnati: R. Clarke & Company, 1871), 243.

41. Ibid., 244.

42. John Cleves Symmes, *Symzonia: A Voyage of Discovery* (New York: J. Seymour, 1820), 92.-93.

43. Ibid., 97.

44. American Traveller, "The New Theory," *Zion's Herald*, May 31, 1826, 3.

45. Robert V. Hine and John Mack Faragher, *The American West: A New Interpretive History* (New Haven: Yale University Press, 2000), 160.

46. American Traveller.

47. National Education Association, *Report of the Committee of Ten on Secondary Education Studies* (New York: American Book Company, 1894), 254.

48. David Hatcher Childress and Richard Shaver, *Lost Continents & the Hollow Earth: I Remember Lemuria & the Shaver Mystery* (Kempton, IL: Adventures Unlimited Press, 1999), 218–219.

49. Richard Toronto, *War Over Lemuria: Richard Shaver, Ray Palmer and the Strangest Chapter of 1940s Science Fiction* (Jefferson, N.C.: McFarland, 2013), 104.

50. Ibid., 112.

51. Ibid., 104.

52. "Discussions," *Amazing Stories*, January 1944, 206–107.

53. Raymond A. Palmer, "The Observatory," *Amazing Stories*, December 1944, 8 [emphasis in original].

54. Raymond A. Palmer, "The Observatory," *Amazing Stories*, March 1945, 8.

55. Richard S. Shaver, "I Remember Lemuria!" *Amazing Stories*, March 1945, 13.

56. Toronto, 4.

57. Shaver, 28–29.

58. Raymond A. Palmer, "The Observatory," *Amazing Stories*, June 1945, 6, 10.

59. Richard S. Shaver, "Thought Records of Lemuria," *Amazing Stories*, June 1945.

60. Palmer's involvement in the early days of the flying saucer craze are outside the scope of this chapter. Palmer was involved in the Maury island Incident (see Chapter 3) and attempted, in *Amazing Stories*, to link the

flying saucers to Shaver's dero and tero. Richard Toronto's *War Over Lemuria* (pp. 158-162) has a detailed account of Palmer's involvement as well as FBI interest in Palmer's involvement in the Maury Island case.

61. Toronto, 171.
62. *Ibid.*, 118–119.
63. *Ibid.*, 135.
64. Sean Casteel, Tim R. Swartz, and Mary Jane Martin, *The Best of the Hollow Earth Hassle*, ed. Timothy Green Beckley, Kindle ed. (New Brunswick, N.J.: Global Communications, 2008), location 111.
65. Fred Nadis, *The Man from Mars: Ray Palmer's Amazing Pulp Journey* (New York: Tarcher, 2014), 257.
66. *Ibid.*, 259.
67. Barkun, 110.
68. U.S. Army Corps of Engineers, *Design of Underground Installations in Rock* (Washington, D.C., 1961), 3.
69. Gretchen Heefner, "Minuteman Missiles: Hidden in the Heartland," The Huffington Post, September 20, 2012, http://www.huffingtonpost.com/2012/09/20/minuteman-missiles-hidden-silos-america_n_1897913.html.
70. Memorandum to Colonel J. M. Chambers from Robert Y. Phillips RE: "Special Facility Preparedness," November 29, 1962, U.S. National Archives, Records Group 396, Declassified P 95 Records, Accession 66A03, Box 6, Folder "Special Facilities Branch."
71. "Raven Rock Mountain Complex (Site R)," *Public Intelligence*, n.d., https://publicintelligence.net/raven-rock-mountain-complex-site-r/.
72. "Who's Who in the Eisenhower Ten," *CONELRAD: Atomic Secrets*, n.d., http://conelrad.com/atomicsecrets/secrets.php?secrets=e15.
73. "FEMA Executive Orders," *The Forbidden Knowledge*, n.d., http://www.theforbiddenknowledge.com/hardtruth/fema_executive_orders.htm.
74. Richard Sauder, *Underground Bases and Tunnels: What Is the Government Trying to Hide?* (Kempton, IL: Adventures Unlimited Press, 1995), back cover.
75. *Ibid.*, 5 [emphasis author's].
76. *Ibid.*, front and back covers.
77. *Ibid.*, 118–119.
78. Don Allen, "Subject: O.H. Krill Intro/README," August 8, 1991, http://wiretap.area.com/Gopher/Library/Fringe/Ufo/krill.txt.
79. Sauder, 121.
80. *Ibid.*, 124.
81. *Ibid.*, 120.
82. Jim Keith, *Black Helicopters Over America: Strikeforce for the New World Order* (Lilburn, GA: Illuminet Press, 1994), 18.
83. *Ibid.*, 43–44.
84. Jon Roland, "Re: What Happened to Michael K. Benn?" Usenet, misc.activism.militia (April 27, 1997).
85. Keith, *Black Helicopters Over America*, 52–53, 79.
86. *Ibid.*, 93–95.
87. Leisa Zigman, "I-Team: The Army's Secret Cold War Experiments on St. Louisans," Ksdk.com, September 25, 2012, http://www.ksdk.com/news/article/339573/3/I-Team-The-Armys-secret-cold-war-experiments-on-St-Louisans.
88. Jim Keith, *Black Helicopters II: The Endgame Strategy* (Lilburn, GA: Illuminet Press, 1997), 33
89. *Ibid.*, 50.
90. *Ibid.*, 80–81.
91. *Ibid.*, 82.
92. *Ibid.*, 54.
93. *Ibid.*, 70.
94. *Ibid.*, 108
95. Sauder, 7.
96. Rodney Cluff, "Our Living Hollow Earth," *Our Hollow Earth*, 2008, http://www.ourhollowearth.com/TheLivingEarth.htm [capitalization in original].
97. Casteel, location 359.
98. *Ibid.*, location 372.
99. Jim Wilhelmsen, "A Hollow Earth," *Echoes of Enoch*, n.d., http://www.echoesofenoch.com/a_hollow_earth.htm.
100. Jim Wilhelmsen, "Two Seeds," *Echoes of Enoch*, n.d., http://www.echoesofenoch.org/two_seeds.htm.

Chapter 6

1. Branton, "The Omega File: Nazi Bases in Antarctica," *The Forbidden Knowledge*, http://www.theforbiddenknowledge.com/hardtruth/omegafil02.htm.
2. Uki Goñi, "Tests on Skull Fragment Cast Doubt on Adolf Hitler Suicide Story," *The Guardian*, accessed March 11, 2015,

http://www.theguardian.com/world/2009/sep/27/adolf-hitler-suicide-skull-fragment.

3. "Adolf Hitler Part 01 of 04," *FBI*, accessed March 11, 2015, http://vault.fbi.gov/adolf-hitler/adolf-hitler-part-01-of-04, 4.

4. Larry Rohter, "Argentina, a Haven for Nazis, Balks at Opening Its Files," *New York Times*, March 9, 2003, sec. International Style / Americas, http://www.nytimes.com/2003/03/09/international/americas/09ARGE.html.

5. "Adolf Hitler Part 01 of 04," 1–3.

6. *Ibid.*, 13.

7. Glenn B. Infield, *Shorzeny: Hitler's Commando* (New York: St. Martin's Press, 1981), 121.

8. Linda Hunt, "US Coverup of Nazi Scientists," *Bulletin of the Atomic Scientists*, no. 61 (1985): 16–24.

9. John Gimbel, "German Scientists, United States Denazification Policy, and the 'Paperclip Conspiracy,'" *The International History Review* 12, no. 3 (August 1, 1990): 441–65.

10. Michael J. Neufeld, "Wernher Von Braun, the SS, and Concentration Camp Labor: Questions of Moral, Political, and Criminal Responsibility," *German Studies Review* 25, no. 1 (February 1, 2002): 57–78.

11. Robert Wolfe, *Analysis of the Investigative Records Repository (IRR) File of Klaus Barbie* (Interagency Working Group, September 19, 2001), http://www.archives.gov/iwg/research-papers/barbie-irr-file.html.

12. Mae Brussell, "The Nazi Connection to the John F. Kennedy," Maebrussell.com, January 1984, http://www.maebrussell.com/Mae%20Brussell%20Articles/Nazi%20Connection%20to%20JFK%20Assass.html.

13. Milton William Cooper, "Cooper Family Targeted by Feds," *Hour of the Time*, July 6, 1998, http://www.hourofthetime.com/targeted.htm.

14. Walter E. Grunden, Mark Walker, and Masakatsu Yamazaki, "Wartime Nuclear Weapons Research in Germany and Japan," *Osiris*, 2nd Series, 20 (2005): 107–30.

15. "The German Space Mirror," *Life*, July 23, 1945.

16. Robert Lamb, "Did the Nazis Have a Space Program?" *Dnews*, http://news.discovery.com/space/history-of-space/did-the-nazis-have-a-space-program.htm.

17. Robert K. Rouse, "Moon and Mars Bases," Usenet, *Alt.Paranet.Ufo* (August 24, 1993).

18. Joseph P. Farrell, *Reich of the Black Sun: Nazi Secret Weapons and the Cold War Allied Legend* (Kempton, IL: Adventures Unlimited Press, 2005), v.

19. *Ibid.*, vi.

20. *Ibid.*, 69.

21. Farrell's citing of Frank Joseph is interesting in itself, due to Joseph's documented connections to the modern neo-Nazi movement. Farrell, to his credit, avoids the outright admiration for Nazism that persists in fringe history of this period. See Jason Colavito, "Fringe History's Frank Joseph Problem," *Jason Colavito*, April 29, 2014, http://www.jasoncolavito.com/1/post/2014/04/fringe-historys-frank-joseph-problem.html.

22. *Ibid.*, 134.

23. *Ibid.*, 163–164.

24. Joseph P. Farrell, *Roswell and the Reich: The Nazi Connection*, electronic ed. (Kempton, Ill.: Adventures Unlimited Press, 2010).

25. Colin Summerhayes and Peter Beeching, "Hitler's Antarctic Base: The Myth and the Reality," *Polar Record* 43 (2007): 1–21.

26. *Ibid.*

27. William Cooper, "Secret Societies/The New World Order," n.d., http://www.theforbiddenknowledge.com/hardtruth/secret_societies_nwo.htm.

28. "FBI Quietly Opens Secret Files That Attest HITLER WENT TO ARGENTINA Rather than Commit Suicide," n.d., http://www.redflagnews.com/headlines/fbi-opens-files-proving-hitler-went-to-argentina.

29. Reginald Phelps, "'Before Hitler Came': Thule Society and Germanen Orden," *The Journal of Modern History* 35, no. 3 (September 1963): 245.

30. Christa Kamenetsky, "Folklore as a Political Tool in Nazi Germany," *The Journal of American Folklore* 85, no. 337 (July 1, 1972): 221–35.

31. Phelps, 261.

32. Peter Levenda, *Unholy Alliance: A History of Nazi Involvement with the Occult*, 2d ed. (New York: Bloomsbury Academic, 2002). 47.

33. *Ibid.*, 60.

34. Becky Branford, "Secrets of Ex-Nazi's Chilean Fiefdom," *BBC*, March 11, 2005, sec. Americas, http://news.bbc.co.uk/2/hi/americas/4340591.stm.

35. Levenda, 325–326.

36. Peter Levenda, *Sinister Forces—A Grimoire of American Political Witchcraft: The Nine* (Waterville, OR: TrineDay, 2005), 143.

37. Nicholas Goodrick-Clarke, *Black Sun: Aryan Cults, Esoteric Nazism, and the Politics of Identity* (New York: New York University Press, 2003), 2.

38. "Jim Wilhelmsen: Time Travel Is Real," *The Prophecy Club*, June 1, 2015.

39. Mark Phillips, "Operation Monarch," *Outpost of Freedom*, February 3, 1993, http://www.outpost-of-freedom.com/operatio.htm.

40. Cathy O'Brien and Mark Phillips, *TRANCE Formation of America*, Revised Kindle electronic ed. (Las Vegas: Reality Marketing, 2005), Location 421

41. David Icke, "Arizona Wilder Interview," n.d., http://www.whale.to/c/wilder.html.

Conclusion

1. Often, the smallest things can be the most confusing and one of these small things is the spelling or typography of Alternative 3, given its life as a television episode, a novel based on the television episode, and its treatment as a factual, historical concept by conspiracy researchers. The convention I have adopted is to use "Alternative 3" to refer to the television episode and *Alternative 003* to refer to the novelization. In quotations referring to it, I will maintain the presentation used by the source.

2. Peter Wright, "Alternative 3 (Review)," *Science Fiction Film and Television* 2, no. 2 (2009): 318–22, 319

3. "Alt3.Txt," Textfiles.com, n.d., http://textfiles.com/sf/alt3.txt.

This document is stored on an archive site that maintains copies of posts from a variety of Bulletin Board Systems from the 1980s and 1990s. While this post is undated, contextual clues (particularly references to "Area 51" and the alleged [and largely conjectural] "Aurora"

aircraft project place it sometime after March of 1990, when Aurora was first mentioned in *Aviation Week and Space Technology*. Aurora has been associated with both the stealth bomber and various claims of "Black Triangle" style UFOs.

4. Cooper, *Behold a Pale Horse*, 213–214 [capitalization in original].

5. *Ibid.*, 221.

6. Mae Brussell, "Book 'Alternative 3,'" *World Watchers International*, March 23, 1979.

7. Jim Keith, *Casebook on Alternative 3: UFO's, Secret Societies and World Control*, 1st ed. (Lilburn, GA: Illuminet Press, 1993), 13.

8. Leslie Watkins, "The Truth About Alternative 3 by Leslie Watkins," Textfiles.com, October 28, 1989, http://textfiles.com/conspiracy/watkins.asc.

9. "150324–03 Exercise Readies SOF for Threats Abroad," March 24, 2014. http://www.soc.mil/UNS/Releases/2015/March/150324–03.html.

10. Kit Daniels, "The Truth About Jade Helm They Don't Want You to Know," *Infowars*, May 4, 2015. http://www.infowars.com/the-truth-about-jade-helm-they-dont-want-you-to-know/.

11. Barbara Starr, "Pentagon Claims It Won't Be Taking Over Texas," CNN, May 5, 2015. http://www.cnn.com/2015/05/04/politics/pentagon-texas-jade-helm-15-takeover/index.html.

12. David Weigel, "Ted Cruz Says He Has Asked the Pentagon for Answers on Jade Helm 15," Bloomberg.com/politics, May 2, 2015, http://www.bloomberg.com/politics/articles/2015-05-02/ted-cruz-says-he-has-asked-the-pentagon-for-answers-on-jade-helm-15.

13. "The Message for America," *Hand of Help*, n.d., https://www.handofhelp.com/vision_1.php.

14. "TPC NEWS Fall of America 2021," *The Prophecy Club*, June 4, 2015.

Bibliography

"About." n.d. http://oathkeepers.org/oktester/about/.

"About David." *David Icke*, n.d. http://www.davidicke.com/about-david/.

"About Us." *America 2050*, n.d. http://www.america2050.org/about.html.

Adcox, Cary. "Cary Adcox." n.d. http://www.randomcollection.info/mcf/v/adcox.htm.

"Adolf Hitler Part 01 of 04." *FBI*, n.d. http://vault.fbi.gov/adolf-hitler/adolf-hitler-part-01-of-04.

Allen, Don. "O.H. Krill intro/README." *Alt.alien.visitors*, August 8, 1991. http://wiretap.area.com/Gopher/Library/Fringe/Ufo/krill.txt.

Allen, Gary. *None Dare Call It Conspiracy*, 2d ed. Saint Louis: GSG & Associates, 1971.

"alt3.txt." Textfiles.com, n.d. http://textfiles.com/sf/alt3.txt.

American Traveller. "The New Theory." *Zion's Herald*, May 31, 1826.

Ansary, Alex. "Mass Mind Control Through Network Television." December 29, 2005. http://rense.com/general69/mass.htm.

Anthony, Dick. "Pseudoscience and Minority Religions: An Evaluation of the Brainwashing Theories of Jean-Marie Abgrall." *Social Justice Research* 12, no. 4 (December 1999): 421–56.

"Arizona Militia Figure Is Shot to Death." *Los Angeles Times*, November 7, 2001. http://articles.latimes.com/2001/nov/07/news/mn-1182.

Barker, Gray. *They Knew Too Much About Flying Saucers*. Liburn, GA: Illuminet Press, 1997.

Barkun, Michael. *A Culture of Conspiracy: Apocalyptic Visions in Contemporary America*. Comparative Studies in Religion and Society. Berkeley: University of California Press, 2003.

Baxter, Irvin. "About Irvin Baxter." *Endtime Ministries*, n.d. http://www.endtime.com/irvin-baxter/.

———. "Global Warming: UN Hoax Driving Us to One World Order." *Endtime Ministries*, April 22, 2014. http://www.endtime.com/blog/global-warming-phenomenon-real-hoax/.

———. "Jade Helm 15." *Endtime Ministries*, May 5, 2015. http://www.endtime.com/prophecy-news/jade-helm-15/.

———. "Mystery Babylon—Who Is It?" *Endtime Ministries*, n.d. http://www.endtime.com/mystery-babylon-who-is-it/.

———. "When Is the End of the World?" *Endtime Ministries*, n.d. http://www.endtime.com/when-is-the-end-of-the-world/.

Beecher, Lyman. *A Plea for the West*. Cincinnati: Truman and Smith, 1835.

Beldo, Jaye. "I Was a Sex Slave for the CIA!!!" *The Konformist*, n.d. http://www.theforbiddenknowledge.com/hardtruth/omegafil02.htm.

Bender, Albert K. *Flying Saucers and the Three Men*. London: Neville Spearman, 1963.

Berman, Ric. *Schism: The Battle That Forged Freemasonry*, electronic ed. Brighton: Sussex Academic, 2013.

Beter, Peter David. "Audio Letter No. 45." n.d. http://www.peterdavidbeter.com/docs/all/dbal45.html.

_____. "Audio Letter No. 46." n.d. http://www.peterdavidbeter.com/docs/all/dbal46.html.

Bilger, Ray. "The True Story about Mark Phillips." July 12, 2000. http://educate-yourself.org/mc/markphillipstruestory12jul00.shtml.

Bishop, Greg. "'They Told Me to Say This!' An Interview with Ufologist Bill Moore." In *Wake Up Down There! The Excluded Middle Anthology*, edited by Gregory Bishop, 37–46. Kempton, IL: Adventures Unlimited Press, 2000.

Bishop, Jason, III. "The Dulce Base." *Sacred Texts*. Accessed June 16, 2015. http://www.sacred-texts.com/ufo/dulce.htm.

Branford, Becky. "Secrets of Ex-Nazi's Chilean Fiefdom." *BBC*, March 11, 2005, sec. Americas. http://news.bbc.co.uk/2/hi/americas/4340591.stm.

Branton. "The Omega File: Nazi Bases in Antarctica." *The Forbidden Knowledge*, n.d. http://www.theforbiddenknowledge.com/hardtruth/omegafil02.htm.

Bratich, Jack. "Injections and Truth Serums: AIDS Conspiracy Theories and the Politics of Articulation." In *Conspiracy Nation: The Politics of Paranoia in Postwar America*, edited by Peter Knight, 133–56. New York: New York University Press, 2002.

Broctune. "William Cooper." *Above Top Secret*, March 6, 2013. http://www.abovetopsecret.com/forum/thread931526/pgl#pid16039938.

Broughton, Richard S. *Parapsychology: The Controversial Science*. New York: Ballantine, 1991.

Brussell, Mae. "The Nazi Connection to the John F. Kennedy." Maebrussell.com, January 1984. http://www.maebrussell.com/Mae%20Brussell%20Articles/Nazi%20Connection%20to%20JFK%20Assass.html.

Casteel, Sean, Tim R. Swartz, and Mary Jane Martin. *The Best of the Hollow Earth Hassle*, Kindle ed. Edited by Timothy Green Beckley. New Brunswick: Global Communications, 2008.

"Cathy O'Brien | The Richie Allen Show." Accessed April 2, 2015. http://richieallenshow.com/cathy-obrien/.

Chambers, Colonel J. M. Memorandum to Colonel J. M. Chambers from Robert Y. Phillips RE: "Special Facility Preparedness," November 29, 1962, U.S. National Archives, Records Group 396, Declassified P 95 Records, Accession 66A03, Box 6, Folder "Special Facilities Branch."

Chardy, Alfonso. "Reagan Advisers Ran 'Secret' Government." *Miami Herald*, July 5, 1987, Final edition, sec. Front.

Cherif, Omar. "The Global Warming Hoax—A Convenient Excuse for a New World Order?" June 4, 2013. http://consciouslifenews.com/global-warming-hoax-convenient-excuse-new-world-order-2/1158164/.

Chick, Jack T. *The Awful Truth*. Ontario, CA: Chick Publications, 2011.

Childress, David Hatcher, and Richard Shaver. *Lost Continents & the Hollow Earth: I Remember Lemuria & the Shaver Mystery*. Kempton, IL: Adventures Unlimited Press, 1999.

Chiniquy, Charles Paschal Telesphore. *Fifty Years in the Church of Rome*. New York: Fleming H. Revell Company, 1886.

CIA v. Sims, 471 U.S. 159 (1985).

Clark, Jerome. *The UFO Book: Encyclopedia of the Extraterrestrial*. Detroit: Visible Ink Press, 1997.

"Climate Change and HAARP—A Working Relationship?" *The Daily Bell*, February 24, 2014. http://www.thedailybell.com/news-analysis/35055/Climate-Change-and-HAARP—A-Working-Relationship/.

Cluff, Rodney. "Our Living Hollow Earth." *Our Hollow Earth*, 2008. http://www.ourhollowearth.com/TheLivingEarth.htm.

Colavito, Jason. "Fringe History's Frank Joseph Problem." *Jason Colavito*, April 29, 2014. http://www.jasoncolavito.com/1/post/2014/04/fringe-historys-frank-joseph-problem.html.

Cole, Dermot. "Air Force Prepares to Dismantle HAARP ahead of Summer Shutdown." *Alaska Dispatch News*. Accessed June 3, 2015. http://www.adn.com/article/20140514/air-force-prepares-dismantle-haarp-ahead-summer-shutdown.

Coleman, John. *The Tavistock Institute of*

Human Relations: Shaping the Moral, Spiritual, Cultural, Political, and Economic Decline of the United States of America. Palmdale, CA: Omni Publications, 1999. http://chomikuj.pl/kuszaba/Polityka/Dr+John+Coleman/Dr+John+Coleman+-+the+Tavistock+Institute+of+Human+Relations,164436080.pdf.

Commander X [pseudonym]. *Underground Alien Bases*. Wilmington, DE: Abelard Productions, 1990.

"Condon Report, Section I: Conclusions & Recommendations." Accessed June 20, 2014. http://files.ncas.org/condon/text/sec-i.htm.

"Conspiracy Theory Poll Results." *Public Policy Polling*, April 2, 2013. http://www.publicpolicypolling.com/main/2013/04/conspiracy-theory-poll-results-.html.

Constantine, Alex. *Psychic Dictatorship in the USA*. Portland, OR: Feral House, 1995.

Cooper, Bill. "Bill Coopers [sic] Reasons for Going Public." n.d. http://textfiles.com/ufo/UFOBBS/1000/1855.ufo.

———. "The Krill Reports Introduction." *UFO Casebook Files*, n.d. http://ufocasebook.com/krillintro.html.

Cooper, Milton William. *Behold a Pale Horse*. Flagstaff: Light Technology Publishing, 1991.

———. "Cooper Family Targeted by Feds." *Hour of the Time*, July 6, 1998. http://www.hourofthetime.com/targeted.htm.

———. "MAJESTYTWELVE." *Hour of the Time*, 1997. http://www.hourofthetime.com/majestyt.htm.

———. "THE SECRET GOVERNMENT: The Origin, Identity, and Purpose of MJ-12." Textfiles.com, May 23, 1989. http://textfiles.com/ufo/mj.12.

Cooper, William. "Secret Societies/The New World Order." n.d. http://www.theforbiddenknowledge.com/hardtruth/secret_societies_nwo.htm.

———. "The Release of the Cooper Material," July 5, 1990. http://textfiles.com/ufo/addit.txt.

———. "The War Of The Worlds," December 17, 1999. http://www.hourofthetime.com/warofthe.htm.

Daniels, Kit. "The Truth About Jade Helm They Don't Want You to Know." *Infowars*, May 4, 2015. http://www.infowars.com/the-truth-about-jade-helm-they-dont-want-you-to-know/.

"Declaration Of Orders We Will Not Obey." n.d. http://oathkeepers.org/declaration-of-orders-we-will-not-obey/.

deHaven-Smith, Lance. *Conspiracy Theory in America*. Austin: University of Texas Press, 2014.

Department of the Army. "DA Civil Disturbance Plan 'GARDEN PLOT,'" August 3, 1978.

———. "DA Civil Disturbance Plan 'GARDEN PLOT,'" February 15, 1991.

Department of Economic and Social Affairs Population Division. *Concise Report on the World Population Situation in 2014*. New York: United Nations, 2014.

"Discussions." *Amazing Stories*, January 1944.

Dolan, Richard. "Introduction." In *The Best of Roswell: From the Files of FATE Magazine*, edited by The Editors of FATE, ix–xii. Lakeville, MN: Galde Press, 2007.

Earman, J.S. "Report on Inspection of MKULTRA." Washington, D.C.: Office of the Inspector General, July 26, 1963.

Ecker, Don. "This Was Written by Don Ecker in the Summer of 1990 for UFO Magazine, in Which It Appeared." Accessed May 1, 2015. http://www.skeptictank.org/files//ufo2/cooperex.htm.

Ehrlich, Paul R. *The Population Bomb*. New York: Ballantine, 1968.

Elbertson Granite Finishing Co., Inc. *The Georgia Guidestones*. Hartwell, GA: The Sun, 1981.

Ellwood, Robert S. "Spiritualism and UFO Religion in New Zealand: The International Transmission of Modern Spiritual Movements." In *The Gods Have Landed: New Religions from Other Worlds*, edited by James R. Lewis. SUNY Series in Religious Studies. Albany: State University of New York Press, 1995.

"FAQ: ICLEI, the United Nations, and Agenda 21." *ICLEI Local Governments for Sustainability USA*, n.d. http://www.icleiusa.org/about-iclei/faqs/faq-iclei-the-united-nations-and-agenda-21.

Farrell, Joseph P. *Reich of the Black Sun:*

Nazi Secret Weapons and the Cold War Allied Legend. Kempton, IL: Adventures Unlimited Pr, 2005.

_____. *Roswell and the Reich: The Nazi Connection,* electronic ed. Kempton, IL: Adventures Unlimited Press, 2010.

FATE, The Editors of. *The Best of Roswell: From the Files of FATE Magazine.* Lakeville, MN: Galde Press, 2007.

"FBI Quietly Opens Secret Files That Attest HITLER WENT TO ARGENTINA Rather Than Commit Suicide..." RedFlagNews.com, n.d. http://www.redflagnews.com/headlines/fbi-opens-files-proving-hitler-went-to-argentina.

Fears, Darryl. "Study: Many Blacks Cite AIDS Conspiracy." *Washington Post,* January 25, 2005. http://www.washingtonpost.com/wp-dyn/articles/A33695-2005Jan24.html.

"FEMA Executive Orders." *The Forbidden Knowledge,* n.d. http://www.theforbiddenknowledge.com/hardtruth/fema_executive_orders.htm.

Fenster, Mark. *Conspiracy Theories: Secrecy and Power in American Culture.* Minneapolis: University of Minnesota Press, 2008.

"150324-03 Exercise Readies SOF for Threats Abroad," March 24, 2014. http://www.soc.mil/UNS/Releases/2015/March/150324-03.html.

Finney, Dee. "MCVEIGH -THE PATSY," December 17, 2006. http://www.greatdreams.com/mcveigh-patsy.htm.

Forstall, Richard L. "Georgia: Population of Counties by Decennial Census." *Census.gov,* March 27, 1995. http://www.census.gov/population/cencounts/ga190090.txt.

"Free Masonry: A Poem. In Three Cantos. Accompanied with Notes, Illustrative ...—Citizen of Massachusetts—Google Books." Accessed April 22, 2015. http://books.google.com/books?id=AVUpAAAAYAAJ&pg=PA166&dq=%22antimasons%22+%22republican+principles%22&hl=en&sa=X&ei=I1GfU9-ULfK_sQS93YCoBA&ved=0CBwQ6AEwAA#v=onepage&q=%22anti-masons%22%20%22republican%20principles%22&f=false.

"Frequently Asked Questions about HAARP." *The High Frequency Active Auroral Research Program,* n.d. https://web.archive.org/web/20130205012118/http://www.haarp.alaska.edu/haarp/faq.html.

Fuller, John G. *The Interrupted Journey.* New York: Dell, 1967.

Genoni, Jr., Thomas G. "Art Bell, Heaven's Gate, and Journalistic Integrity." Accessed May 21, 2015. http://www.csicop.org/si/show/art_bell_heavenrsquos_gate_and_journalistic_integrity/.

"The German Space Mirror." *Life,* July 23, 1945: 78–79.

Gimbel, John. "German Scientists, United States Denazification Policy, and the 'Paperclip Conspiracy.'" *The International History Review* 12, no. 3 (August 1, 1990): 441–65.

Goñi, Uki. "Tests on Skull Fragment Cast Doubt on Adolf Hitler Suicide Story." *The Guardian.* Accessed March 11, 2015. http://www.theguardian.com/world/2009/sep/27/adolf-hitler-suicide-skull-fragment.

Goodrick-Clarke, Nicholas. *Black Sun: Aryan Cults, Esoteric Nazism, and the Politics of Identity.* New York: New York University Press, 2003.

"GRILL FLAME Program Session Report." U.S. Army, INSCOM, n.d.

"GRILL FLAME Program Session Report." U.S. Army, INSCOM, n.d.

Grunden, Walter E., Mark Walker, and Masakatsu Yamazaki. "Wartime Nuclear Weapons Research in Germany and Japan." *Osiris,* 2nd Series, 20 (2005): 107–30.

Gulyas, Aaron John. *Extraterrestrials and the American Zeitgeist: Alien Contact Tales Since the 1950s.* Jefferson, N.C.: McFarland, 2013.

Haberman, Clyde. "An Idaho Family, and Federal Tactics, Under Siege." *New York Times,* October 27, 2014.

Hainaut, Olivier. "Hale-Bopp Companions?!?" January 22, 1997. http://www.ifa.hawaii.edu/images/hale-bopp/tholen-sep1/.

Hall, Manly P. *The Secret Teachings of All Ages: An Encyclopedic Outline of Masonic, Hermetic, Qabbalistic and Rosi-*

crucian Symbolical Philosophy. Courier Corporation, 2010.

Hatonn. "Martial Law Plans for USA." *The Phoenix Liberator*, July 7, 1992.

Hatonn, Gyeorgos C. *Space—Gate: The Veil Removed*, 3rd ed. Las Vegas: Phoenix Source, 1993.

Heefner, Gretchen. "Minuteman Missiles: Hidden in the Heartland." *The Huffington Post*, September 20, 2012. http://www.huffingtonpost.com/2012/09/20/minuteman-missiles-hidden-silos-america_n_1897913.html.

Highland1. "HAARP Being Used to Create Floods to Destroy World's Food Supply." *The One Truth*, February 11, 2014. http://jandeane81.com/threads/2041-HAARP-being-used-to-create-floods-to-destroy-World%EF%BF%BDs-food-supply?s=9c3aaa69f06bd11b72f7f3dc9f08b819&p=13138&viewfull=1#post13138.

"A Hoax of Hate: The Protocols of the Elders of Zion." *The Antidefamation League*, n.d. http://archive.adl.org/special_reports/protocols/protocols_intro.html#.VYhYwRNVhBc.

Hodges, Dave. "The Agenda 21 Depopulation of Rural Areas Will Give Obama Stalin-Like Control Over Food." *The Common Sense Show*, August 26, 2014. http://www.thecommonsenseshow.com/2014/08/26/the-agenda-21-depopulation-of-rural-areas-will-give-obama-stalin-like-control-over-food/.

_____. "We Won't Get Fooled Again!" July 22, 2012. https://www.freedomsphoenix.com/Article/115348-2012-07-22-we-wont-get-fooled-again.htm.

Hofstadter, Richard. "The Paranoid Style in American Politics." *Harper's Magazine*, November 1964.

Hunt, Linda. "US Coverup of Nazi Scientists." *Bulletin of the Atomic Scientists* xli (1985): 16–24.

Hunter, Edward. *Brainwashing: The Story of Men Who Defied It*. New York: Farrar, Strauss and Cudahy, 1956.

_____. *Brain-Washing in Red China*. New York: Vanguard Press, 1951.

Hynek, J. Allen. *The UFO Experience: A Scientific Inquiry*. New York: Da Capo Press, 1998.

Icke, David. *Alice in Wonderland and the World Trade Center Disaster*. Wildwood, MO: David Icke Books, 2002.

_____. "Arizona Wilder Interview." n.d. http://www.whale.to/c/wilder.html.

_____. *The Biggest Secret: The Book That Will Change the World*. Scottsdale: Bridge of Love, 1999.

_____. *Children of the Matrix: How an Interdimensional Race Has Controlled the World for Thousands of Years-and Still Does*. Ryde, Isle of Wight: David Icke Books, 2001.

_____. *Human Race Get Off Your Knees: The Lion Sleeps No More*. Ryde, Isle of Wight: David Icke Books, 2010.

_____. *I Am Me I Am Free: The Robots' Guide to Freedom*. Poway, CA: Bridge of Love, 1996.

_____. *The Perception Deception*. Ryde, Isle of Wight: David Icke, 2014.

_____. "Problem-Reaction-Solution Explained." Davidicke.com, September 8, 2014. http://www.davidicke.com/headlines/david-icke-problem-reaction-solution-explained-2/.

_____. *The Robots' Rebellion: The Story of the Spiritual Renaissance*. Bath: Gateway Books, 1994.

_____. *Tales from the Time Loop: The Most Comprehensive Expose of the Global Conspiracy Ever Written and All You Need to Know to Be Truly Free*. Wildwood, MO: Bridge of Love, 2003.

_____. *Truth Vibrations—David Icke's Journey from TV Celebrity to World Visionary: An Exploration of the Mysteries of Life and Prophetic Revelations for the Future of Humanity*, rev. electronic ed. Dublin: Gill and Macmillan, 2014.

I.M. Feddup [pseudonym]. "Behold a Stale Horse." n.d. https://web.archive.org/web/20000510202212/http://home.worldonline.nl/~karel/ufo/people/cooper-lear/stale-horse.html.

The Imperial Japanese Mission 1917: A Record of the Reception Throughout the United States of the Special Mission Headed by Viscount Ishii. Washington, D.C.: Carnegie Endowment for International Peace, 1918.

Infield, Glenn B. *Shorzeny: Hitler's Com-*

mando. New York: St. Martin's Press, 1981.

Intergovernmental Panel on Climate Change. *Climate Change 2014: Synthesis Report. Contribution of Working Groups I, II and III to the Fifth Assessment Report of the Intergovernmental Panel on Climate Change*. Core Writing Team, R.K. Pachauri and L.A. Meyer, eds. Geneva: IPCC, 2014.

Internal Revenue Service. "Internal Revenue Bulletin—April 4, 2005—Rev. Rul. 2005-21." April 4, 2005. http://www.irs.gov/irb/2005-14_IRB/ar13.html.

Israel, Jonathan. *Democratic Enlightenment: Philosophy, Revolution, and Human Rights, 1750-1790*. New York: Oxford University Press, 2011.

Jacobs, David M. *The Threat: Revealing the Secret Alien Agenda*. New York: Simon & Schuster, 1999.

Jessup, Morris K. *UFO and the Bible*. New York: Citadel Press, 1956.

"John Lear Tells All—02." *Bibliotecapleyades*, April 2008. http://www.bibliotecapleyades.net/sociopolitica/sociopol_lear03b.htm.

Jones, Columbia. "Editorial." *MKZINE*, Spring/Summer 2003.

Kamenetsky, Christa. "Folklore as a Political Tool in Nazi Germany." *The Journal of American Folklore* 85, no. 337 (July 1, 1972): 221-35. doi:10.2307/539497.

Keith, Jim. *Black Helicopters Over America: Strikeforce for the New World Order*. Lilburn, GA: Illuminet Press, 1994.

_____. *Black Helicopters II: The Endgame Strategy*. Lilburn, GA: Illuminet Press, 1997.

_____. *Casebook on Alternative Three: UFO's, Secret Societies and World Control*. Lilburn, GA: Illuminet Press, 1994.

_____. "Jim Keith on The Biggest Secret." n.d. http://www.konformist.com/1999/icke-keith.htm.

_____. *Mind Control, World Control*, 2d ed. Kempton, IL: Adventures Unlimited Press, 1998.

_____. *Saucers of the Illuminati*. Kempton, IL: Adventures Unlimited Press, 2004.

_____, ed. *Secret and Suppressed: Banned Ideas & Hidden History*. Portland, OR: Feral House, 1993.

Kell, Kate. "Kerry's Royal Roots Will Give Him Victory, Says Burke's." *The Guardian*, August 17, 2004. http://www.theguardian.com/world/2004/aug/17/uselections2004.usa1.

"Key Texts." *The Tavistock Institute*. Accessed October 16, 2014. http://www.tavinstitute.org/who-we-are/key-texts/.

Keyhoe, Donald. *The Flying Saucer Conspiracy*. New York: Henry Holt and Co, 1955.

_____. *Flying Saucers: Top Secret*. New York: Putnam, 1960.

Knight, Peter. *Conspiracy Nation: The Politics of Paranoia in Postwar America*. New York: New York University Press, 2002.

Kollipara, Puneet. "How a Group of Conspiracy Theorists Could Derail the Debate over Climate Policy." *Washington Post*, January 22, 2015. http://www.washingtonpost.com/news/energy-environment/wp/2015/01/22/how-a-group-of-conspiracy-theorists-could-derail-the-debate-over-climate-policy/.

Kramar, John W. "GRILL FLAME Protocol." United States Army, Materiel Systems Analysis Activity, July 7, 1978.

Krupey, G.J. "AIDS: Act of God or the Pentagon?" In *Secret and Suppressed: Banned Ideas and Hidden History*, edited by Jim Keith, 241-55. Portland, OR: Feral House, 1993.

kyviecaldegs. "William Cooper." *Above Top Secret*, March 6, 2013. http://www.abovetopsecret.com/forum/thread931526/pg1#pid16040172.

Lamb, Robert. "Did the Nazis Have a Space Program?" *DNews*. Accessed March 14, 2015. http://news.discovery.com/space/history-of-space/did-the-nazis-have-a-space-program.htm.

Lear, John. "Statement Released by John Lear." December 29, 1987. http://textfiles.com/ufo/alear1.txt.

Levenda, Peter. *Sinister Forces—A Grimoire of American Political Witchcraft: The Nine*. Waterville, OR: TrineDay, 2005.

_____. *Unholy Alliance: A History of Nazi Involvement with the Occult*, 2d ed. New York: Bloomsbury Academic, 2002.

Light, Edmund. "Beginnings of the Mind

Control Forum." n.d. http://www.random collection.info/mcf/light2.htm.

———. "Ed Light: Mind Control Forums' Founder." 1995. http://www.random collection.info/mcf/v/light.htm.

Lindemann, Michael. "Courtney Brown Speaks on Hale-Bopp Photo Hoax." January 16, 1997. http://www.theanomalies channel.com/archive/cni-news/CNI.0619.html.

Lohr, Steve. "Bush, They Say, Is Indeed a Connecticut Yankee From King Henry's Court." *New York Times*, July 5, 1988, sec. U.S. http://www.nytimes.com/1988/07/05/us/bush-they-say-is-indeed-a-connecticut-yankee-from-king-henry-s-court.html.

M0JFK. "Re: David Icke Update on settlement......The Warman Case Is over—Here Is the Background." Accessed April 21, 2015. http://projectavalon.net/forum4/showthread.php?80600-David-Icke-update-on-settlement......The-Warman-case-is-over-here-is-the-background&p=941556&viewfull=1#post941556.

"Majestic 12." *FBI*, n.d. http://vault.fbi.gov/Majestic%2012.

Mason, Fran. "A Poor Person's Cognitive Mapping." In *Conspiracy Nation: The Politics of Paranoia in Postwar America*, 40–56. New York: New York University Press, 2002.

"Matthew Cooke Manuscript." n.d. http://en.wikisource.org/wiki/Matthew_Cooke_Manuscript.

May, Elaine Tyler. *Homeward Bound: American Families in the Cold War Era*. New York: Basic, 1990.

McBride, James. *Pioneer Biography: Sketches of the Lives of Some of the Early Settlers of Butler County, Ohio*. Cincinnati: R. Clarke & Company, 1871.

"Megaregions." *America 2050*, n.d. http://www.america2050.org/content/megaregions.html#more.

Melley, Timothy. "Brainwashed! Conspiracy Theory and Ideology in the Postwar United States." *New German Critique* 103 (January 1, 2008): 145–64.

"The Message For America." *Hand of Help*, n.d. https://www.handofhelp.com/vision_1.php.

Miller, Christian. "None Dare Call It White Genocide." *Majority Rights*, August 25, 2010. http://majorityrights.com/weblog/comments/none_dare_call_it_white_genocide/.

Miller, Edith Starr. *Occult Theocrasy*. Abbeville, France: F. Paillart, 1933.

Monteith, Stanley K. "The Georgia Guidestones," n.d. http://www.radioliberty.com/stones.htm.

Moore, William L. "UFOs and the U.S. Government: Part I." *MUFON UFO Journal*, November 1989.

———. "UFOs and the U.S. Government: Part II." *MUFON UFO Journal*, December 1989.

Morgan, William. *Illustrations of Masonry by One of the Fraternity*. Batavia, N.Y.: David C. Miller, 1827.

Moseley, James W., and Karl T. Pflock. *Shockingly Close to the Truth: Confessions of a Grave-Robbing Ufologist*. Amherst, N.Y.: Prometheus, 2002.

Mumford, Michael D., Andrew M. Rose, and David A. Goslin. "An Evaluation of Remote Viewing: Research and Applications." The American Institutes for Research, September 29, 1995.

Nadel, Alan. *Containment Culture: American Narratives, Postmodernism, and the Atomic Age*. Durham: Duke University Press, 1995.

Nadis, Fred. *The Man from Mars: Ray Palmer's Amazing Pulp Journey*. New York: Tarcher, 2014.

National Education Association. *Report of the Committee of Ten on Secondary Education Studies*. New York: American Book Company, 1894.

National Security Council. "Implications of Worldwide Population Growth for U.S. Security and Overseas Interests." December 10, 1974.

Neufeld, Michael J. "Wernher von Braun, the SS, and Concentration Camp Labor: Questions of Moral, Political, and Criminal Responsibility." *German Studies Review* 25, no. 1 (February 1, 2002): 57–78. doi: 10.2307/1433245.

Nino, Florencia Soto. "Climate Change Threatens Irreversible and Dangerous Impacts, but Options Exist to Limit Its

Effects." *UN and Climate Change*, November 2, 2014. http://www.un.org/climatechange/blog/2014/11/climate-change-threatens-irreversible-dangerous-impacts-options-exist-limit-effects/.

O'Brien, Cathy, and Mark Phillips. *ACCESS DENIED For Reasons Of National Security: Documented Journey From CIA Mind Control Slave To U.S. Government Whistleblower*, 2d ed. Reality Marketing, 2014.

———. *TRANCE Formation of America: True Life Story of a Mind Control Slave*, 16th English ed. Reality Marketing, 2014.

"Opening the Times [sic] Capsule." *The Geogia Guidestones*, n.d. http://www.thegeorgiaguidestones.com/When.htm.

"Operation Vampire Killer 2000." n.d. http://www.lawfulpath.com/ref/vk2k.shtml.

Palmer, Raymond A. "The Observatory." *Amazing Stories*, December 1944.

———. "The Observatory." *Amazing Stories*, March 1945.

———. "The Observatory." *Amazing Stories*, June 1945.

Peebles, Curtis. *Watch the Skies!: A Chronicle of the Flying Saucer Myth*. Washington, D.C.: Smithsonian Instiution Press, 1994.

Phelps, Reginald. "'Before Hitler Came': Thule Society and Germanen Orden." *The Journal of Modern History* 35, no. 3 (September 1963): 245–61.

Phillips, Mark. "Operation Monarch." *Outpost of Freedom*, February 3, 1993. http://www.outpost-of-freedom.com/operatio.htm.

Pipes, Daniel. *Conspiracy: How the Paranoid Style Flourishes and Where It Comes From*. New York: Touchstone, 1999.

Potok, Mark, Larry Keller, and David Holthouse. "The Second Wave: Return of the Militias." Montgomery, Alabama: Southern Poverty Law Center, August 2009.

"PrimeTime: McVeigh's Own Words." March 29, 2001. http://abcnews.go.com/Primetime/story?id=132158&page=1&singlePage=true.

Project MKULTRA, the CIA's Program of Research in Behavioral Modification. Washington, D.C., 1977.

Puthoff, H. E. "CIA-Initiated Remote Viewing at Stanford Research Institute." n.d. http://www.biomindsuperpowers.com/Pages/CIA-InitiatedRV.html.

"A Relic of the War: How the Pope Recognized the Southern Confederacy—His Letter to Jeff. Davis." *New York Times*, August 18, 1876.

Risselada, David. "Human Depopulation Is the Real Agenda." *Freedom Outpost*, August 9, 2014. http://freedomoutpost.com/2014/08/human-depopulation-real-agenda/.

Robison, John. *Proofs of a Conspiracy*. New York: George Forman, 1798.

Rohter, Larry. "Argentina, a Haven for Nazis, Balks at Opening Its Files." *New York Times*, March 9, 2003, sec. International Style / Americas. http://www.nytimes.com/2003/03/09/international/americas/09ARGE.html.

Roland, Jon. "Re: What Happened to Michael K. Benn?" Usenet. *Misc.activism.militia*, April 27, 1997.

Ronson, Jon. "Jon Ronson on David Icke." *The Guardian*. Accessed April 6, 2015. http://www.theguardian.com/books/2001/mar/17/features.weekend.

———. *Them: Adventures with Extremists*, reprint ed. New York: Simon & Schuster, 2003.

Rosenbloom, Joe, III. "Waco: More than Simple Blunders?" *Wall Street Journal*, October 17, 1995.

Rouse, Robert K. "Moon and Mars Bases." Usenet. *Alt.paranet.ufo*, August 24, 1993.

Sauder, Richard. *Underground Basese and Tunnels: What Is the Government Trying to Hide?* Kempton, IL: Adventures Unlimited Press, 1995.

Shaver, Richard S. "I Remember Lemuria!" *Amazing Stories*, March 1945.

———. "Thought Records of Lemuria." *Amazing Stories*, June 1945.

"STAR GATE [Controlled Remote Viewing]." *Federation of American Scientists*, December 29, 2005. http://fas.org/irp/program/collect/stargate.htm.

Starr, Barbara. "Pentagon Claims It Won't Be Taking over Texas." *CNN*, May 5,

2015. http://www.cnn.com/2015/05/04/politics/pentagon-texas-jade-helm-15-takeover/index.html.

Sterling, Robert. "Konformist: Jim Keith (AKA Commander X) 1949–1999." *Konformist Newswire*, September 24, 1999. https://groups.yahoo.com/neo/groups/konformist/conversations/messages/703.

Stormer, John. *None Dare Call It Treason*. Florissant, MO: Liberty Bell Press, 1964.

Strieber, Whitley. *Communion: A True Story*, rev. ed. New York: Avon, 1988.

Sullivan, Randall. "American Stonehenge: Monumental Instructions for the Post-Apocalypse." *Wired*, April 20, 2009. http://archive.wired.com/science/discoveries/magazine/17-05/ff_guidestones?currentPage=all.

Summerhayes, Colin, and Peter Beeching. "Hitler's Antarctic Base: The Myth and the Reality." *Polar Record* 43 (2007): 1–21.

Symmes, John Cleves. *Symzonia: A Voyage of Discovery*. New York: J. Seymour, 1820.

Taylor, Brice. *Thanks for the Memories ... The Truth Has Set Me Free! The Memoirs of Bob Hope's and Henry Kissinger's Mind-Controlled Slave*. Landrum, SC: Brice Taylor Trust, 1999.

Thibodeau, David, and Leon Whiteson. *A Place Called Waco: A Survivor's Story*. New York: HarperCollins, 1999.

Thomas, Kenn. "Foreword." In *Saucers of the Illuminati*, 5–6. Kempton, IL: Adventures Unlimited Press, 2004.

———, and Jim Keith. *The Octopus: Secret Government and the Death of Danny Casolaro*, rev ed. Port Towsend, WA: Feral House, 2003.

Toronto, Richard. *War over Lemuria: Richard Shaver, Ray Palmer and the Strangest Chapter of 1940s Science Fiction*. Jefferson, North Carolina: McFarland, 2013.

"Trust in Government." *Gallup*, n.d. http://www.gallup.com/poll/5392/trust-government.aspx.

U.S. Army Corps of Engineers. *Design of Underground Installations in Rock*. Washington, D.C., 1961. http://hdl.handle.net/2027/coo.31924004600700.

"U.S. Global Climate Change Weapon Called HAARP." *PRESS Core*, December 31, 2010. http://presscore.ca/haarp-responsible-for-the-accelerated-melting-of-the-glaciers-aka-global-warming.

U.S. Senate Select Committee to Study Governmental Operations with Respect to Intelligence Activities. *Final Report of the Select Committee to Study Governmental Operations with Respect to Intelligence Activities: Book 1, Foreign and Military Intelligence*. Washington, D.C.: Government Printing Office, 1976.

Vallee, Jacques. "The Bill Cooper Briefing." *Bibliotecapleyades*, n.d. http://www.bibliotecapleyades.net/sociopolitica/esp_sociopol_cooper14.htm.

Warman, Richard. "The Official Website of Richard Warman." Accessed April 21, 2015. http://www.richardwarman.ca/.

Watkins, Leslie. "The Truth About Alternative 3 by Leslie Watkins." Textfiles.com, October 28, 1989. http://textfiles.com/conspiracy/watkins.asc.

Weigel, David. "Ted Cruz Says He Has Asked the Pentagon for Answers on Jade Helm 15." Bloomberg.com/politics, May 2, 2015. http://www.bloomberg.com/politics/articles/2015-05-02/ted-cruz-says-he-has-asked-the-pentagon-for-answers-on-jade-helm-15.

"Who Is Ed Dames?" *Learn Remote Viewing*. Accessed October 20, 2014. http://www.learnrv.com/eddames.cfm.

"Who We Are." *The Tavistock Institute*. Accessed October 16, 2014. http://www.tavinstitute.org/who-we-are/.

"Who's Who in the Eisenhower Ten." *CONELRAD: Atomic Secrets*, n.d. http://conelrad.com/atomicsecrets/secrets.php?secrets=e15.

Wilhelmsen, Jim. "Echoes of Enoch." n.d. http://www.echoesofenoch.org/.

———. "Two Seeds." *Echoes of Enoch*, n.d. http://www.echoesofenoch.org/two_seeds.htm.

"William Cooper Predicted 9/11 Less Than 11 Weeks Before Attacks Happened—June 28, 2001–." June 11, 2014. http://www.sott.net/article/280317-William-Cooper-predicted-9-11-less-than-11-

weeks-before-attacks-happened-June-28-2001.

Winter, Alison. "Manchurian Candidates: Forensic Hypnosis in the Cold War." *Grey Room*, no. 45 (Fall 2011): 106–27.

Wolfe, Robert. "Analysis of the Investigative Records Repository (IRR) File of Klaus Barbie." Interagency Working Group, September 19, 2001. http://www.archives.gov/iwg/research-papers/barbie-irr-file.html.

Wright, Peter. "Alternative 3 (review)." *Science Fiction Film and Television* 2, no. 2 (2009): 318–22. doi:10.1353/sff.0.0071.

Young, Mary De. *The Day Care Ritual Abuse Moral Panic*. Jefferson, N.C: McFarland, 2004.

Zigman, Leisa. "I-Team: The Army's Secret Cold War Experiments on St. Louisans." Ksdk.com, September 25, 2012. http://www.ksdk.com/news/article/339573/3/I-Team-The-Armys-secret-cold-war-experiments-on-St-Louisans.

Index

Numbers in ***bold italics*** refer to pages with photographs.

Abbot, Greg 200
Adamski, George 77–78
Adcox, Cary 125–126
Aerial Phenomena Research Organization (APRO) 72–74, 86
AFOSI *see* Air Force Office of Special Investigations
Agenda 21 141–144
Air Force Office of Special Investigations 86, 116
Alhazen 23
Aliens 17, 36, 62–64, 70, 79–81, 87–97; abduction phenomenon 65, 73, 80–83, 86–90, 100, 108, 158, 163, 166, 167, 169–173, 194; "Grays" 80, 89, 170, 173; and the "inner Earth" 159, 168, 170; and mind control 113, 121–122; and underground bases 161–162–163
Allen, Gary 46, 49
Allen, Richie 118
Alternative 003 (book) 197–200
"Alternative 3" (television program) 196–200
Amazing Stories (magazine) 154–157
America 2050 142–145
America Unearthed (television program) 15
American Medical Association (AMA) 153
American Party 29
American Psychiatric Association 153
American Stonehenge *see* Georgia Guidestones
Ancient Aliens (television program) 15
Annunaki 36
Anthroposophic Society 64
Anti-Catholicism in conspiracy theories 6, 14, 22–24, 29–33, 57–58, 110, 168, 193–196
Anti-Communism in conspiracy theories 33–34, 45, 64
Anti-Jewish conspiracies *see* Anti-Semitic conspiracies
Anti-Masonic Party 29
Anti-Masonry in conspiracy theories 6, 24–29, 32–36, 57–58, 64, 188,
Anti-Saloon League 33
Anti-Semitic, sentiment in conspiracy theories 6, 14, 37, 43, 57, 63, 68
Aquinas, Thomas 22

Area 51 10, 13, 88
Aristotle 22
Arnold, Kenneth 71, 82
ARTICHOKE (CIA program) 105
Atlantis 35–36, 42, 155
Aurora Colorado theatre shootings 57

Bacon, Roger 23
Barbie, Klaus 182
Barker, Gray 79
Barkun, Michael 3, 9–11, 13, 19, 110, 123, 158–159
Bavarian Illuminati *see* Illuminati
Baxter, Irwin 140–141
Beecher, Lyman 30–31
Bell, Art 64–65, 127–128, 131–132
Bender, Albert K. 78–79
Benn, Michael 164
Bennewitz, Paul 86–89, 92, 96, 158
Beter, Peter ***46–48***, 174, 180
Bilderbergers 46, 57, 166
Bin Laden, Osama 68
Bishop, Greg 86, 89
Bishop, Jason III 92
Black helicopters 51, 70, 90, 158, 163–167, 199
Boxcar Willie 107, 112
Brainwashing 98–104, 113, 163, 174
Branch Davidian Standoff 54–54
Brennan, William 106
Branton (pseudonym of Bruce Alan Walton) 173–174
Braun, Eva 175
British Broadcasting Corporation (BBC) 34
British Green Party 34–35
British Union of Fascists 33
Brooks, Jack 50
Brooks-Baker, Harold 39
"Brotherhood" 36–41; *see also* Icke, David
Brown, Courtney 19, 132–133
Brussell, Mae 183, 198
Buchanan, Lyn 128
Bureau of Alcohol, Tobacco, and Firearms (BATF) 55
Bush, George H.W. 39–40; announcement of "New World Order" 58–59; role in mind control conspiracies 109–111

225

Index

Bush, George W. 40
Byrd, Robert 111

Casolaro, Danny 114–115
Catholicism *see* Anti-Catholic conspiracies
Cattle mutilations 70, 87, 90, 163, 164
Central Intelligence Agency (CIA) 12–13, 18–20, 77, 92, 117; and mind control 100–115, 122, 193; and remote viewing 127–129
CFR *see* Council on Foreign Relations
Chardy, Alfonso 49
Charles, Prince of Wales 41
CHATTER (CIA program) 105
Chem trails 144, 146, 148
Cheney, Dick 18, 99, 111–112
Chick Publications 32
Chiniquy, Charles 31–32
Church, Frank 49
Church Committee 49
CIA v. Sims (1985) 106
Climate change *see* Global warming
Clinton, Bill 18, 55, 99, 109, 111, 146, 164
Clinton, Hillary 112
Coast to Coast AM 127, 131, 189
COINTELPRO 116
Colavito, Jason 213n21
Cold War 6, 21, 45, 48, 73, 76–77, 98–101, 113, 134, 159–162, 181, 195
Coleman, John 119
Colonia Dignidad 192–193
"Commander X" 92, 96; *see also* Keith, Jim
Committee for Scientific Investigation of Claims of the Paranormal (CSICOP) 132
Communism *see* Anti-Communist conspiracies
Condon, Edward *see* Condon Committee
Condon, Richard 98, 102
Condon Committee 72
Confederate States of America 31–32
Connell, Richard 112
Constantine 35
Constantine, Alex 122
Containment 77
Cooper, Milton William 10, 20, 40, 50, 61–69, 116–117, 121, 141, 159, 161, 165–167, 183, 188, 198 ; and UFO movement 88–97
Council on Foreign Relations 46, 48, 57, 92, 166, 188
Cruz, Ted 200

Dames, Edward A. 131–133
Dark Skies 82
Davis, Jefferson 31
Defense Intelligence Agency (DIA) 110
deHaven-Smith, Lance 3, 6, 9, 11–14, 27, 195
della Mirandola, Giovanni Pico 23
Dero *see* Shaver, Richard
De Rothschild, Guy 42
Descartes, René 23
Dewey, John 94
Diana, Princess of Wales 41

Dickinson, John 27
Doctor Who 197
Dolan, Richard 82
Duduman, Dumitru 201
Dukakis, Michael 39
Dulce, New Mexico *see* Dulce Base
Dulce Base 17, 19, 88–89, 92, 158–162, 173–174, 180
Dulles, Allan 104

Earman, J.S. 104
EBE *see* Aliens
Ecker, Don 91, 162
Edwards, Frank 74–76
Eherlich, Paul 139, 149
Eichmann, Adolph 176, 180, 193
Eisenhower, Dwight D. 161
Elizabeth II 40
Emerson, Willis George 154
Endtime Ministries *see* Baxter, Irwin
English, William S. 89, 95
Enlightenment Era 22–27, 171
Executive Order 9066 49
Extraterrestrials *see* Aliens

Farrell, Joseph 174, 185–187, 190
Farsight Institute *see* Brown, Courtney
FATE (magazine) 157
Federal Bureau of Investigation (FBI) 54–55, 84–85, 102, 176–177, 183, 189–190
Federal Emergency Management Agency (FEMA) 49–51, 60, 87, 143, 161, 166
Federal Reserve System 37, 46, 81
Fenster, Mark 3, 8–10, 13
First World War *see* World War I
Flying saucers *see* UFO
Ford, Gerald 49, 110,-*111*
Ford, Susan *see* Taylor, Brice
Forrestal, James *83*
Freedom of Information Act (FOIA) 106, 181
Freeh, Louis 55
Freemasonry *see* Anti-Masonic conspiracies
French Revolution 24–25, 27
Friedman, Stanton 81

Garden Plot (military operation) 50–54, 56
Garman, Ron *see* Gurudas
Georgia Guidestones 19, 148–150
"Global Education 2000" 113
Global warming 135–141, 145–146
Gore, Al 145–146
Gottlieb, Sidney 102–103
Grace, John 90–91, 159
"Gray" aliens *see* Aliens, "Grays"
Green, Harold R., Jr. 60
Greenwood, Lee 112
GRILL FLAME (government program) 128–129
Groom Lake *see* Area 51
Gun control 57, 141
Gurudas 115–116, 118

Index

Gutenberg, Johannes 23
"Gyeorgos Ceres Hatonn" 50–51

HAARP (High Frequency Active Auroral Research Program) 144–146, 148
Hale-Bopp Comet 131–132
Hall, Manly Palmer 65–66
Heaven's Gate 132
Helms, Richard 48, 102–105
Hersh, Seymour 48–49
Hill, Barney 79–80
Hill, Betty 79–80
Hitler, Adolf 42, 174–195
HIV/AIDS, conspiracy theories about 146–148
Hofstadter, Richard 6–10, 13
"Hollow Earth" theories 70, 92, 136, 152–158, 167–171, 194; *see also* Shaver, Richard; Symmes, John Cleves
Hoover, J. Edgar 177, 179, 183
Hope, Bob 18, 107, 118
House Un-American Activities Committee 6, 76
HUAC *see* House Un-American Activities Committee
Hunter, Edward 100–102
Hussein, Saddam 128

Icke, David 20–21, 34–44, 61, 108, 121–122, 141, 167, 195, anti-Semitism 37–39, 42–43
ICLEI-Local Governments for Sustainability 144
Illuminati 22–29, 37–39, 41, 43, 63–65, 92–96, 166, 173, 188, 194–195
Illustrations of Freemasonry by One of the Fraternity 28
In Search of... 197
Independence Day 71
Inouye, Daniel 103
Inslaw 115
Intergovernmental Panel on Climate Change 137–138
Internal Revenue Service (IRS) 38, 117, 183
International Flying Saucer Bureau (IFSB) 78–79
Iran-Contra Affair 50, 115, 167

Jacobs, David M. 80–81
Jade Helm 15 200–201
Jesuit Order *see* Anti-Catholicism in conspiracy theories
Johnson, Lyndon B. 119
Johnson, Stan 201
Jones, Alex 87, 200
Joseph, Frank

Keith, Jim 20, 34, 60, 92–93, 96–97, 117, 164–167, 199
Kennedy, John F. 12–13, 15, 17, 20, 61, 81–82, 183
Kennedy, Robert F. 17, 20
Kerry, John 40

Keyhoe, Donald 73–78; *see also* National Investigations Committee for Aerial Phenomena (NICAP)
KGB 63, 176
King, Martin Luther, Jr. 17, 20
Kissinger, Henry 99, **111**, 118–119, 146
KKK *see* Ku Klux Klan
Knights Templar 16, 25, 64, 188
Know Nothing Party *see* American Party
Korean War 98–102
Koresh, David 55
KRILL Document 90–91, 93, 95
Ku Klux Klan 116

Lazar, Bob 161; *see also* Area 51
Lear, John 87–93, 95, 99–100, 159
Lemuria 42, 154–156
Lessing, Gotthold 26
Levenda, Peter 174, 190, 192–194
LeVesque, Tal 168–169
Lincoln, Abraham 31–32
Livestock mutilations *see* Cattle mutilations
Lizard People *see* Reptilians
Lloyd, John Uri 154
Lorenzen, Coral 73–74; *see also* Aerial Phenomena Research Organization (APRO)
LSD 18, 40

Mack, John 80
Majestic 12 *see* Majestic Twelve; MJ-12
Majestic Twelve 83, **84–85**; *see also* MJ-12
"MAJESTYTWELVE" 63–66, 95
Malcolm X 17
The Manchurian Candidate (book) 98, 102
The Manchurian Candidate (film) 98, 102
Marshall, Thurgood 106
Martin, Mary Jane 157–158
Masonic Lodges *see* Anti-Masonic conspiracies
The Matrix 41, 126
Matthew Cooke Manuscript 25
McCarthy, Joseph 6, 76
McMoneagle, Joe 127, 131, 133
McVeigh, Timothy 9–10, 56
Men in Black 78–79, 90
Mengele, Joseph 176, 180, 193, 195
Merovingian bloodline 42
Militia movement 55–60, 66–68, 95, 164, 201
Miller, Edith Starr 32–34,
Miller, David C. 28
Mind Control Forum (website) 123–127
MJ-12 61, 83–85, 87–90, 173–174
MKDELTA 104–105
MKNAOMI 105
MKULTRA 100, 102–107, 110, 113, 116, 117–118, 121–122, 126–127, 143, 166, 193, 199
MKZINE 126
Mondale, Walter 48
Monroe Doctrine 27
Monteith, Stanley 149–150
Moore, William 81, 83, 86–89, 92, 95–96, 159

Index

Morgan, J.P. 46
Morgan, William 28
Moseley, James W. 72
Mu 154–155
Multiple Personality Disorder (MPD) 110, 118, 122, 124
Mutual UFO Network (MUFON) 73, 92
Mutwa, Credo 40
"mystery schools" 40, 64, 66, 68

National Education Association (NEA) 153
National Investigations Committee for Aerial Phenomena (NICAP) *see* Keyhoe, Donald
National Security Act of 1947 106
National Security Agency (NSA) 173
National Security Council (NSC) 131, 143–144, 146, 150
Nazi Party *see* Nazism
Nazism 100, 119, 135, 172–174, 183–185, 190, 194; and mind control 100, 119, 122, 172–173, 193–195 ;and secret societies 42, 190–194; secret weapons of 183–187
Nephilim 36, 170
Neu Schwabenland 170, 185
New World Order (NWO) 19, 22, 25, 38, 44, 50–51, 58–60, 65, 81, 92–93, 95–96, 108, 112–115, 120, 135, 137, 158, 163–165, 171, 173–174, 183, 190
Nichols, Terry 56
9/11 attacks 43
Nixon, Richard M. 8, 46, 48, 81
North, Oliver 49

Oath Keepers 59–60
Obama, Barack 57, 142, 146, 200–202
Obama Administration *see* Obama, Barack
O'Brien, Cathy 19, 40, 99, 107, 109, *111*–127, 194
O'Brien, Earl 110
O'Brien, Kelly 109, 114, 115
Occult Theocrasy 32–34, 64
O.H. KRILL *see* KRILL Document
Oklahoma City Bombing 56–57, 183; *see also* McVeigh, Timothy; Nichols, Terry
Operation Vampire Killer 2000 58–59
Order of the Golden Dawn 119
"Organic Robotoids" *47*–48, 174, 180

Palmer, A. Mitchell 33
Palmer, Ray 154–158, 167–168
Paranet 87
Patriot movement *see* Militia movement
Philadelphia Experiment 38
Phillips, Mark 109–110, 112, 114–115, 117, 120–121, 124–125, 194–195
Pinochet, Augusto 193
Pipes, Daniel 24
Pius IX 31
Plato 22, 25
The Population Bomb see Eherlich, Paul
Population control 19, 58, 139, 141–150

Post Traumatic Stress Disorder (PTSD) 110
Powers, Francis Gary 76
Princess Diana *see* Diana, Princess of Wales
Prince Charles *see* Charles, Prince of Wales
Project Monarch 105, 109–110, 113–114, 117–118, 121–122, 125–126, 194; *see also* O'Brien, Cathy; Taylor, Brice
Project Paperclip 180–183, 193
Prophecy Club see Johnson, Stan
Protestant Reformation 23, 33
Protocols of the Elders of Zion 37–39, 63, 68, 204n35
Puthoff, Hall 127
Pythagoras 22, 25

Quadrant sign code 60

Rand Corporation 147
Remote viewing 99, 127–136
Reno, Janet 55–56, 183
Rense, Jeff 115–118
Reptilians 21, 39–44, 64, 121, 141, 196,
Reptoids *see* Reptilians
Revolution of 1688 *see* Glorious Revolution
REX-84 50–51, 54, 56, 59–62, 143, 166, 200
Rhodes, Stewart 59; *see also* Oath Keepers
Robison, John 27
Rockefeller Commission 49, 102
Rockefeller family 46, 48–49, 57
Rockefeller, John D. 46
Rockefeller, Nelson 49
Roman Catholicism *see* Anti-Catholic conspiracies
Ronson, Jon 42–43, 56–57
Roosevelt, Franklin 49
Roswell, New Mexico *see* Roswell Incident
Roswell Incident 17, 20, 38, 73, 81–83, 87, 90, 94–95, 135–136, 143, 187
Rothschild family 42, 46
Ruby Ridge Standoff 54–58, 67

Satanic Ritual Abuse 114, 118, 120, 208n29
Satanism 33, 41–42; *see also* Satanic Ritual Abuse
Sauder, Richard 162–164, 167
Schaefer, Paul 193
Schramek, Chuck 132
Second Great Awakening 29
Second World War *see* World War II
Senate Select Committee on Intelligence 103; Investigation into MKULTRA 103–104
September 11 attacks *see* 9/11 attacks
Shandera, Jaimie 83
Shaver, Richard 154–158, 167–170
The Shaver Mystery *see* Shaver, Richard; *see also Amazing Stories*; *FATE*; Palmer, Ray
"Silence Group" 77–78
Sitchin, Zecharia 36
Skorzeny, Otto 180
Skull and Bones Society 166, 189
Smith, William 49

Southern Poverty Law Center 59
Soviet Union 33, 45–48, 98–101, 113, 128, 131, 147, 159–160, 174–175, 180, 182, 184, 191, 193, 195
Speer, Albert 183
Stanford Research Institute (SRI) 127–128, 209n64
STAR GATE (government program) 128, *130*
Star Trek 65–66
Star Wars 66
Stormer, John 45–46
Strieber, Whitley 80, 162
Swann, Ingo 127
Symmes, John Cleves 151–154
Szabo, Ladislas 188

Targ, Russell 127
Tavistock Institute of Human Relations 119
Taylor, Brice 19, 107–111, 118–126
Tax protest movement 66, 205n39
Technical Remote Viewing *see* Remote Viewing
Tero *see* Shaver, Richard
Theosophical Society 64, 170, 192; *see also* Theosophy
Theosophy 170, 188, 192
They Live 40
Thibodeau, David 56
Thomas, Kenn 96
Thompson, Linda 51, 55, 159, 165–166
Thule Society 173, 187, 191–192
TRANCE Formation of America see O'Brien, Cathy
Trevor-Roper, Hugh 180
Truman, Harry S. *83*
The Truman Doctrine *see* Containment
Turner, Stansfield 103–104
Tuskegee syphilis experiments 147

Underground bases 17, 19, 21, 26, 42, 62, 70, 87–89, 92, 156, 160–162, 167, 170–174, 180, 184, 196

Unidentified Flying Objects (UFO) 10, 35, 38, 116–117, 121, 132, 135, 139–141, 159, 161–164, 168–169, 174–175, 190; early history 70–73; and global conspiracies 92–97; in the 1950s and 1960s 73–78; in the 1980s and 1990s 79–92; and William Cooper 61–63
Union of Soviet Socialist Republics *see* Soviet Union
United Nations (UN) 9, 14, 17, 21, 45, 57–60, 71, 140–142, 150, 159, 165, 194; and climate change 137–138
United States President's Commission on CIA Activities Within the United States *see* Rockefeller Commission
University of Colorado UFO Project *see* Condon Committee
USSR *see* Soviet Union

V 40
Vander Jagt, Guy 109
Vietnam War 7, 192
von Braun, Werner 182

Walton, Bruce Alan *see* Branton
Warburg family 46
Warren Commission 12, 193
Watergate 7–9
Watkins, Leslie 199
Weaver, Randy 54–56; *see also* Ruby Ridge Standoff
Weishaupt, Adam 26–27
Wells, Orson 94
Wilhelmsen, Jim 168–170
Winthrop, John 29
World War I 33, 46, 94, 191
World War II 17, 21, 32–33, 45, 160, 172, 186, 188, 190–195; Japanese-American internment during 60
Wunderwaffe ("wonder weapons) *see* Nazi-era Germany, secret weapons of

The X-Files 82

www.ingramcontent.com/pod-product-compliance
Ingram Content Group UK Ltd.
Pitfield, Milton Keynes, MK11 3LW, UK
UKHW041946140426
5217IPUK00014B/679